AMAZON
UP CLOSE

The Passionate Adventurer's Guide To The Brazilian Amazon & The Pantanal

Pamela Bloom

HUNTER
PUBLISHING

HUNTER PUBLISHING, INC.
130 Campus Drive
Edison NJ 08818-7816, USA
Tel (908) 225 1900; Fax (908) 417 0482
E-mail: hunterpub@emi.net
Website: www.hunterpublishing.com

1220 Nicholson Road
Newmarket, Ontario L3Y 7V1, CANADA
Tel (800) 399 6858; Fax (800) 363 2665

ISBN 1-55650-780-1

© 1997 Pamela Bloom

Every effort has been made to ensure that the information in this book is correct, but the publisher and authors do not assume, and hereby disclaim, any liability to any party for any loss or damage caused by errors, omissions, misleading information or any potential problem caused by information in this guide, even if these are a result of negligence, accident or any other cause. All opinions expressed in this book stem from the author's personal experience only or from those of her contributors; consequently, neither she nor the contributors can be held accountable for a reader's personal experience while traveling.

Maps by Kim André

Cover photo: Bora Indian Boy by Danny Lehman, Westlight. The Bora tribe was one of the first to inhabit the Brazilian Amazon. All other images by author unless noted otherwise.

Acknowledgments

As part of the research I completed, both for this book and my other guide, *Brazil Up Close* (Hunter Publishing, 1997), I owe much gratitude to literally hundreds of forest spirits, who guided me through this wonderful, exasperating and unforgettable country.

Especially in the Amazon, I would like to thank the tourist boards of the states of Pará and Amazonas, as well as those of the cities of Belém and Manaus for supporting my work. Special thanks go to André von Thuranyi of Expeditours, whose passionate commitment to ecology and the soul of the forest kept me inspired through some rough and rugged adventures. Many thanks go to John C. Jones for his contribution on fly-fishing in the Amazon.

Cheers to Beatrice Imbiriba in her position as Secretary of Tourism of the city of Santarém, a true Amazon warrior in the best tradition. May you succeed in all your dreams for the forest and its peoples.

The deepest of gratitude is extended to the special contributors of this guidebook, Dr. Trish Shanley, Dr. Mark Plotkin and especially Prof. M.C. Meyer, all outstanding scientists who are doing what we all should be: changing the course of our planet's history for the better. Their dedication, brilliance and indefatigable energy continue to be true gifts to mankind.

Many thanks for the tireless efforts of a translating assistant, LLR. Also much gratitude to Judge Alvarina Miranda de Almeida of Manaus for her efforts on behalf of the Amazon.

Deep appreciation is also extended to Varig Airlines for their continued support of this project.

Thanks also go to Michael Hunter of Hunter Publishing and Kim André for seeing the continued worth of this work and helping me realize it.

And finally, to my mother, Mitzie Bloom, my late father, Dr. Manuel G. Bloom, and my brothers, Kim and Kerry, and their families for always supporting me through my wildest dreams.

About The Author

Pamela Bloom is a music and arts critic, travel and fiction writer, whose work has appeared in *The New York Times*, *The Chicago Tribune*, and *The Los Angeles Times*, as well as *High Fidelity*, *Musician*, *Downbeat*, *Seven Days*, *Connoisseur*, and *Elle* magazines, among others. She received a B.A. in comparative literature from Trinity College (Hartford, CT), attended Dartmouth College, and also studied opera at Indiana University and the Juilliard School of Music. She taught the history of Brazilian jazz at the New School for Social Research in New York, and has presented multimedia lectures on Brazilian music and culture at the Ballroom Club in Manhattan for their annual Brazilian jazz series.

A world traveler, Pamela Bloom has pursued writing assignments in China, Spain, Greece, France, Belgium and the Caribbean, as well as throughout the U.S. As a dedicated Brazilophile, she has danced in Rio's Carnaval with the Portela Samba School, interviewed the country's top musicians and traveled extensively within Brazil. A native of Houston, Texas, she now resides in New York City.

Author, Pamela Bloom

Important! A Word About Money

Brazil has had a crazy history of enormous inflation and to predict its future would be foolhardy. However, the present currency, called the *real* (pronounced ray-ow) was instituted on July 1, 1994 to be more or less equivalent to the American dollar. Since that time, fluctuations have not been absent but they have not reflected the monumental dives of other years. Unfortunately, such an economic move has made traveling through Brazil no longer inexpensive, in relation to some other Latin American countries. However, nothing is predictable in Brazil, and prices quoted in this edition should be considered only a fair estimate.

Throughout the text, restaurants and hotels are listed in price categories as defined in the following table:

Hotels

Price is for standard double, without tax, most often including breakfast buffet. Sometimes 10% service charge is added to the bill.

Very Expensive	Over $200
Expensive	$100-$180
Moderate	$50-$100
Inexpensive	Under $50

Restaurants

Price is for one person, without drinks.

Expensive	Over $25
Moderate	$10-$25
Inexpensive	Under $10

We Love To Get Mail

Anyone who would like to be considered as a contributor for future editions or who would like to offer comments or suggestions is invited to write the author: Pamela Bloom, c/o Hunter Publishing, 130 Campus Drive, Edison, NJ 08818-7816. Alternately, readers may e-mail Pamela directly at BrazilBust@aol.com

> *"I believe tourism is a process in which travelers have the right to know the global reality of the place they will visit –the culture, the food, the habits, passions, sins, even its crime – and if we do it in tourism, then to be a tourist will become an exercise in citizenship."*
>
> Edward Sanovicz, Department Chief of Tourism, City of Santos (São Paulo, Brazil)

To My Readers

Picture this: I'm 10 years old, a definite non-camper stuck in the backwoods of Texas, and I'm facing what was for me – then – the epitome of horror: an outdoor latrine. No amount of soothing from my Scout leader could console me, so I spent the entire weekend whining and about to throw up. Little could my troop leader imagine that some umpteen years later, I would grow up to eat, sleep, and tramp joyously through the Amazon forest.

Why the Amazon? My love affair started with Brazil itself, an irresistibly beautiful, exotic, exasperating country that seeped into the core of my being from the moment I stepped onto its soil. A country that's perpetually about to fall apart, but will never do so until it first throws an unforgettable party. A country born to sing and dance, to love, to fight, to lie on the beach, to do everything to avoid going to work – a country where it's simple to find a lover who will inspire in you a thousand moments of *saudade*, or unrequited longing. All that inspired me to write my first guidebook on Brazil (originally titled *Fielding's Brazil*, now available in its most recent incarnation as *Brazil Up Close*, Hunter Publishing). And considering the positive feedback, I think I can safely say my guides have inspired a lot of people to give themselves fully over to that wild and woolly "Brazilian experience."

The reality is, you can't truly know Brazil without knowing its environmental core – the Amazon rainforest and the Pantanal swamplands in the west. As most people are aware by now, these two ecological systems and their delicate balance support not only Brazil, but the entire planet. The Amazon forest and the Pantanal are two of the greatest natural patrimonies on this earth, and the opportunity to meet them face to face is an unusually precious privilege of living in this modern, Concordized era. Sadly, and this is the very real state of our planet at present, if you don't take up this opportunity now, there may not be time in the future, so delicate is their preservation and so fast is their destruction.

A *New York Times* critic once described my first Brazil guidebook as "idiosyncratic" (was she being complimentary??!!), but the fact is, I love to write idiosyncratic books. In my opinion, whenever you commit yourself to leaving home and traveling abroad, you should absolutely surrender and throw yourself in hook, line and sinker. That means you need to learn everything you can, like who's fighting whom, who's destroying what, and who's banding together and struggling to survive. When you travel, I believe you have to engage yourself body and soul in the life-and-death dramas that create environments on every level – political, social, economical and spiritual. And in that way, you will return from your trip a different person, a transformed person, and you will be able to contribute that much more to your community.

And yet my first edition of *Amazon Up Close* is dedicated to an even more advanced kind of ecotourism – what I personally have called *interactive ecotourism*. These days it is not enough just to look, research, and ponder; it has become essential to give back as well. As such, I have included several articles by some of the finest scientists in the world who have not only researched the Amazon, but have gone back to share the fruits of their labors with local communities, both indigenous and non-indigenous – from Dr. Mark Plotkin, who works with Brazilian medicine men in Suriname, to Professor M.C. Meyer, a physician who was exotically initiated into the Sateré-Mawé tribe, to Dr. Trish Shanley, who works with forest dwellers to develop entrepreneurial self-sufficiency. The range of hands-on involvement by these scientists is changing the future of the planet, all the while teaching us something about transcultural sharing. At the very least, I guarantee that after you read these articles you will not look at a tree or a plant, or even an Amazonian resident, in the same way.

For Amazonian factniks, this new edition also offers a plethora of up-to-date info that should help you begin to separate the forest from the trees – like what the Amazon Basin looked like before it split off from Africa billions of years ago, how the early explorers and scientists traipsed through the forest smeared with crocodile grease, how the early native population fought for centuries to stave off the inevitable invasion. You'll discover what is really happening behind the closed doors on Indian reservations and what you can do to support the political struggles of native peoples, rubber tappers and nut gatherers. For nature buffs, there are guides to the fauna and flora of both the Amazon and the Pantanal, and there is also a look at the folklore, legends and crafts of the regions. For fishermen, there is a special new section on fly-fishing in the Amazon, written by John C. Jones, an internationally acclaimed fishing expert. There is also in-depth travel information that tells you where to go, what to do and how to get safely home in one healthy piece. My *Health Guide to the Tropics*, especially researched for Amazon travel, should be studied months before a trip.

What can you do with this book besides read it, you might ask. If you sit on it, stomp on it and squeeze it a few times, it will easily fit inside your knapsack. You can burn it for firewood if you lose all your energy bars. You can pull it out on one of those long, soporific barge rides down the Amazon when you realize you've forgotten that fat, juicy novel. You can even shred it and feed it to piranhas when you've mistakenly jumped into a bloody river full of just-gutted fish. Or you can simply sit back and enjoy it (and never even go to the Amazon) because there are lots of travel-adventure narratives that will keep you enthralled for hours. (Two readers of my guidebook on Brazil actually called me to say that they had gotten into bed and read parts of it out loud to each other!) Well, I can't claim that *Amazon Up Close* is as sexy as *Brazil Up Close*, but I can guarantee you will feel a certain frisson when you read about the peculiar mating habits of culex mosquitoes.

In the final analysis, I have come to believe that anybody can go to the Amazon jungle. I wouldn't have thought so before I actually did, but there exists, in these regions, an adventure and mode of travel for every level of physical ability. Before you go, of course, you should take my *Should I Go to the Amazon?* quiz (see below), but if you fail it, don't worry – you will still own an interesting book. If you decide to go, make a promise to me right now that you will become the best eco-conscious traveler ever: that means traveling light, not unduly disturbing fauna and flora above or under the sea, and disposing of garbage properly. *Preserva natureza* (preserve nature) and by doing so, we'll preserve the planet.

Not much else to say for now, so just go out and get your hammock, your hiking boots and the strongest insect repellent you can find and join me in an adventure you will never forget. As they say in Brazil, *Vai com Deus*, (Go with God) and as I like to add, "Don't let the bedbugs bite."

PAMELA BLOOM

Should I Go To The Amazon?

Take the following quiz to determine if you are a good candidate for an Amazon adventure. Don't cheat or it will come back to haunt you. If you rate more than six "Trues," sign up immediately; you'll probably actually enjoy yourself.

1. You are in good physical shape (heart and lungs), though you needn't be able to jog five miles.

2. You are able to withstand heat and humidity while trekking through a rugged forest on relatively flat land.

3. You do not flinch in the face of flying bugs, ticks, gnats, ants or spiders, and will not falter in the face of a dead snake (screaming in the face of a live one is permitted, but not encouraged).

4. You can endure less than haute cuisine for a few days, and travel on a boat in severely cramped quarters.

5. Seasickness is not a problem for you, nor are you scared of small canoes with bad motors.

6. You are not overly allergic to bees or bug bites and are prepared to return with arms and legs eaten up by mosquitoes.

7. You like mud.

8. You can handle intense, frequent rain.

9. You know how to psych yourself to withstand "green overload," fear of the unknown, and that kind of squishy, moldy feeling that comes from being rained on and not being able to change your clothes immediately.

Dedication

To the spirits of the rainforest:
May they teach us to cherish each other and the planet.

Contents

Important! A Word About Money v
Should I Go To The Amazon? ix

AMAZÔNIA
Introduction.. 1
A Bird's-Eye View...................................... 3
Facts, Myths & Legends................................. 5
History 8
The Indian Issue 18
    Open Letter From A Yanomami Indian............... 26
A Quick Rainforest Tour 29
What's What: A Guide To Fauna & Flora................. 34
Future Of The Forest 65
    A Healing Pharmacy by Dr. M. C. Meyer 65
Voices From The Amazon................................ 73
    A Shaman's Apprentice: Interview with 73
    Dr. Mark Plotkin, Ph.D............................
    Amerindian Initiation Into Sacred Science 85
    by Dr. M. C. Meyer...............................
    Where Are The Fruit Trees? by Dr. Trish Stanley 103
Culture 115
    Cuisine... 115
    Festivals....................................... 122
    Handicrafts..................................... 123
Options For Travel 125
    Fly-Fishing 126
The Amazon Survival Kit 132
Where To Go In Amazônia
Santarém 138
    History... 139
    A Bird's-Eye View 140
    Sights.. 141
    Excursions...................................... 144
    River Cruises 146
    Lodge Expeditions............................... 149
    Where To Stay 149
    Where To Eat 150
    Nightlife 152
    Shopping.. 153
    Hands-On Santarém 154

Belém 158
   History 158
   Bird's-Eye View 159
   Sights 160
   Excursions 169
   Where To Stay 173
   Where To Eat 174
   Nightlife 177
   Shopping 178
   Hands-On Belém 180
Manaus 183
   A Bird's-Eye View 185
   History 186
   Sights 187
   Beaches 190
   Museums 190
   Jungle Excursions 193
   Cruise Packages 194
   Riverboat & Jungle Touring 195
   Excursions 196
   Where To Stay 197
   Where To Eat 204
   Nightlife 207
   Gay Manaus 208
   Shopping 208
   Hands-On Manaus 210
Alta Floresta 215
   Culture 216
   Where To Stay 218
   Hands-On Alta Floresta 218

THE PANTANAL
   Introduction 221
   A Bird's-Eye View 221
   History 225
   Culture 227
   What's What: A Guide to Fauna & Flora 232
   Options for Travel 246
      Lodges 246
      Botels & Boat Cruises 250
      Independent Travel 251
   Pantanal Survival Kit 252
  Where To Go In The Pantanal
   Cuiabá 256

A Bird's-Eye View 257
Sights 257
Museums & The Zoo. 258
Where To Stay 259
Where To Eat 260
Nightlife 261
Shopping. 261
Healers. 262
Hands-On Cuiabá 262
Chapada Dos Guimarães 266
History. 267
A Bird's-Eye View 267
Sights 268
Where To Stay 271
Where To Eat 272
Shopping. 273
Healers. 273
Hands-On Chapada Dos Guimarães 274

CONTACTS & MORE
Specialty Tours 277
Travel Agencies & Tour Operators. 280
Ocean Line Cruises 281
Health Kit For The Tropics 285
Books & Films 293
Books 293
Films 298
Selected Discography. 300
Language 306

Maps

Amazônia & The Pantanal 3
The Pantanal 222

*"When it's noon in the Amazon and your motor
has just died, the only thing to do is smile."*
Pamela Bloom

AMAZÔNIA

"The Amazon is the last unwritten page of Genesis."
Euclides da Cunha, geographer and novelist

"Imagine if the people in Amazônia decided in the next decade not to treat the places they lived in as a commodity but as a sacred place."
Ailton Krenak, Krenak Indian

"Amazônia is simply nothing more than a piece of paradise embedded in Brazil, in which entangled together are preciousness, exuberance, fascination, mystery and beauty – all ingredients of the unbelievable!"
Alvarina Miranda de Alemida, Amazonian Magistrate and Indigenous Activist

"How do I convey the scent of wet forest, as ineffable as a mixture of crushed herbs?" Loren McIntyre, photojournalist

To travel through the great Amazon River region is a nature experience you will never forget. The innate wisdom of the forest – its voluptuous beauty, the life-and-death dramas of millions of species – are realities that will literally enter your bones as you tramp through the rainforest, cruise down the tributaries, or raft over rapids. The Amazon is about challenge, and ever since the first explorers set foot on the banks of the continent, the dark, mysterious rainforest has inspired countless numbers to sacrifice life and limb for a little excitement and the promise of treasure.

These days, of course, travel through the Amazon need not be life-threatening, though it's still exciting, unpredictable and full of challenge. Despite all the recent political controversy, there's still a lot of poetry left in the rainforest: the liquid rustle of treetops, the elusive shadows of animals, the cries of unseen birds. But for most travelers, the most memorable part of a jungle adventure is the people – the locals who toil day by day in the jungle; *caboclo* fishermen who live like Indians along the river shores; old ladies who have fled to the jungle to escape city violence; little girls who paddle to school every morning and brush their teeth in the river. There are also Indians, those living on protected reservations, and others trying to survive halfway between "civilization" and tribal security. Add to that botanists, biologists, and scientific photographers who are trying to capture the miracle of the ecosystem. And finally, there are the gold miners, rubber tappers, ranchers, and industrialists – all, in their own way, attempting to bend the will of nature to their own commercial desires. A circus of cross-purposes, yes, but no matter what one's political allegiance is, each "jungle" person you meet will only add to your understanding of what the Amazon rainforest is – a fragile paradise.

Traveling through the Amazon is not for couch potatoes, and you may have to do some solid soul-searching to see if you'll make a good candidate. (The *Should I Go to the Amazon?* quiz will separate the gnats from the no's.) The best way to indoctrinate yourself is to rent a few videos (*The Emerald Forest, Arachnophobia, At Play in the Fields, Medicine Man*) or dive into travel-adventure narratives and novels that will let you feel the thrills without the thorns. Some of the best books are *Tales from a Shaman's Apprentice* by Mark Plotkin, *Running the Amazon* by Joe Kane, *The Cloud Forest* by Peter Matthiesson, *Amazon Beaming* by Petru Popescu, *Amazônia* by Loren McIntyre, and (for laughs) *Holidays in Hell* by P. J. O'Rourke.

A BIRD'S-EYE VIEW

Maybe it was all those Tarzan movies, but to most people the phrase "The Amazon" has come to suggest a vast, humid jungle. Technically, "The Amazon" refers only to the river itself, including more than 1,000 tributaries that stretch some 4,000 nautical miles from the Atlantic Ocean to its source, Lago Lauricocha, high in the Peruvian Andes. Resembling a large funnel, the Amazon flows in a Y-shaped system into which its headwaters, the **Negro-Branco,**

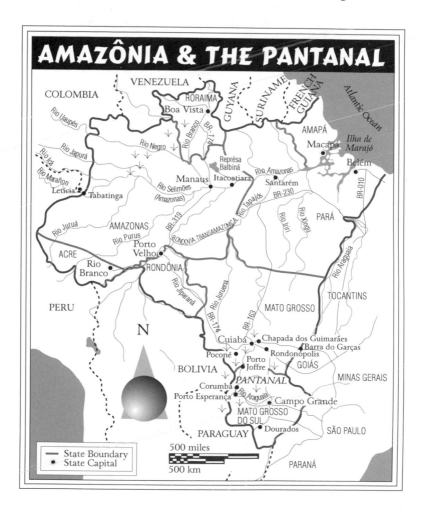

from the northwest, and the **Madeira**, from the southwest, converge. When the main trunk reaches the Brazilian border, it turns into the **Solimões**, a so-called "white river," dense with silt and microorganisms, until it meets the darker and clearer **Rio Negro**. Long a point of fascination among visitors, the "dark" and "light" rivers run parallel for several miles without mixing. They finally blend, forming the pale-brownish Amazon, which empties into the Atlantic. The term *Amazonas* refers to Brazil's largest state (of which **Manaus** is the capital), which is part of **Amazônia**, a vast basin of forests and wetlands occupying about half of the South American continent (75% of Brazil, as well as parts of Venezuela, Ecuador, Peru, Suriname, Guyanas and Colombia). Within Brazil itself, Amazônia embodies the states of Amazonas, Acre, Rondônia, parts of Pará, Mato Grosso and Maranhão, and the territories of Roraima and Amapá.

FACTS, MYTHS & LEGENDS

Facts

- Amazônia is the world's largest rain forest, covering 2.5 million square miles.
- The Amazon River system is the planet's largest body of fresh water.
- The Amazon Basin, with 6 million square kilometers of river and jungle, is the world's largest in terms of volume. The basin holds two-thirds of the world's flowing water.
- Besides the Amazon River, there are 1,100 tributaries (17 of which are more than 1,000 miles long). All totaled, there are 48,000 miles of navigable rivers.
- The Amazon River is at times so wide (up to seven miles) that you can't see the other side of the shore.
- The flow of the Amazon River is 12 times that of the Mississippi.
- There are 15,000 known animal species, 1,800 species of butterflies, 1,200-2,000 species of fish, four types of big cats and 200 mosquito species. One-quarter of the world's 8,600 bird species live in the Amazon.

Myths

- **Myth 1: Western fast-food chains like McDonald's are responsible for the destruction of the forest because of their use of cheap tropical beef.**
  Forests in Brazil are primarily cleared for pasture. Amazonian cattle ranching has no connection to the Western penchant for hamburgers. In the Amazon, cattle are used as an excuse for claiming land that often has little to do with the profitability of ranching. In fact, the Amazon is a beef *importer*.

□ **Myth 2: The Amazon's worst destroyers are small settlers and peasants who set fire to the forest for small-scale agriculture.**
In truth, large-scale landowners and corporations are the biggest destroyers of the forest, often setting massive forest on fire to clear land for ranching and mining.

□ **Myth 3: If cultivated properly, the Amazon forest could feed the world.**
This myth is left over from the 19th century. Amazon soil, due to its monocultural system, is most often poor and requires vast sums of fertilizers and insecticides to yield suitable crops. According to present-day scientists, if a vast array of agricultural techniques are utilized, including agroforestry and the exploitation of areas of fertile soil, it is conceivable that a large population could actually survive by living off the forest.

□ **Myth 4: The Amazon Basin is full of plants, not minerals.**
The Amazon Basin is loaded with mineral reserves, 97% of Brazil's bauxite reserves, 49% of manganese, 77% of its atanho and 60% of its kaolin. The Amazon has the world's largest iron ore deposit, and also produces gold and oil.

□ **Myth 5: Nobody lives in the forest.**
As late as a Census Bureau report in 1985, it was generally believed by the Brazilian public that there were no people in the Amazon forest. In truth, there are over two million people, including Indians, rubber tappers, river dwellers, nut gatherers and herb collectors who inhabit the forest.

Legends

Legends and superstitions seem to lurk behind every plant or animal in the Amazon jungle; don't hesitate to ask locals about their folk beliefs.

□ Among the most "enchanted" of jungle beings are *botos*, or dolphins, who are thought to transform themselves at night into white-suited cads and seduce young virgins. It's even said that *botos* are particularly attracted to the scent of menstrual blood – a folk belief so powerful that girls often refuse to bathe in the river during their periods.

☐ The **japiim**, an Amazonian bird, also enjoys a notorious reputation. Legend has it that in the early days of the jungle, the japiim had a very beautiful voice, which secured him a place in heaven right next to God. One day he came to earth and tried imitating the songs of the other male birds. When he started attracting all the females, their enraged spouses told him to get lost or reap the punishment. Desperate, the japiim turned to the bees for help, who allowed him to make his nest right next to theirs. As such, you can always find a beehive near the nest of a japiim, whose song is often mistaken for that of other birds.

☐ The mystical origin of the **lily pad** is particularly evocative. Once a beautiful but ambitious girl named Arari wanted to be just like the moon. She tried climbing a great mountain to reach it, but finally jumped to her death from despair, falling into a glimmering lake. The moon, who had a bigger heart than most imagined, took pity on the girl and decided to transform her into a part of the forest. Hence was born the lily pad, which is formed from a blossom that sinks to the bottom of the river, then resurfaces.

HISTORY

Conquest Of The Amazon

"With eyes wide open,the conquistadors lived in a lucid and endless delirium."
Jean Desola

A billion years ago there was no South America, not even an Amazon jungle. Over one single planetary landmass called **Pangea**, seas simply advanced and retreated; the only life forms were bacteria and algae. What would eventually become known as **Amazônia** (today called the Brazilian and Guianian shelf) were merely the two highest points of land – massifs of ancient gneissic and granitic rock that formed a V-shaped flank. Almost 280 million years ago, as Pangea broke into north and south sectors, Amazônia became a vast inland sea opening to the Pacific. Some 150 million years later, the area called **South America** began to disconnect from **Africa**, and drifted westward, giving birth to the **Atlantic Ocean**. Then, a mere two to four million years ago, the Andes heaved themselves skyward, breaking through the soft hills of the two "shields" and initiating a flow to the Atlantic. Sediment and sand from the weathering massifs created a diverse basin floor, what is today termed *terra firme* (the solid floor of the forest). During the Pleistocene Era, some 1.6 million years ago, the forest itself, with its tall slender trunks, tangled canopy, and leaf-littered soil finally emerged into being.

Some scientists believe that the first humans arrived in the Amazon some thirty thousand years ago as they fled the advancing ice cap over the Bering land bridge. At that time Amazônia must have seemed a warm inviting refuge in contrast to the cold, empty highlands that offered little sustenance. Most assuredly, the first inhabitants encountered luxuriant plant life, copious fish, manatees and giant turtles, which they heartily consumed. Most likely, these early native tribes were also hunter-gatherers, living off the fruits of the jungle and practicing the slash-burn technique of shifting agriculture that is still used in the region today. By the time the first Europeans arrived in the late 15th century, there were probably around six million native people scattered all over Brazil.

Since the moment the New World was sighted, however, the Old World marched in mercilessly to conquer, subjugate and exploit;

neither human nor animal nor plant life were spared. **Christopher Columbus'** 1942 discovery of the Americas opened Pandora's box, and in 1493, a papal decree was already divvying up the world between the two major powers: **Portugal** received control of all territory east of the longitude line running through Cape Verde Island, while **Spain** retained the western half. No less than a year later, the Treaty of Tordesillas moved this division 370 leagues to the west, giving Portugal even more control of a vast space that seemed to do nothing more than protect the Crown's claims in the South Atlantic. Once word of a new continent had been spread, hungry adventurers – from Spain, Britain, France, Holland and the Holy Roman Empire – all stood poised to raise forts and missions along the confluences of rivers and significant tributaries.

What first inspired the early European explorers to traipse wearily through a hot, humid forest, was myth, pure and simple. Four centuries ago, the most prevailing legend was that of **El Dorado**, a tribal chieftain whose wealth was so vast that he supposedly tattooed his body daily with gold dust. In 1540 **Gonzalo Pizarro**, the brother of the conqueror of Peru, launched an expedition with Ecuadorian general **Francisco Orellana** to conquer the lands of El Dorado and his "Cinnamon Forests" – a huge country so magical that it was rumored to be carpeted with the aromatic spice so beloved back home. The trip itself proved disastrous, but the threat of disease and imminent starvation finally compelled Orellana to break from the main troops and scavenge the jungle with his own party, eventually discovering the mouth of the Amazon.

It's from Orellana's own journal that we first hear reports of a fierce tribe of women warriors who once a year invited male adults to participate in their mating rituals. In fact, Orellana even used the fact of sighting them as the primary excuse for never returning to Pizarro's troops. Whether Orellana's sighting was real or merely a mirage born of jungle fever has never been determined, but the tale, soon bloated from retelling, came to inspire thousands of booty-seekers called *bandeirantes* to follow in his footsteps. Later, Spanish scholars dubbed the region and its massive river "The Amazon," in honor of the women warriors in Greek mythology who removed their right breast so they could more skillfully use a bow and arrow.

From the earliest expeditions, **Jesuit priests** made their way across the ocean to subjugate the so-called native "heathen" and establish the sovereignty of the Church under the Crown's blessing. With little or no sensitivity to the integrity of native customs and spiritual traditions, the missionaries systematically stripped the subjugated tribes of their lifestyles, indoctrinating them, however feebly, in Christian mores, and sometimes even dressing them up as Europeans. Jesuit priests could often be astute observers, as was one **Father Cristobal de Acuñã**. His eight-month sojourn from Quito to Belém in 1638-9 with the Portuguese explorer **Captain Pedro Teixeira** provided a wealth of insights. In his journal published under the title of *A New Discovery of the Great River of the Amazons*, Father Acuñã wrote glowingly of 10-foot jungle giants, dwarfs no bigger than tender babies, and humans with their feet turned backwards (the latter is still accepted as belief by forest people). As was the tradition at the time, Acuñã even had his own female warrior sighting, claiming the fierce tribe of women he had glimpsed had not released their weapons until they were confident of their male visitors' peaceful intentions. More importantly, Acuñã recorded the fishing and hunting customs of various tribes and nearly identified the principal resources of the region, which remain to this day its most viable products.

Jungle travel, however, was not limited to men. One of the greatest tales of grit and courage was that of the 18th-century **Madame Godin**, who faithfully waited in Quito for over 15 years for her husband to return from a French scientific expedition. Upon hearing reports of a rescue party on the upper Marañon, she staunchly set off over the Andes with her two children, brother and several servants in tow. When she finally arrived at the village where she expected to find her husband, she discovered it had long ago been decimated by smallpox. She was forced to continue on foot. Soon everyone except Madame Godin died from starvation or exhaustion. After nine days struggling alone in the jungle, Madame Godin was found by Indians, who took her to the mission village. Finally, after a 19-year separation, this courageous lady, who had been to "green hell" and back, was finally reunited with her husband in Belém.

By the end of the 17th century, the Amazonian pie had been carved and served – Spain and Portugal being the only real contenders. By the mid-1700s, scientists had caught up with adventurers, and in one of the most memorable expeditions a team of botanists, astronomers and respected intellectuals set forth down the Amazon River with **Charles Marie de la Condamine**, a brilliant young French mathematician who was determined to prove whether the earth bulged at the equator and flattened out at the poles, or vice versa. Regarding Amazonian lore, La Condamine's insights were invaluable; he found Indians (the **Omaguas** on the Solimões River) who pierced their ears, used *cahuchu* (a form of rubber) to make unbreakable vessels, and partook enthusiastically of a hallucinogenic powder made from the *cucupá* plant. More fantastical, however, were his claims that famed women warriors of the region had finally moved and settled in the heart of Guiana.

As new discoveries of land and sea were made, navigational maps began to shed some of their mystical references, to be replaced by freshly drawn demarcations and boundaries. Perhaps the most momentous geographical discovery was that made by **Alexander von Humboldt** in 1800 of the **Casquiare River**, following the flow from its confluence with the **Rio Negro** to its starting point on the **Orinocco**. That this waterway was truly navigable was earth-shattering news in the Industrial Age, since it provided the access to expand trade on both sides of the Atlantic.

The 19th-century travelers who visited Amazônia were a different breed from the elegant noblemen and the rough-and-ready *bandeirantes* who preceded them. Spurred by public enthusiasm, crowned heads of various European countries organized scientific expeditions led by some of the greatest minds of the century. In a hotbed of novelty like the tropical forest, botanical discoveries could often seem like magic. For example, in the 1840s, **Robert Schomburgh** stumbled upon a gigantic water lily, some six feet across, that looked like an enormous pie plate. It was testimony to his political loyalties that he christened the flamboyant green, pink and red flower *Victoria regis*, in honor of the British sovereign Queen Victoria.

Two of the most dedicated Amazonian scientists were **Henry Walter Bates** and **Alfred Russel Wallace**. When they first met to share their jungle fever, one was an apprentice to a hosiery manufacturer and part-time bug collector, and the other was a schoolteacher. The **British Museum** commissioned the pair to compile a collection of insects and plants – three pence for every specimen received in "salable condition" – and in 1848 they arrived in Belém, eager but penniless. The entomologist Bates, who would become the founder of protective mimicry, walked through the forest looking like a human pincushion, collecting over 114,712 species (8,000 of which were new to science). Wallace, determined to solve the problem of the origin of the species, spent four years on the Rio Negro, later contributing significantly to Darwin's resolution of the matter before the Linnaean Society in London. And yet as analytical as he was, Wallace could also wax poetical about Amazonian wonders, as his journal attests: *"The beauty and brilliance of this insect are indescribable, and none but a naturalist can understand the intense excitement I experienced when I at last captured it. On taking it out of my net and opening the glorious wings, my heart began to beat violently, the blood rushed to my head and I felt more like fainting than I* *have done when in apprehension of immediate death. I had a headache the rest of the day..."*

Scientific glee, however, didn't succeed in warding off the massive threat of jungle life. Humboldt's own adventure became a living hell when the crocodile grease he daily smeared on his body failed to do its job. Bates himself was attacked by innumerable insects and blood-sucking bats, almost overcome by malaria, and was even robbed by an Indian assistant who left him shoeless for an entire year. He even reported being deeply unnerved by the screeching of howler monkeys and other mysterious jungle sounds, like the clanging of iron, that woke him in the middle of the night. Perhaps the most poignant description of frustration came from the English botanist, **Richard Spruce**, who wrote in his diary: *"Save willing Indians to run like cats or monkeys up the tree for me... the only way to obtain the wildflowers and fruits was to cut down the tree, but it was long before I could overcome a feeling of compunction at having to destroy a magnificent tree, perhaps centuries old, just for the sake of gathering flowers."*

Rubber Boom & Bust

It was **rubber**, not gold, that transformed the face of Amazônia. Contrary to popular belief, the rubber trade in Amazônia started long before Charles Goodyear accidentally discovered rubber in 1839. As early as 1750, **Dom José** was sending his boots to be waterproofed in Pará, and by 1800 Belém was exporting rubber shoes to New England. The famous Amazonian rubber boom, however, was actually fueled by the debt peonage of isolated *serengueiros* (rubber tappers) and *caboclos* (backwoodsmen), who sold their balls of latex to the trading post for a mere pittance. It's been estimated that in 1850 there were 5,200 rubber workers; by 1912 when the boom peaked, no less than 190,000 Brazilians were tapping 88% of the world's rubber. During these giddy years, **Manaus** became a boom city, its wealth concentrated in the hands of about 100 men – so-called "rubber barons" – who drank Hennessey brandy, dined on Irish linen, and built palatial homes. Soon, electricity was installed and the first tramway in South America initiated. The crowning glory in Manaus was a massive customs building modeled on that of New Delhi, prefabricated in England, and shipped to Brazil piece by piece.

In 1870, a young Englishman named **Henry Wickham**, in cahoots with the Royal Botanical Gardens at Kew, conspired a scam that would totally puncture the rubber future of Brazil. Working with the **Tapiu Indians**, a "detribalized" tribe, Wickham raced to gather hevea seeds at their prime, smuggled them past customs with a large dose of charm, then nursed them across the Atlantic to Le Havre, where a special chartered train delivered them to Kew. From there, the seedlings were rushed to Ceylon, where in the swampy fields of Sri Lanka, the few that survived came to form the basis of the great rubber plantations of Malaysia. In a mere 24 years the trees matured, outstripping the Amazonian market, which totally burst in 1923. With frightening speed, tycoons, speculators, traders and prostitutes departed from the tropics, leaving behind decayed palaces, a boarded-up opera house, and cobblestones full of weeds. The only beneficiaries were the native people, who would be left in peace for another half-century.

It was only a natural extension of the modern pulse that the 20th century would witness the veritable "pushing back of the jungle" or at least, determined attempts to tame it. In 1912 one of the region's most illustrious visitors was **Theodore Roosevelt**, who voyaged down the basin's southern tributaries. A river discovered on that mission, first called **River of Doubt**, was later renamed **Rio Roosevelt**. Traveling intimately with local tribespeople, Roosevelt developed a greater respect for native intelligence than some of his predecessors, but his attitude toward wildlife, alligators in particular, was hardly allied to conservation. He wrote: *"The ugly brutes lay on the sandflats like logs... it is good to shoot them. I killed half a dozen and missed nearly as many – a throbbing boat does not improve one's aim."*

Even as late as the 20th century, tall tales were still coming out of the Amazon, and the tallest came from **Percy Fawcett**, a retired English army colonel sent to the upper Amazon in 1906 to resolve the overlapping claims of Bolivia and Peru arising from the rubber boom. Fawcett fueled rumors of anacondas swallowing cattle whole and picking men right out of canoes at night. He even claimed he once smelled a penetrating fetid odor emanating from one. *"Probably its breath,"* he wrote, *"which is known to have a stupendous effect."* Fawcett also complained about the anacondas' melancholy wails at night – a phenomenon never proven by scientists. Certainly a colorful figure, Fawcett never carried a radio during his expeditions, which didn't seem to matter since several spiritualists, including his wife, claimed to be in psychic contact with him. Ever in search of the lost city supposedly discovered by the Portuguese explorer Francisco Raposo in 1754, Fawcett was eventually found dead near the mouth of Xingú River, most likely murdered by Kalapalo tribesmen.

Only a few years later, in 1927, another world-famous American would also leave his mark in the Amazon. A most curious jungle saga began when automobile mogul **Henry Ford**, after researching sites around the world, decided that the **Tapajós Valley** was the best region in which to cultivate rubber trees on an international scale. (Curiously, no Brazilian had ever given it much thought.) Capitalizing on a contract that awarded him 110,000 kilometers of forest for 50 years, Ford actually transported an entire prefabricated city into the jungle, complete with all the modern facilities. The community, appropriately named **Fordilândia**, was light-years ahead of other cities in the Amazon Basin. Workers reaped the benefit of free housing, electric lights, running water, telephones, schools, theater, nurseries, orchards and the best equipped hospital in the state of Pará.

What Ford didn't anticipate was an explosion between the social classes, including an outbreak (known as the "**saucepan breaking incident**") when the native workers demanded back their old food – beans, manioc flour and cachaça – instead of the protein-enriched American rations. The real downfall of the enterprise, however, was attributed to a fungus known as **leaf blight** that devastated the plantation. In 1934, the same venture was attempted in another tract of land 60 kilometers south of Santarém called **Belterra**, but it, too, was attacked by the fungus, as well as by **caterpillar blight**. Today, ecologists understand that the root of the disasters was **monoculture** – the lack of any other species that could balance the delicate ecosystem of the jungle. After 27 years the Ford company finally gave up the enterprise and "presented" the government of Brazil with the remains of the two communities for $250,000 (a loss of more than $20 million). Today, Fordilândia, though still inhabited, resembles a ghost town, with its deserted sheds surrounded by picket-fences and crumbling houses– a mere shadow of the imposing structures erected during the twenties and thirties.

From the time when hunting/gathering natives first followed the massive prehistoric mammals into the lowlands to the bitter end of the rubber boom, the commercial attitude toward the Amazon's resources was almost exclusively extractive. The concept of making an investment was entirely foreign – the *modus operandi* was simply to take, pick up, or dig out what was there. Henry Ford was actually the first major investor to encounter serious nationalist opposition, culminating in the 1940s when **Gétulio Vargas** seized power of the federal government and urged the nation away from Atlantic shores toward occupying – even exploiting – their own vast space. The military coup of March 31, 1964 threw the country into a right-wing dictatorship for more than 20 years, which stabilized the nationalistic tendencies of the Brazilian Army. Although conflicting attitudes about Amazônia did surface at this time, the prevailing notion continued to favor the concept of occupation as a principle of national security.

In the face of threatening foreign domination, especially from North America, the government initiated the building of the **Carretera Marginal**, a Trans-Andean highway that opened up rich new lands on the eastern slopes of the Peruvian Andes. In 1965 President Castello Branco implemented **Operation Amazônia**, which included the issuance of several laws that would inspire development. Although Brazilian leaders in the late sixties more or less ignored the idea of small-farmer colonization in Amazônia, **President Juscelino Kubitschek**, as part of his 50-years-in-5 progress program, began a road to serve as the east-west counterpart of the Belém-Brasília Highway, linking the town of Cuiabá in Mato Grosso with Porto Velho. It was down this road, overgrown with jungle the moment it was completed, that pioneers valiantly trod, jumping off their trucks to clear jungle with their own hands and building primitive shacks along the highway. As a result, when a mineral rush of cassiterite and tin ore was discovered in 1952, **Porto Velho** became an overnight boom town, creating the kind of rough-and-ready frontier that made the jungle itself seem an "oasis of tame." A sign on the classic Porto Velho Hotel said something about the usual clientele: "Spit neither on the floor, nor on the walls, nor beside the bed."

Highways have been the bulldozers of primitive culture and in 1970 **President Emilio Garrastazu Médici**, shocked by the poverty in the Northeast, decided to build a road that would provide refuge in the fertile Amazônia. The **Trans-Amazonian Highway** ran east to west from the town of Marabá on the Tocatins River, due south of Belém, clear across to Benjamin Constant on the Solimões at the border with Columbia. An additional plan was to settle one million families at selected spots along the highway, where it felt there was good farming. Despite promises of easy credit, health, education and technical assistance, substantial obstacles arose: malaria epidemics, poor soil and lack of social integration. Soon, larger commercial enterprises superseded concern for the individual migrant, and by the mid-1970s cash development for largescale enterprises pushed the rate of Amazonian deforestation sharply up as virgin forests were cleared for cattle grazing.

The Last Great Gold Rush

In 1979 **Gensio Ferreira de Silva**, the owner of a two-bit cattle ranch, discovered that his scrubby grasses and skinny cows were astride the most important gold strike in Amazonian history. By 1985, over 500,000 prospectors were toiling up and down the vast pits dug into the mountainside – a frightening tableau of human mudmen right out of a Breughel painting. The federal government, worrying about the potential danger of so many unruly men near Carajás, the largest iron development in the world, finally sent in troops. In May, 1984, the military occupied the **Serra Pelada**, led by Major Cúrio, who, descending from his helicopter, flashed his magnum and cried, "*The gun that shoots loudest is mine.*" Though the military occupation brought a much needed health center, bank, post office, telephone line and wholesale government store, the *garimpeiros* (gold miners) staged a rebellion down the Bélem-Brasília Highway, eventually forcing the government to retreat.

The last two decades of Amazonian history have erupted in an openly bloody conflict among all inhabitants of the forest as goals, life-styles and environmental concerns have collided in cross-purposes. As international environmental organizations, backed by the warnings of eminent international scientists, have protested to preserve the rainforest in the face of irrevocable planetary destruction, those who live and work in the forest have struggled to maintain their own individual lives. At least in the Brazilian segment of the Amazon forest, this socioeconomic dilemma must be understood against the backdrop of the enormous financial crisis threatening the entire country. The overweening inflation, along with natural disasters, such as severe droughts in the Northeast, forces Brazilians to eke out a living in any way they can. Consequently, many who become gold miners (the life of which is difficult, dirty and often without payoff), are forced to do so because of even worse circumstances back home. Nevertheless, their merciless invasion into government-sanctioned Indian reserves have increasingly erupted in violent clashes with tribal peoples; the deadly pollution of their rivers and streams with mercury continues to devastate not only wildlife, but human life.

One of the most prominent names in recent Amazonian activism was that of **Chico Mendes**, a poor rubber tapper born in Seringal, Cachoeira. Illiterate until the age of 18, he gained most of his worldly education from listening to Radio Moscow, Voice of America and the BBC Portuguese Service; when he finally learned to read, he discovered the price of rubber was being outrageously exploited by the *seringalistas*. As ranchers and settlers came to clear the rainforest, the rubber tappers were forced to leave, but Chico refused, urging his fellow workers to unionize. With no knowledge of Gandhi or Martin Luther King, Mendes hit upon the idea of nonviolent resistance, and in 1976 organized a series of human standoffs that prevented work crews from using their chainsaws. In 1989, Indians joined the lobby in favor of extractable reserves set aside for use by rubber tappers and gatherers of nuts, fruits and fibers; today over a million acres of forest have been preserved. In December 1988, after returning home from a labor-organizing trip, Mendes stepped into his backyard and was fatally blasted by a shotgun at close range. The 31-year-old son of a rancher who hated Mendes finally confessed to the murder, but general opinion conceded that the father, **Darli Alves**, was to blame. In 1993, father and son escaped from a loosely secure prison in Rio Branco, Acre, and have not been found. Following the murder of Mendes, Hollywood descended on his family and his wife, Ilzamar.

The 1990s will be decisive for Amazônia. Before the dawning of the third millennium, planners and policy-makers must decide whether the world's largest remaining area of tropical rainforest will follow much of Africa and Asia down the path of irreversible destruction, or whether the resources for this vast region will be harnessed for the benefit of Brazilian society and the world as a whole. The Brazilian portion of the Amazon Basin occupies two-thirds of the entire region's 4.2 million square kilometers. By the end of 1988, it was estimated that 12,000 square kilometers of forest, equivalent to the size of Belgium, had already disappeared from the face of Amazônia; that is to say, 12% of the total forested area.

For more information on the history of the Indians in Brazil, see the following chapter.

THE INDIAN ISSUE

The real history of the Amazon region belongs to its native peoples – a subject that deserves not a few paragraphs, but tomes (among the best of which are *Red Gold* and *Amazon Frontier: The Defeat of the Brazilian Indians*, both by John Hemming). When the first explorers arrived in 1500, there were six to nine million Indians in the Amazon Basin; today there are less than 200,000. Like all North American Indians, those of the **Amazon Valley** descended from **Paleo-Mongoloids** somewhere between 30,000-70,000 years ago, having crossed from Siberia to Alaska on a temporary land bridge over the frozen Bering Strait. Their features, still apparent today, were clearly Mongoloid, with high cheekbones, black eyes and an epicanthic fold of the eye; characteristically, they had no beard, eyebrows or eyelashes. Indeed, so strong was their connection to the East that many of their artifacts – blowgun, penis sheath, and panpipe – as well as the habit of chewing lime or ashes with a narcotic, can be found in indigenous Asian cultures. The Indian peoples who entered the New World were already accomplished hunters, used to stalking game, mastodons, mammoths, ground sloths, giant cats and even camels. As they moved slowly (one kilometer a year), it took these tribal people 40,000 years to reach the rainforest, gradually evolving from nomadic hunters to farmers. As they fanned out and became isolated, four major linguistic groups developed – **Tupi Guarani, Jí, Karib** and **Aruak**. A few of the most remote tribes like the **Trumai** and **Yanomami** invented languages that have no relation to others spoken in the Amazon Basin, or, indeed, anywhere else in the world.

When Pedro Alvares Cabral, the Portuguese explorer credited with "discovering" Brazil in 1500, first set foot on soil in what is now the state of Bahia, the native people who shyly met his boat were friendly enough, even generous in their innocence. They were Tupi-Guarani, short and bronze-colored, with long, straight black hair. The Tupis tended toward cannibalism (they ate the first bishop to arrive in Bahia), but they were also true masters of tropical survival. They decorated themselves with intricate body designs made from the juice stains of plants. Although they were not equal in culture to the sophisticated Aztecs of Central Mexico, the Mayas of Yucatan and Guatemala, or the Incas of Peru, they did develop a strong tradition of spirituality, in which the *pajé*, or medicineman, communed with nature spirits and prescribed herbal medicines culled from the forest. Though these *pajés* were known to be deeply visionary, they were unfortunately unable to foresee their own imminent destruction by white invaders.

Today the characteristic multi-ethnicity of the Brazilian people – a mixture of Portuguese, African and Indian roots – owes its origins to those early white colonists who mixed freely with the Indian population. Among the first white men the Indians encountered were often *degredados* – exiled criminals ordered to live among the Indians and learn their language. Since Portuguese women were excluded from the first colonies, the conquerors, who were already accustomed to the dark-skinned beauty of the Moorish, African and Asian females, soon discovered a veritable paradise. Some men, like

Diogo Alvares (renamed Caramuru), sired an entire village of miscegenational offspring with Indian women. As a result, a new race quickly appeared – the *mameluco* or *caboclo* – a blend of European and Indian blood well adapted to the physical demands of living in the tropics. In return, the Indian taught the white man the best methods for farming and hunting, introduced him to new crops like manioc, and showed him the best way to pass the night in the tropical heat – in a swinging hammock.

Beautiful Amazonian features on a young girl.

As ship captains bartered with Indians, exchanging trinkets for brazilwood, a temporary truce between them was enjoyed. But soon enough, **Jesuit missionaries** set out to convert the "heathens." At the same time, the arriving colonists, supported by daring explorers, were rounding up conquered Indians as candidates for forced labor. In time, the Jesuits would severely antagonize the Court with their viewpoint that the enslavement of Indians was contrary to Christian intent, but the fathers themselves managed to violate the native population's basic human dignity. Institutionalized in missions called **Reductions**, the Indians were forced to adapt to a spartan routine of work and worship. (One Amazonian historian suggested that the transition to the rigid discipline of the Reductions was made easier for the Indians by the fact that, long before the Jesuits' appearance, flagellation had played an important part in their religious and erotic lives.) Nevertheless, though some Indians became acculturized, most either rebelled or ran away, or, more frequently, succumbed to death when their immune systems proved too weak to fight even the slightest Western cold germ. Fortuitously, in 1769, under pressure from business interests, the **King of Portugal** threw the Jesuits out of the Amazon. In the 20th century, the **Salesians**, who are Roman Catholic, are still making converts. This is also true of the nondenominational Summer Institute of Linguistics, begun in the 1930s to teach indigenous populations to read and write in their own tongue, with the ultimate goal of translating the New Testament. In 1977, **FUNAI**, the federal Indian protection agency, canceled the Salesians' permit under suspicions they were a CIA front.

The Jesuit missionaries were only one form of unnatural control. What truly undermined the Indian was *cachaça* (sugarcane liquor), happily provided by the *bandeirantes* (rough-and-hardy pioneers), who soon discovered it was the only way to press-gang the natives into submission. The tribes that escaped such ignominy, including the rape of their women, the theft of their children, and a legacy of incurable alcoholism, retreated deeper and deeper inside the forest.

Journals of the early scientists very often revealed the depth of Western prejudice toward meeting "uncivilized" tribes. In 1854 Alfred Wallace Bates, an entomologist, discovered an unspoiled village in Marari, what he called "a miserable little settlement of Mura Indians." As he inspected the 20 slightly built "mud hovels," he discovered several women who were employed cooking a meal. As he wrote in his journal: *"Portions of a large fish were roasting over a fire made in the middle of the low chamber and the entrails were scattered about the floor, on which the women with their children were squatted. They offered us no civilities; they did not even pass the ordinary salutes, which all the semi-civilized and savage Indians offer on a first meeting. The men persecuted Penna for cachaça, which they seemed to consider the only good thing the white man brings with him."*

Although many scientists held similar disdain, one group of 19th-century Portuguese explorers, armed with awe, talent and respect, did make a momentous journey through the Amazon, compiling an invaluable collection of illustrations documenting the life of Indians and fauna. A doctor of natural philosophy, **Alexandre Rodrigues Freire** and his companions were artists from the Royal Natural History Collection in Lisbon. This team covered over 24,800 miles in nine years, painting and drawing a variety of Indian tribes with such magnificence that their work became true journalistic art.

By depicting the everyday tools and weapons of the Indian, Freire and his men came to deeply respect the ingenuity of the tropical Indian who had learned how to extract and use the best from the plant world. Through trial and error, the natives had learned that reeds could be used for arrows, that toxic vines beaten in the water could daze fish, that the seeds of the *Beixa orellana* smeared on the skin could give it a bright red color; and that resins or infused leaves, when ingested, could produce hallucinogenic symptoms.

A typical story of native development and demise is that of the **Xavantes**, once one of the proudest tribes in Amazônia. At the turn of the 18th century, 2,000 *bandeirantes* led by **Captain Moto** settled on the **Rio das Mortes**, in the heart of Xavante country, winning confidence by giving gifts. One day, however, a *bandeirante* killed a Xavante, and the next day, the entire settlement of pioneers was wiped out. In 1765, the governor of the state of Goiás sent a man named **Tristão de Cunha** to reestablish friendly relations; he eventually persuaded a few thousand Indians to settle closer to the city of Goiás, but when the Indians managed to eat all the food in the city; the order was given to Portuguese troops to drive them away. Half the Xavante community was killed; the rest retreated behind the Rio das Mortes and killed every white man in sight. They remained an isolated and feared tribe until 1842, when they allowed an anthropologist to study them.

Of the 260 Amazon tribes that were identified by studies in 1900, only 143 remain today, totaling about 250,000 individuals. In western Amazônia, several villages of **Amahuaca Machiguenga** and the head-hunting **Jivaros** live well back from the main river. In Acre, along the Peruvian frontier, are the **Mayoluno**, and some of the more remote **Mayarunas**, in Amazonas the **Macu** and several other small groups. In Rondônia live the **Caheça-Secas**, some of the **Surui**, and some of the **Cintas-Largas**. In the northeastern state of Pará, there are three **Kayapó** and one **Kreen-Akroare** village and several in Mato Grosso. (This is only a partial list.)

In the second half of the 20th century, the onslaught of "progress" has continued to devastate the native population. The construction of the two highways – the Transamerica and the Cuiabá-Santarem– dislocated over 10,000 families and disease nearly wiped out the tribes of the Araba, Parkana, Kreen Akroare and Txucurramai. In 1969, three Brazilian-born brothers named **Orlando, Claudio** and **Leonardo Villas-Boas** persuaded the government to create a national park for the **Xingú** tribe, whose lands during World War II were invaded by the construction of military airstrips connecting

Amazonian Indians caught at the crossroads of civilization outside Manaus.

Rio to Manaus. Entranced by Indian life, the Villas-Boas brothers not only fought for native rights, but also managed to live with various tribes for many years. (Today the **Xingu National Park** covers 12,000 square miles in Mato Grosso and houses 18 tribes living traditionally.) Until they succumbed to old age and malaria, the brothers fought valiantly to secure the government's protection of the area from the rubber tappers, journalists, hunters, industrialists, missionaries and even anthropologists. In 1971, however, builders overrode public sentiment and drove Highway BR-080 right through the park.

Today Brasilian Indians are championed by FUNAI, the successor of the Indian Protection Service founded in 1910 by **Colonel Candido Mariano da Silva Rondon**, who himself was part Indian. The organization tries to mediate conflicts between Indians and *civilizados*, rubber tappers and nut gathers, skin hunters, *caboclos*, gold miners and ranchers. They also contact remote tribes, explaining they are citizens of a country named Brazil and set up posts from which medicine, tools, clothing, fishing lines and other products are distributed. A controversial agency which is always dodging fire from all sides, FUNAI itself was implicated several years back in the wholesale slaughter of Indians by dynamite, machine guns and sugar laced with arsenic.

In the late fifties and sixties, contact with some native tribes proved to be tragic. A telling example is that of the **Kreen-Akroare**, a primitive, semi-nomadic group on a territory of 5,000 square kilometers southwest of the Air Force base at Cachimbo in the state of Pará. The Kreens are mostly hunters, who until lately couldn't even make pots or manioc bread, and had never seen a gun. In 1957 their traditional enemies, the **Menkranoti**, armed with shotguns, attacked their villages; by the time the defenseless Kreens could flee, 15 of their tribesmen were dead. In 1961 the Kreens killed **Richard Mason**, an English botanist working near the Air Force base. Six years later, a two-engine Air Force plane flew over another village. Kreens took aim and brought the plane down, killing 20. In 1968 they were again attacked by Menkranoti, who killed 25 of them, and when the Kreens approached the air base with corpses in hand, the commander panicked, fired shots in the air, and sent them running back into the forest. A year later, as two highways were being built through their lands, the Villas-Boas brothers, who had been nominated for the Nobel Prize for setting up the Xingú National Park, spotted some Kreens on the other side of the river. The brothers had other natives with them, who shouted to the Kreens in 14 different tongues, but the latter disappeared from sight.

In 1970 Claudio Villas-Boas returned bearing gifts, waiting for one year in the clearing without moving. Finally in February 1971, three Kreens appeared to Claudio and Orlando, who threw down their guns, paddled over and embraced them. One tribesman gave a speech for an hour, despite the fact that nobody but his own tribe understood him. Later, being showered with gifts, 40 more Kreens showed up with women to dance. Claudio, knowing full well that the highways would kill the Indians, didn't finish the "contract" by entering their village, but later, another *sertanista* did. By 1972, 40 Kreens had died of pneumonia contracted from road crews building the Cuiabá-Santarem Highway, now only two kilometers from their village. Soon the tribe was reduced to eating urucum seeds, from which their red body paint is derived; a picture in Rio's *Globo* newspaper showed a devastatingly sad photo of several starving Indians on their knees begging for food.

In December 1974 only 70 Kreens were left; three-quarters had been killed by pneumonia, flu and malaria. The Villas-Boas brothers arranged for them to move to Xingú National Park, where the Kyabi agreed to give them their village of Prepuri, along with some plantations. The Kreen had much to learn, however, like how to fish with hook and line instead of arrows and to cook manioc, instead of eating it in its poisonous raw state of toxic prussic acid. Eventually, they had to move in with the Txucurramai because other Xinguano tribes would visit and eat their food, trying to intermarry and dominate them. They finally moved to a third village. In January 1976, only 64 remained, with only 10 women able to bear "socially acceptable" children.

In the last decade, Indian activism and international press coverage reached a record high. During the 1980s Indians began to display political self-determination when a group of Txucurramai from the Xingú National Park held the director of the park hostage, demanding demarcation of their land, severed from the rest of the park by Highway BR-080. For a short term, a Xavante Indian chief even enjoyed his own seat in **Congress**. In February of 1989 in the town of **Altmira**, over 500 Indians from Amazon tribes gathered together with international environmentalists to protect the Brazilian Eletronorte's Xingú Dam Scheme. Few who were present (or saw the documentary film) will ever forget the sight of a Kayapó woman brandishing a machete at Eletronorte's CEO and fervently crying, *"Do you think we are so stupid that we don't know what your plans are for us, for this forest?"*

In the last few years, a Kayapó Indian chief – **Paulinho Paiakan** – has emerged as a worldwide icon of native power. Touted as Brazil's wealthiest Indians, the 5,000 Kayapó Indians earn millions of dollars a year in royalties from **gold** and **mahogany reserves** in central Brazil. In recent years, the chief solicited the support of the rock star Sting, who founded **The Brazilian Rainforest Foundation**. He even managed to sell brazil-nut oil to **The Body Shop**, an international cosmetic chain. But on the eve of a \$40 million movie to be made of his life (not to mention numerous international awards), Chief Paiakan was abruptly arrested when the 19-year-old white Portuguese language tutor of his children accused him of rape. In Brazil, a national furor erupted, turning environmentalists against feminists (the latter enraged that rapists rarely are punished in Brazil) and raising the ire of the Indian rights movement.

Among the most tragic native situations at the present moment is that of the **Guarani-Kalowá** of Jaquapiré, Mato Grosso, whose legally demarcated lands are being invaded by ranchers. As such, finding themselves without land and forest, considered the center of their religion, the 250 Guarani pledged to commit collective suicide if they were expelled from their homeland. In 1992 the area they occupied was declared their permanent possession by an act of the Minister of Justice, but ranchers persist at ever-increasing rates to clear the forest for pasture. As a result, many have already committed suicide, and in 1994 and 1996, their chief passionately addressed conferences sponsored in New York by the Amanaka'a Network, where she pleaded for international assistance.

Perhaps the most highly publicized tribe in the last few years has been the **Yanomami** tribe. The largest indigenous tribe in the Amazon, the Yanomami until the 1980s was one of the most isolated tribes in the Amazon. Today, approximately 9,000 Yanomami live in the northern state of Roraima and another 12,000 across the border in Venezuela.

The name "Yanomami" means "human being." They live in small villages, grouped by family and kin in one large communal dwelling called a **shabono**. This disc-shaped structure inside an open-air center plaza is an earthy version of their gods' abode. They hunt and fish over wide ranges and tend large gardens, cultivating the forest.

A deep-seated animism lies behind the Yanomami's sacred traditions, a belief that the natural and spiritual world are a unified whole; nature is the source of all, and therefore sacred. They believe that their fate, and the fate of all people, is inescapably linked to the fate of the planet. Destroying the environment is, to the Yanomami, tantamount to suicide.

In the 1980s, the isolated lands of the Yanomami were mercilessly invaded by miners in search of gold, diamonds and tin. In 1989, **President Sarney** brought national attention to the plight of the Yanomami Indians when their 9,000-square-kilometer reserve on the border between Brazil and Venezuela was overrun by 40,000 gold miners bringing sickness and disease. Military troops were sent in, but the army simply refused to subdue 45,000 burly *garimpeiros* (gold miners), even though they were poisoning the Yanomami River with mercury and attracting new strains of malaria. Today, some 70% of the Yanomami reservation has already been confiscated by mining concerns, but even more tragic has been the physical devastation brought on by constant contact with the outside world. The first case of AIDS has already been reported.

In recent years a devastating massacre of a Yanomami community brought international attention to their plight, but the

Children of the Amazon region face an uncertain future.

government failed to act in retaliation and attempts were made to discredit first-hand reports. Tribesmen who escaped the massacre were loathe to testify for fear of reprisal. Today, international organizations have started to galvanize support, one of the most active being the New York-based **Amanaka'a,** who raises money for the Yanomami Health Project (also supported by Oxfam and Medicine San Frontiers). Presently the leader of the Yanomami, **Chief Davi Kopenawa Yanomami,** has emerged not only as an international spokesman for his people, but as a spiritual voice for the planet. In 1988 he received the Global 500 Award from the United Nations for his efforts in preserving the environment. (See his *Open Letter* below.)

At the moment, however, the fate of the Amazonian Indian is trapped between a rock and a hard place. Despite valiant efforts by activist groups (including the Rainforest Action Network, the Rainforest Alliance, and others), the future of Indian tribes will more than likely depend on how well they can self-empower themselves and span thousands of years to step into the 21st century. Eternal protection in this age of the ubiquitous bulldozer will more likely prove itself to be a pale fantasy. Perhaps the only future is one of studied cooperation, a possible program, which is put forth in a later chapter called *The Future of the Forest.* Beyond threat of disease and loss of cultural identity, what the native population of the rainforest stands to lose in the inexorable forward push of "progress" can hardly be grasped by dimmed Western eyes. Perhaps the best answer was given by a Waura chief named **Taxapuh** who, when asked how he could return to his village after having been exposed to the wonders of São Paulo (he had been flown there for an emergency hernia operation), replied with stunning conviction:

"How can you breathe this foul air or sleep with these noises? How can you eat this food made to have tastes not its own? Why would men want to have intercourse with these women who are afraid to be women and hide themselves and cover their eyes? Who are these men with guns who stand in the paths of the village?"

(For more about indigenous Brazilian tribes, see *A Pantanal Indian Speaks Out* in the Pantanal section, see page 228.)

Open Letter From A Yanomami Indian

The chief spokesman for the Yanomami tribe, Davi Kopenawa Yanomami was born in the 1950s in the Yanomami region of Toototobi, in the state of Roraima, in the northern Amazon rainforest. His father-in-law initiated him into training as a shabori, or shaman. He first became active in the Western world as an interpreter for FUNAI. In 1974 he helped form the **Commission for the Creation of the Yanomami Park** (CCPY), an independent organization that has been instrumental in fighting for the demarcation of Yanomami territory.

Currently, CCPY and Davi are constructing **The Demini Health Outpost,** a clinic that will serve the 10,000 Yanomami in Davi's home region, and are campaigning for a second outpost in Balawau village.

Dear Friends,

I am Yanomami. We Yanomami used to think that Whites were good to us. Now I am seeing that is the last invasion of indigenous lands, all land. Foreigners are teaching Brazilians to destroy our place. The same thing happened to our Indian brothers and sisters in America.

The government is not respecting us. It thinks of us as animals. We have the right to speak out. Foreign people help us, but if we ourselves don't do anything, they cannot help. If we send them letters, they will put pressure on our government to change something.

The government knows that we are the oldest Brazilians, that we were born here. Our name is known to the world. We know nothing about money, shoes, clothes and few Yanomami undestand what is happening. The government got us by surprise.

The government does not know our customs, our thoughts. We too do not understand the government. All it understands is money. Our thought is the Earth. Our interest is to preserve the Earth, or there will be sickness for all the people of Brazil, not only the Indians.

The rivers, fishes and the forest are asking for help, but the government doesn't know how to listen. It says we will all die of hunger if mining is closed off. But, if they stop mining, we will plant macacheira (manioc), banana, taioba, papaya, sugarcane, pupunha and no one will die of hunger anymore. We Yanomami want our land. We do not want our customs to die. Until today, we have not lost our tongue and our Earth. That is why we fight. We Yanomami are dying of diseases that Indians don't know, brought by miners from the outside. Pajé (medicine men) can cure Indian illnesses, but white people's sicknesses, we cannot cure.

In our land, there are many mountain ranges. In the mountains live the Xapuri and Hekura, the spirits of nature. Between the mountains are the Xapori's path, but no one sees them, only the pajé knows about these connections. The mountain ranges are sacred places, where the first Yanomami were born, where their ashes were buried. Our elders left their spirits in these places. We've been using these spirits for years, they will never end. We call on the Hekura to cure our ills. Omam left these spirits to defend the Yanomami people. Omam gave their origin to everyone, to the whole world. This is why it's important to preserve the mountain where his spirit lies. We want to preserve these places in order not to finish with our history. I'd like white people to understand this ancient story, so they respect it.

Davi Yanomami

The letter is reprinted with permission from Amanaka'a's Amazon Network Newsletter, Update #1, Summer 1993.

UP CLOSE TRAVEL ALERT: Travel to Indian reserves is expressly prohibited by the Brazilian federal government, except for special projects, which must receive permission from FUNAI and other agencies. Isolated tribes have no resistance to flu, pneumonia, measles, tuberculosis or even the common cold. A sneeze from a tourist could wipe out a whole tribe. Furthermore, when a village is seized with an epidemic, the food-gathering system itself breaks down and more actually die of starvation than the original disease. Please take caution.

A QUICK RAINFOREST TOUR

To the uninitiated, the jungle looks like so much green mess, but actually the terrain that runs through the Amazon River System is extremely diverse. Some soils are deeply fertile, others approach bleached sand; along the Negro River, the vegetation is stunted, whereas in southeastern Pará, the forest, with its purplish-red soil, abounds with wildlife. There are also huge areas of wetlands and large expanses of savannah.

The rainforest itself grows in distinct layers, a natural hierarchy formed by the access (or lack of access) to the sun. Most of the activity take place in the luxuriant **canopy**, 100-130 feet above the forest floor, where plants compete for sunshine and where the majority of animals and birds live. Above the canopy poke the trees that form the **skyline** of the forest. A poorly defined middle layer of **understory** merges with the canopy, hosting a variety of epiphytes – plants that derive moisture and nutrients from the air and rain, but live on the surface of other plants. About 50 to 80 feet above ground spreads a tangle of seedlings, saplings, bushes and shrubs. On the forest floor, plant life is limited because the thick vegetation of the canopy blocks out all but one or two percent of available sunlight. Ants and termites live here among the scattering of leaves and decaying plant matter.

Types Of Forest

There are three types of Amazon forest: *várzea*, or floodplain, regularly flooded by the rivers; the *igapós*, which are occasionally flooded; and the *terra firme*, generally unflooded land that forms the majority of the surface area. Much of the terra firme is high forest, where animal life exists as much in the canopy as on the ground. When the forest is destroyed, the land turns to scrub since its fertility is bleached out.

Why Preserve The Forest?

Rainforests are intimately tied to **global weather conditions**, and their preservation helps prevent the global warming trend known as the **Greenhouse Effect**. **Deforestation** causes up to 30% of all human-produced carbon dioxide to the atmosphere, as well as unknown amounts of methane and nitrous oxide gases that exacerbate global warming and threaten the quality of life worldwide. Rainforests also provide a **natural defense** against hurricanes, cyclones and typhoons, absorbing the punch of howling winds and preventing storm tides from eroding beaches.

The products that come from the rainforest are part and parcel of our daily lives. As a fantastic natural pharmacy, the forest is home to thousands of medicinal plants that can be turned into antibiotics, painkillers, heart drugs, and hormones. The National Cancer Center in the US has identified 3,090 plants as having anti-cancer properties – 70% of which come from the rainforest. Other products that can made from the forest's resources without destroying it range from cosmetics to automobile tires.

Tropical forests also provide the planet with much of its **biological diversity**. Every species that lives there is a living repository of genetic information, i.e., the building blocks of life. If the food chain that binds them together in a complex web of relationships is disturbed, it is not possible that humankind itself could survive. At the very least, we'd be facing the future with a shrunken world, a hostile climate, and a genetic base vulnerable to mutations.

Last but not least, the forest is home to millions of **indigenous people** who have known no other way of life for thousands of years. Within their memory banks is a trove of natural wisdom, including how to use plants medicinally, that can never be duplicated once they pass from the earth. With very few exceptions, the forced relocation of indigenous forest people in the face of the bulldozer has invariably spelled disease, despair and death.

ECO ALERT: Mercury Contamination

The amount of mercury released by Amazon gold miners has been reduced by 50% in the last decade, but travelers should still be aware of the possibility of severe contamination. Scientists are now finding out, however, that avoiding mercury contamination is not as simple as avoiding sites of contamination. Contrary to general expectation, the most dangerous spots are not strictly limited to gold mining properties.

In recent years, the main culprits of contamination in Brazil have been, of course, **gold miners**, who use about 60-80 tons of liquid mercury each year to bind together fine particles of gold they dredge up from the country's rivers. In order to purify the gold, mercury is added and then burned, a process that releases mercury vapor into the atmosphere. Any excess liquid mercury escapes into the river with the sluice water.

Scientists have long determined that mercury vapor hangs in the atmosphere, then is blown and dispersed by the wind until it eventually falls back to earth with the rain.

According to **Geraldo Guimarães**, a biochemist at the **Center for Tropical Medicine** in Belém, scientists are only now learning how far the vapor travels and what happens when it falls.

And far it is traveling. Scientist **Bruce Forsberg** and his colleagues at the **National Institute for Amazon Research** in Manaus have discovered high levels of mercury contamination at sites where there has been little or no gold mining. Other researchers have found high levels of contamination in fish in Canadian and northern US lakes – far from contamination sites.

Research also showed that mercury vapor seems to stay aloft in the atmosphere long enough – up to six months – to spread fairly equally over the planet. That means that, theoretically, Chicago could receive as much mercury fallout as Manaus.

Even more alarming is the fact that while most soils contain clay that binds the mercury, some thinner, sand-like soils, including the humus-covered Amazon soils, rapidly leach the toxic heavy metal back into rivers and lakes.

Mercury levels in fish and sediments are highest in the rivers and lakes that border those thinner soils. These rivers are usually marked by their dark colors, caused by the leaching of organic material from the soil as well as by mercury.

It is along those black rivers – especially at hot spots near mining camps – that mercury poisoning cases are surfacing in Brazil.

Wolfgang Pfeisser, an environmental biophysicist at the **Federal University of Rio de Janeiro**, claims that people showing up at special clinics in Santarém and Rondônia are manifesting two to three times the level of safety as specified by the World Health Organization – a contamination level that exceeds 150 parts per million.

Surprisingly, the majority of patients are not gold miners, but fishermen who live downstream from mining camps and depend on the fish they catch to feed their families. Other victims are gold-shop workers who inhale the escaping mercury vapor.

In an interview with a *Chicago Tribune* reporter, Pfeisser said it has been extremely difficult to determine just how many people are being poisoned by mercury. Symptoms of mercury contamination are many and varied, and some mimic malaria and yellow fever.

Unless a doctor is specifically trained to spot mercury poisoning, a patient may be misdiagnosed.

According to Guimarães, mercury as a contaminant is most insidious, not only because it lingers without bio-degrading into the environment, but because it also can be passed from mother to child in utero.

As such, travelers to the Amazon should be careful where they fish for food and should avoid lingering for any length of time at a gold miner's camp.

Is Eco-Tourism Kosher?

Many eco-conscious travelers ponder whether joining the rank and file of tourists tramping through the rainforest will ultimately endanger it further. Truly in Brazil, the word eco-tourism has become the buzz word for the 1990s, though in many cases it's merely a marketing device referring to any outdoor adventure, be it beach, mountain or forest. There are a select number of travel agencies and operators, however, who are deeply dedicated to preserving not only the forest (as well as other ecosystems), but also the country's native peoples. Among these are **Expeditours** in Rio, **Lago Verde Turismo** in Santarém, and **Ariaú Jungle Tower** outside Manaus. However, generally in Brazil these days the prevailing philosophy is that eco-tourism actually serves to preserve the forest by giving its residents another way of making a living besides cutting down trees. Of course, one need only imagine the trash and debris that could clog the mighty Amazon and its tributaries when gum-chewing, cigarette-smoking, beer-drinking tourists hit its banks. The nightmare needn't happen, however, if each traveler takes responsibility for his or her actions.

How Not To Destroy The Rainforest

The best way to preserve a rainforest is to travel with a conscience. Here are some Do's and Don'ts for visiting natural reserves.

- □ Don't give food to the local animals. It disturbs their immune systems as well as the ecological balance of the environment. It might also be dangerous.
- □ Don't hunt.

- ☐ Don't destroy trees or break branches.
- ☐ Don't throw litter.
- ☐ Don't kill or mistreat fish, birds or other animals, except in self-defense.
- ☐ Don't make a fire.
- ☐ Do have a reliable guide who respects the environment.
- ☐ Do not cross into Indian reserves without special permission from FUNAI (nearly impossible to get). This law protects native peoples from unwanted diseases and cultural disturbance.

Federal law prohibits the killing of dolphins, turtles, alligators, *peixe boi* (cowfish), tortoises, birds and capybaras. Any animal that lives in the forest belongs to the state. Anyone caught red-handed by authorities is sent to prison for three months to a year. You do not want to languish in a Brazilian jail for any amount of time.

WHAT'S WHAT: A GUIDE TO FAUNA & FLORA

When you first set foot in the forest, you may be sorely disappointed. The only animals you may see are ants, mosquitoes and a few transparent butterflies, surrounded by the sounds of crickets and cicadas, which create a kind of permanent background buzz. Unlike the zoo, animals don't exist in the forest to be seen – many are extremely well **camouflaged**. To really make a write-home-about sighting, you should be prepared to stay for weeks or months crouched silently behind a bush. Simply, camouflage is the art of jungle survival, developed over millions of years. Bits of bark, green leaves, dead leaves, all sorts of leaf fragments with holes in them, broken twigs, even pendant-like drops of water have been imitated by the animal kingdom.

And forget looking for an elephant, rhinoceros, hippopotamus, zebra or giraffe in the Amazon. They don't exist. The largest animals, which are all actively hunted, include **tapirs, peccaries** (both the collared and white-lipped species), **brockets** (about the size of the European roe deer), and the larger **marsh deer** in the southern border regions. **Raccoons, coatis, American potto**, and the lesser-known **olingos** belong to a family completely native to the Americas. **Armadillos, anteaters** and **tree sloths** are the last survivors of the *edentates*, a very ancient South American order of mammals. Cats like the **jaguar, puma** and **ocelot** have become rare. Scientists still ponder why there were many species of large animals throughout the neotropical region during the tertiary period, the last representatives of which died out during the Pleisticene era. One theory is that the advent of the first humans led to their extinction when they were not able to defend themselves.

To experience the Amazonian animal world firsthand, it's best to hire a boat for a day trip and be paddled or pooled down one of the numerous tributaries by a reliable and knowledgeable guide. It's best to choose a river that not only flows through the forest, but also has side streams and areas of still water covered with floating plant life.

If you are lucky, one of the first visitors to trail behind your canoe may very well be a **sweetwater dolphin**, which can grow to a length of 10 feet. This species is nearly blind and has to find its way through echo-sounding. Other species to inhabit the Amazon River and its tributaries include creatures that originated in the ocean, among them the **sweetwater ray**, whose sting is greatly feared, as well as **herrings, garfish, croakers**, and even **sole** – all of which have their sweetwater equivalents.

One of the great icons of the river region is the **black vulture**. Whenever a dead creature is washed ashore, you will inevitably see these large black birds, the size of hens, gathering to scavenge. Often hanging about such kills will be another bird, whitish with dark wings, called the **yellow-headed caracará**, which belongs to the family of vulture falcons. **Turkey vultures**, which are also prominent, are among the very few birds that have an excellent sense of smell.

It is usually at the confluence of a small tributary with a larger one that animal and bird life become more varied. South America is the richest region in the world, not only in fish species, but also in birds. (According to Michael Goulding, a leading scientist for the Rainforest Alliance, the Amazon Basin is home to at least 950 bird species – a tenth of the of the world's entire avian biodiversity, and almost half are endemic, to be found nowhere else.) Unfortunately, you will see few of the larger birds as their populations have been decimated by hunters. Among those prized by hunters are the **Orinoco goose**, the **muscovy duck** (which is the original form of the South American domestic duck), the **Brazilian teal**, and the **whistling** or **tree duck**. Other birds hunted enthusiastically are the larger **herons** and **storks**, as well as **spoonbills** and **squacco cranes**. (Note: many of these birds are described in the chapter *Fauna in the Pantanal*, page 39.)

The Central American jacaná, the fin foot and the sun bittern are all that remain of prehistoric birdlife and ought to be protected as effectively as possible. These loners stand in contrast to the huge groups of other neotropical varieties, such as **hummingbirds** (233 species), **nuthatches** (211 species), **tyrant flycatchers** (315 species) and **tanagers** (179). The **Central American jaçaná**, with its incredibly enlarged feet, is splendidly adapted to moving about in the perpetually swaying undergrowth of floating plants in the calmer areas of the rivers. One special bird is the **fin foot**, which is a very good diver, capable of swimming on the water like a small duck, while carrying its young on its back. The **soul bittern** resembles a small heron, but with a slightly longer tail, easily recognized by its tranquil flight and the large red-brown markings on its rounded wings.

One favorite riverbank bird that you should search for is the **kingfisher**; there are many species in Amazônia. They all boast similar colorings, but are different in size. **Swallows** are omnipresent, flying around the river looking for food, or perching on sticks and roots that emerge from the water. A relative of the woodpecker, called a **swallow wing**, looks like a black and white swallow, but breeds in small holes in the earth near the riverbank. Another frequent inhabitant of the bush growth along the riverbank is the **anis** or cuculiform – a bird that resembles the European blackbird, but with a bigger beak. It builds its own nest in which several females lay eggs that they hatch together.

A little extra luck is needed to see the **hoatzin**, also known as the gypsy hen – sociable hens that live in bushes and trees along the riverbank in small flocks. Before seeing them, you may hear a kind of wheezing snore or panting. They feed exclusively on leaves, which they prepare for eating and store in their large crops, since their stomachs are very small. When the crop is full, they become top heavy and while sitting the breast has to be supported on the ground; hence, the species has developed a special callus for that purpose. Fossil remains date the hoatzin back to the Oligocene era, about 40-50 million years ago; an astonishing discovery was made recently, claiming that the hoatzin was related to the cuckoo.

In the woods along the riverbank, you might encounter a fowl-like bird, which attracts attention by making a loud cackling noise. This call sounds as if it were made by one solitary bird, but is, in fact, the joint call of a male and female couple. Their sounds are so well matched that they produce a perfectly regular *u-du-aa-ra-ku* motif, incessantly repeated. This is the call of the **chacala**, a smaller member of the neotropical Cracidae family, to which belong a number of large and very shy forest birds, such as the **helmeted curassow** and the **razor-billed curassow**.

Lizards abound in Amazônia; most frequently found on the riverbanks are the **ameivas** that belong to the *telid* family. Among the larger ones are the **red tegu**, which can grow to 1.4 meters (4.3 feet) and the **caiman lizard**, which reaches up to 1.25 meters (3.9 feet). The caiman lizard leads a largely aquatic life in flooded woodland and is able to crack open the hard-shelled water snails with its strong jaw filled with stone-like teeth. Another even more multiform family of American lizards is that of the *iguanid*, the most common species being the **iguana**, a typical denizen of the riverbanks, which can grow up to 3.2 meters (10 feet). They often lounge for hours on branches overhanging the riverbanks and let their horny legs dangle.

Butterflies in profuse quantities are one of the great blessings of the Amazon; their appearance in swarms always seems somehow magical. They are to be found everywhere in Amazônia; both on riverbanks and in cultivated areas. Many like to light on damp sand in order to suck up the moisture, and whenever possible, they choose places where mammals have left urine. In some spots, vast swarms can be seen hovering closely together for hours. Most of the butterflies are whites (*Pieridae*), but some are exquisitely colored flambés and swallowtails. Sometimes, near a group of white and yellow butterflies, a small group of brown-black species will gather together. During the mating season, butterflies spread their wings and fly around each other in pairs so that the various species may be readily identified by the color patterns peculiar to them. In Amazônia, many varieties take their nourishment from rotten fruit, carrion, excrement and urine traces.

Butterflies swarm magically around a canoe.

Pollination in the Amazon occurs not so much through insects but through birds. The king of pollinators is the **hummingbird**. The largest are the size of a swallow and the smallest no bigger than a large bumble bee. All are accomplished in the art of hovering, capable of suddenly interrupting their whirring flight and lighting quietly on a blossom to extract small insects and nectar. Most hummingbirds make an identical round each day, during which they visit in exactly the same order the individual flowers they have come to know. If you are taking photos, note the exact time you see a hummingbird so you can catch him at the same time the next day.

Basking in the riverbanks will most likely be some **crocodiles**. The **black caiman**, which can grow to a length of almost five meters (15 feet), has long since been exterminated in settled areas because of the value of its skin. Also along the banks can be spotted **water tortoises**.

At about five o'clock in the evening, the **capybara** (water hog) leaves the thicket that protects him from the daytime heat. Since they are not hunted for food in Amazônia, capybaras are more frequently seen and they are not shy. The capybara is the largest rodent that has survived to date, reaching a length of 1.25 meters (4 feet). Another large rodent is the **paca**, which is hunted everywhere for its excellent meat.

Towards evening (or at dawn), you may see **parrots**, particularly the **aratinga**, which fly strictly in pairs, though in large groups. (I made a particularly wonderful sighting of this phenomenon at Ilha dos Papagaios, a little outside Belém, where green parrots fly off at dawn en masse squawking loudly). As nightfall approaches the croak of frogs intensifies into a bass symphony of grunts and gurgles. Included in the voicing are the croaking of the large **tree frog** and the bark-like hooch of the **giant piping frog**. The large number of piping and tree frog varieties is one of the things that gives the amphibious fauna of South America its distinctive flavor; of almost 2,000 kinds of frogs in the world, nearly half live in the tropics. In Amazônia, the lightly colored and sometimes very poisonous **dendrobatidae**, also known as the colored tree frog or tree climber, should be avoided.

Sometimes at sunset, you can hear the loud sound of the **six o'clock cicada** and, shortly afterwards, the first **bats** will leave their daytime hiding places. You also might glimpse the archenemy of the bat, the **bat hawk**. Many bats eat insects which they catch during flight, while others are fruit eaters or take nourishment from flowers. There are even fishing bats which, through an echo-sounding process, can so perfectly analyze the waves made by fish on the surface of the water that they can catch them by reaching out and seizing them with their elongated legs. South America is also the home of the **vampire** bat, a medium-sized sized bat that feeds on blood. They land at night on a sleeping mammal and approach it on all fours. With razor-sharp teeth, they make a small, painless incision and then lick the blood that flows from the wound. Cows become greatly weakened by this nightly blood loss, and there is also the possibility of rabies transmission. Dogs usually notice bats immediately and bite them to death. (Ethnobotanist Mark Plotkin in his fascinating book *Tales from a Shaman's Apprentice* recalls a true Stephen King moment when his native guide had to cut the head off a vampire bat which had sunk its fangs into Mark's ankle!)

As twilight settles in the forest, swallows also awaken. The **paraque**, or **cacho**, is particularly common on cultivated land and near rivers and makes a loud *o-to-hu* sound. As darkness descends you may also hear a more melodious birdsong that consists of four or five descending notes on the scale, almost human sounding, from the common **potoo**, or as the Brazilians call it, *ayamama* ("mother of the dead") or *urutau*. In native folklore, the melancholy sound is thought to be a lament.

Waking up in the jungle at dawn is delicious. You will wish you had brought your cassette recorder to tape the symphony of wake-up calls that stir from the innermost recesses of the forest. As the sun rises it's probably a good idea to check your hammock for any creepy crawlies that might have snuggled up with you.

Fauna

Mammals

Anteater

Tamandua retradactyla
TAMANDUA-DE-COLETTE *or* TAMANDUA-MIRIM
Confined to Central and South America, the aboreal anteater has no teeth, a long snout and tubular mouth, and a tongue that can be extended for some distance. It prefers to scavenge during the night, sleeping most of the day. It feeds on wild bees, ants and termites, which it finds in hollow tree trunks or on the ground. The anteater opens hard clay mounds with its powerful claws, drawing in the ants with its sticky tongue, and then swallowing them whole. The Great Anteater, about eight feet in length, lives on the ground; the Lesser Anteater, about half the size, lives in trees, aided by a prehensile tail, which helps it swing through branches. The anteater's biggest love is honey.

Jaguar

Pantera onca onca
ONÇA
The jaguar is the western hemisphere's biggest cat, weighing up to 250 lbs. Many Indian tribes claim they are descended from jaguars; in the Andes, the animal's pelt is still used for ritual dancing. In 1967 Brazil instigated a hunting ban which failed to save half a million felines that were slaughtered for pelts. Today, the two-to-three kittens in each litter are more heavily protected by international controls. Up close, a jaguar in pose is exquisite, with an apparent calmness of expression. Although it seems to be a heavy animal, its

suppleness and elegant bearing are easy to perceive, yet it is vicious enough to successfully attack a crocodile.

Giant Otter

(Brazilian giant) otter
Pteronura brasiliensis
This otter is a very rare species, confined to the slow-moving rivers and streams of South America. Also called saro and margin-tailed, the otter has completely webbed feet and usually brown fur with a large whitish chest patch. Marvelous swimmers, they sleep at night in dens tunneled into the riverbanks and spend days diving beneath floating vegetation to catch fish. Giant otters may eat up to three tons of fish a year, competing with fishermen who attack them with machetes and rifles.

Early explorers claimed their canoes were surrounded by barking otters. Extremely playful, they enjoy sliding down a steep bank of mud, but occasionally fall prey to jaguars, pumas and anacondas. In 1971 they were declared protected, and are now among the 23 most endangered species in the world.

Manatee

Trichechus ingunguis
PEIXE-BOI
Called *peixe-boi* or cowfish, this aquatic mammal weighs up to 1,300 pounds and reaches 10 feet in length. Since manatees are slow swimmers, they are easily caught as food by *caboclos* (backwoodsman), who harpoon them at night, then suffocate them by stuffing wooden plugs into their nostrils when they surface to breathe. Commercial exploitation started in the 16th century with the arrival of Europeans, who fried manatee meat in its blubber, then shipped it home. After an era of tanning hides, the manatee became an endangered species. Today, the Brazilian conservation agency INPA employs *caboclos* to capture manatees who have been abandoned so that they may be brought back to their laboratories for renewal.

Maned Wolf

Guará
CHRYSOCYON BRACHYURUS
With legs like a pelican, the *guará* is not a wolf, but a dog so tall that locals have dubbed it "fox-on-stilts." It is usually golden brow or reddish-brown in color, with black stripes on its legs. A solitary, non-threatening creature, the *guará* roams at night and mainly feeds on rodents. Today, the *guará* is a vanishing species, since it

unconsciously courts its own demise by pausing to look back at pursuers. Its height, however, allows it to see over the tall savannah grasses that cover the expanse of the Amazon.

Puma

Felis concolor
SUCURANA
The puma, one of seven species of smaller cats, is highly adaptable, and roams such habitats as tropical forests and the desert. It is best identified by tracing its tracks in the sand or mud. The puma is noted for its uniformly brown color, in contrast to the ocelot and jaguar. As a couple, the male and female stay together for about two weeks. After a gestation period of 90 days, two or three kits are born, always in very well protected places, such as a cave. The mother suckles her young for three months or more, although they begin to eat meat before they are six weeks old. Around the age of two, they master tracking small animals and become independent, finally leaving the mother.

Sloth

Bradypus tridactylus
PREGUIÇA
The name "sloth" originates from the extreme slowness of this mammal's movement, which results from a very sluggish metabolism. Although slow moving on land, it is a very fast swimmer. It sleeps hanging from a branch on its four legs, its head between its forearms, curled like a ball. Its fur harbors an immense variety of parasites, including two kinds of ticks. The shoots and tender leaves of the trumpet *(cecropia)* are its favorite food. Sloths seldom descend to the ground, and because they cannot walk, they pull themselves along the ground with their claws, thus becoming easy prey for jaguars and other larger animals.

There are six living species of sloths in tropical South and Central America.

Peccary

Tayassu spp.
CATITU, PORCO DA MATA
Few animals that live in the dense forests are as feared as peccaries, whose sharp, knife-edged tusks have forced many a local up into a tree for hours. Also known as the wild pig, this mammal travels about in small groups led by a male elder. The litter generally consists of two suckling pigs that follow the mother a few hours after birth. Peccaries are accustomed to feeding in the morning and

evening and eat various kinds of animals, such as insects, worms, snakes and frogs, as well as roots, fruits and nuts. Frequently, its presence is noted by the peculiar odor emitted by a gland on its rumps or by rooted-up soil.

Amazonian Skunk

Coneptus
FUINHA
A genus of skunk endemic to the Amazon forest, it belongs to the hog-nosed skunk family, named for its characteristically long, naked snout. Its coarse fur is black with a white tail and its body length ranges from 12-20 inches. Like all skunks, it is noted for its offensive odor produced by glands on either side of its anus. Most species exhibit a characteristic warning behavior, such as foot stomping; if the threat continues, the animal turns its hindquarters toward the target and ejects a fine spray of yellow, odoriferous liquid as far as 12 feet. Primarily nocturnal, they feed on rodents insects, eggs, birds and plants. Their litters, gestating from 42-72 days, contain 2-10 young.

Tapir

Tapirus terrestris
ANTA
The tapir, which attains a weight of several hundred pounds, is the largest indigenous land mammal and is much sought after for its meat. With heavy bodies and short legs, tapirs are about six-eight feet long. Their eyes are small, their ears short and rounded, and their snout extends into a short fleshy proboscis or trunk that hangs down over their upper lip. The young of all tapirs are dark brown, streaked and spotted with yellowish white. They are shy inhabitants of the deep forest, or swamps, traveling on well-worn trails, usually near water. When disturbed, they usually flee, crashing through undergrowth and often seeking refuge in water. Their main enemy is man, though in South America it is the jaguar.

Ring-tailed Coati

Nasua Nasua
QUATIS
Related to raccoon-like carnivores, coatis are found throughout South America. Between 29 and 54 inches in length, they have long flexible snouts and coarse gray to reddish-brown fur with light underparts and light facial markings. Early morning or at dusk, alongside grassy marches, or at the edge of the forest, one might glimpse groups of seven to ten females with their tails erect,

searching for food. The males are solitary and join the groups only during the short mating season. Coatis eat birds, eggs, insects and fruit, and they also root in the humus looking for worms and larvae. They tend to love sweets and when thrown some in a group, they fight and squeal over the booty.

Capybara

Hydrochaeris hydrochaeiris
CAPIVARA
The capybara, the largest rodent in the world, looks like a giant guinea pig, and may weigh up to 100 pounds. It lives along the Amazon and its tributaries and is an excellent swimmer and diver. Its flesh, though considered a delicacy, is used for food and is frequently dried for shipment to market; its hide is made into high-quality leather. Often as large as a real pig, it reaches up to four feet in length and can weigh 75 pounds. It sports webbed feet, small ears, coarse brown hair, and no tail. When it snoozes among water plants with just the top of its nose above water, it is not easy to find. Capybaras live on vegetation growing both in and out of the water. Other common rodents found in the region are paca, agouti, spitty rat and a species of squirrels, rats, mice and porcupine.

Deer

Mazama americana
VEADO-MATEIRO
In the Tupi language, deer are generally called *çu-assú*, which means meat, much food, or big game. These graceful deer, also called *suassupita*, belong to the genus *Simplicornis*. Instead of branched antlers, they have single horns, no more than 12 centimeters long (5 inches). They live in the forest, and also like to graze at dawn and at nightfall, sleeping during the day in the dense woods. In regions where hunters seldom go, they don't always run from visitors, and may often come to peer intently at them.

Primates

The darlings of the jungle, monkeys – called *macacos* in Portuguese – are animals with an almost human appearance and social habits. If you have the chance to inspect them up close, you will be thrilled, if sometimes appalled, at their human similarities. Their tails may reach twice their body length and function as an additional hand and point of support. They feed on fruits and insects, and when showered with human attention while in captivity, they can develop intense attachment. (One tiny monkey I saw at the Eco Park in Manaus had become so attached to a park employee that he refused to let go of him.) The large consumption of monkey meat and fur in the Amazon has significantly reduced the population. There are 30 species unique to the region. Among them are the following:

Spider Monkey

Ateles paniscus
MACACO-ARANHA, CUATA
This monkey has a slender body with forelegs shorter than its hind legs. Its prehensile tail is longer than its body and provides mobility and support. It can mostly be found in bands high up in the forest trees. Spiders are thoroughly adapted to life in the treetops and can do more things at one time than a human juggler – hold fruit in one hand, pick up more with a foot, place food in mouth with a second hand, and walk and swing from branches with the other foot and tail. They are known to break off branches and throw them at human invaders. Still, they are gentler than other species. They are the prey of eagles and other predatory animals.

Marmoset

Callithrix jacchus
SAGÜI
The world's smallest monkey, the marmoset is kept as a pet by Indians who wear them in their hair to remove lice. Because of their size and behavior, they often seem more like squirrels than monkeys. They live in troops, climbing up in forest trees, feeding on fruits and insects and occasionally uttering chirping noises. The white-eared marmoset is known for its thick and silky fur and white tufted ears, which make it resemble Albert Einstein. Marmosets bring forth two or three young at a time. One marmoset kept in captivity was noted never to have washed its face, hands, or coat, with one exception: an almost violent obsession to groom its tail, which was twice as long as he was.

Squirrel Monkey

Saimiri sciureus
MACACO DE CHEIRO
Squirrel monkeys are the most common primate in the region; they command the food supply simply because of their numbers. With a black snout, black upper head and white rims around the eyes, it resembles a stuffed toy; the head and short trunk are extremely rounded. Squirrel monkeys live in the same jungle as howlers,

wooly monkeys, spider monkeys and capuchins. This small primate boasts yellow-grayish fur and a black spot around the mouth.

Woolly Monkey

Lagothris
MACAO-BARRIGUDO
This primate has a strong large body and prehensile tail, which helps it to swing playfully though the forest trees. To move along the ground, it uses its hind legs, swinging its forelegs to keep its balance. Woolly monkeys are quite large and are covered with a dense coat of woolly fur. They are gray or reddish in color.

White-faced Capuchin

Sapajou
MACACO-CABLUDO
 This monkey has a stout body covered with rather woolly fur. The head is round and the eyes large and bright. Often it's been described as looking like a little old man as seen through the wrong end of a telescope. Capuchins usually eat insects by examining crevices in trees and withered leaves, seizing the largest beetles and munching them with great relish. This species is very fond of eggs and young birds, and plays havoc with nestlings. Capuchins tend to travel in troops, but scatter when one is shot by a hunter.

Owl or Night Monkey

Aotus vociferans
MACACO DA NOITE
As opposed to other monkeys who are active by day, the owl monkey hides and sleeps in a hollow tree during the day and roams at night in search of insects, small birds and other small animals and fruit. It occasionally utters "cat calls" to herald its coming. A small quadruped monkey with a long, large body and round eyes, it uses its forelegs and feet to propel itself along the ground. Its eyes are particularly noticeable, extremely large and yellowish in color, a condition often developed by nocturnal animals. Their senses are so developed that when a person passes by a tree in which a number are concealed, he or she may be startled by the sudden appearance of a group of little striped faces crawling into a hole in the trunk.

Howler Monkey

Alouatta caraya
GUARIBA-PRETO
The opera singer of the forest, the howler monkey emits cries of such depth and volume that it can be heard from two miles away. It has

a naked face and retreating forehead, with its hair slicked back 50s style. Its body is robust, reaching up to 27 inches with a tail almost as long. Early explorers dubbed it the ugliest monkey in the forest because of its protruding jaw and bulbous eyes. From their perches high up in the treetops, some have been known to scatter urine and dung on passersby. The peculiar screaming voice is produced from an enlarged windpipe. Traveling in troops of four to 35, they communicate with strong gesticulations and a variety of sounds, which includes the deep metallic cluck of the male leader, the wail of a mother, and the squeal of the playing young. A howling group of monkeys can sound louder than the roar of a lion.

Birds

Parrots

Amazona
PAPAGAIO
There is an enormous variety of parrots in the Amazon, from the **red-fronted Amazona**, which is predominantly green, with a red area on its beak and tail, to the **blue-fronted Amazona**, which is predominantly green, with its upper wings colored red. **Chiriri parakeets** are small and green, while **canary-winged parakeets** are green with yellow feathers at the base of their wings.

Parrots vary in length from 3-40 inches, including their tail. The short neck and sturdy body, along with the stout feet and thick bill, give them a bulky appearance. Pointed wings and a long tail are usually found in species that travel long distances. Their green plumage is marked with other bright colors, chiefly on the upper head; the sexes look alike. They live in the rainforests and are difficult to breed. They may become aggressive as well as squawky. Parrots use their toes and hands in manners similar to humans, but their extremely powerful jaws can be quite dangerous. Most are gregarious and noisy, forming small groups. Parrots are monogamous and their courtship techniques have included vocalizations, bill-caressing, mutual preening, head bowing, wing-raising, tail-spreading, and feeding the mate.

Of 81 genera recognized in the 1937 revision of the taxonomy of parrots, the neotropical region (South and Central America) has 28, none of which are found elsewhere.

Toucans

Ramphastidae
TUCANO
Along with the hornbill, the toucan enjoys the distinction of having the largest bill for the size of its body of any bird. The horny sheath, however, is only about 1/30-1/50" thick and the inside is filled with air and a delicate filigree of bone. The beak is used to pick fruit from trees and capture insects. Soft fruit is cut by the serrated edges of the bill, while the smaller morsels are held by the tip of the beak, tossed into the air, then gulped. One species utters a call that resembles the Brazilian word "tucano." One peculiar characteristic is the presence of a ball and socket joint that hinges the tail to the body so that the tail can be bent up over the back. Nearly an icon of the Amazon, the **white-chested toucan** has a beak sometimes longer than its body and emits a sound similar to a scream, which drives people to address it as "You crazy bird!"

Curassow

Cacaidae (order Galiformes)
Any number of tropical American birds belong to the above family, but the term "curassow" refers to seven to 12 species in which the male is glossy black (often with white belly) and has a curled crest of feathers and brightly colored bill ornament; the female, lacking the ornament, is smaller and brownish. It is a game bird, and its flesh is considered a delicacy; however, the **razor-billed curassow** of the Amazon is critically endangered. A noisy, terrestrial bird, the curassow makes its nest in trees, feeding on fruit and small animals.

Cock-of-the-rock

Rupicola
GALO-DA-SECA
The cock-of-the-rock belongs to one of two species of brilliantly colored birds, noted for the male's flattened circular crest extending over the bill. During much of the year the males display in open glades near the forest floor, maintaining and defending communal areas. Much of the movement consists of static posturing interspersed with stylized eye-catching movements, especially when the female is visiting. To perform courtship dancing the male clears spaces on the forest floor. Indian trappers search for the secret little dance halls and strew them with mud and twigs, coated with resin, which stick to the birds' feet and inhibit flight, not to mention mating. The female builds her nest of plant materials plastered with mud against a rock wall.

King Vulture

Sacroramphus papa
URUBU-REI
Known as the "condor of the tropical forest," the *urubu-rei* sports a bizarre face and beak, and its huge flapping wings can scare monkeys and humans alike. It is smaller than the Andean bird and has appeared in ancient manuscripts of the Mayan civilization as the glyph of Cip, the 13th day of the month. Like a true king, this vulture always presides over a carrion feast; lesser vultures wait until it is finished. Vultures are considered the garbage collectors of the jungle and their presence nearly always signifies carcasses.

Great White Heron

Ardea cocoi
GARÇA
This magnificent white heron lives in swamps, as well as in occasionally flooded fields. At the time of reproduction, it acquires nuptial feathers and makes a ritual out of choosing its mate. Nests are built in colonies where both parents look after their young, and are generally located in rough platforms of sticks constructed in bushes or trees near water. These herons usually feed while wading quietly in the shallow waters of marshes and swamps, catching frogs, fish and other aquatic animals. Acrobatic masters, they fly with legs loosely bent and their head held back against their body, instead of stretching their necks out front as most birds do.

Hoatzin

Opisthocomus hoazin
CIGANA
The strongest of Amazon birds, the hoatzin differs so much from other birds that its kinship is doubtful, but it is most closely related to the game birds. Although sporting wings, it prefers to creep among the branches of trees in which it lives, rather than fly. The flight from tree to tree is slow and labored. The adult is about the size of a mourning dove – dark olive with white streaks above and rufous streaks below – and it uses its wings like arms, climbing awkwardly about trees. In order to digest mangrove tree leaves, its gullet is 50 times larger than its stomach. It feeds on fruit and leaves of certain tropical trees that grow along the riverbanks. The flesh of the bird is particularly disagreeable in odor, resembling that of raw hides, leading locals to dub it a "stinking pheasant."

Reptiles

Black Caiman

Melanosuchus niger
JACARE-AÇU
Once extremely populous, the black caiman is now nearly extinct. Henry Walter Bates once figured the number of caiman in the Amazon in the 1850s to be *"as thick as tadpoles in a summer pond in England."* By the mid-20th century most had been killed by poachers. The few that are left leave their river habitat to lay eggs adjacent to a termite nest. The termites incorporate the eggs into the nets where the eggs mature at perfect temperatures for each sex: cool for female, warm for male. They rarely attack humans unless provoked and instead feed on a variety of fish, mammals and birds, which are usually eaten in the water. Today, they are under great threat by poachers, who can kill up to 12 in an hour. Flank skins are sold to dealers, with each skin going for about a dollar.

Bushmaster

Lachesis muta
JARARAGA
The bushmaster is the largest of all Amazonian vipers, reaching a length of 12 feet. It is rumored to be extremely aggressive, but in truth, fatal bites rarely occur. The bushmaster inhabits tropical Central and South America, especially damp, steamy forests, where it frequents holes in the ground made by armadillos and other animals. It is usually reddish-yellow with dark crossbars, and a black stripe extends from the jaw to the eye. Bushmasters roam mostly at night, hiding under roots and logs while they hunt for mammalian prey. Following a good feeding, they will remain in the same spot while digesting their prey, a process that may take two to four weeks. A bold snake, it behaves as if it were conscious of its power; indeed, because of its long fangs and large amount of poison, it is extremely dangerous. Most vipers bring forth their young alive, but the bushmaster lays eggs.

Pit Viper

Viperidae
JARARACA, SURUCUCU
Pit vipers are the most feared snakes in the jungle. They have big triangular-shaped heads and short slender tails. Large sensory holes between the eyes allow heat receptivity, which registers infrared radiation, thus helping to locate prey. All vipers have highly

evolved, well-developed teeth used to inject venom into victims. The poison primarily affects the blood and initial symptoms include local pain, vomiting, sweating, headache, and swelling. When not treated, pit viper venom can cause death in about 7% of the population, as a result of hypertension, renal failure or intracranial bleeding.

Boa Constrictor

Sucuri
ANACONDA
The biggest snake in the world, the anaconda can grow to nearly 40 feet. It's a venomless boa constrictor that kills by wrapping around and strangling its prey. Silvery-green in color, it feeds generally on fish, birds, mammals and alligators. Underwater, it flicks its tongue constantly to obtain chemical information about the environment. Also called a water boa, it often lies in the rivers with only its head above the surface waiting for a luckless bird or animal to pass by. After strangling its victim, the boa swallows it under the water. The most common boa in Amazônia is the **Rainbow Boa** (*epichrates cencrhia*), which is hunted by local farmers because it preys on chickens.

   Extra Caution: Be aware that some animals mimic rainforest plants in order to hide from predators or sneak up on prey. Snakes, in particular, love to look like vines. For protection, wear ankle-high boots and tuck your pants into them.

River Turtles

Podocnemis expansa
TARTARUGA
The **South American River Turtle** (*Podocnemis expansa*) migrates along rivers in masses that may impede the passage of boats. The turtles gather on the sandbars of large rivers to lay their eggs. **Sea turtles**, on the other hand, migrate over long distances to lay their eggs on special beaches and then disperse over a wide area. The **arrau**, or **side-necked turtle**, gets its name from the method of protecting the head and neck by bending them to the side, rather than withdrawing them backward into the shell as most turtles do. It grows into a shell length of about 30 inches, and its eggs have been a source of human food. Among several turtle species in the Amazon Basin is the world's largest freshwater turtle, the **tartaruga**, which reaches 150 pounds. The **matamata**, a bizarre turtle, has a distinctive nonretractable neck so it must swing its head under its carapace sideways. When prey approaches, it opens its mouth, creating suction that pulls the victim into its throat. **Green turtles**

(*Chelonia mydas*), which deposit their eggs along the coast of Costa Rica in Central Mexico, disperse through the Gulf of Mexico and the West Indies, and have been recovered on the coast of Brazil 4,000 miles away.

Hunted by river people for their meat and eggs, Amazônia's turtle population has been badly depleted, a fact that was predicted by Henry Walter Bates a century before. Turtles of all species, have been seriously threatened by the destruction of floodplain vegetation. Natural predators include catfish, dolphin, caiman, vultures, ibises and storks. The **giant Amazon turtle** is the most endangered species. During the 19th century, large nesting grounds were discovered along both the Rio Madeira and the Amazon River itself, but today they are severely limited to the protected sites in the Rio Xingu and Rio Trombetas in Pará.

The island of Fernando de Noronha and the resort of Praia do Forte in Bahia are leaders in their preservation. (For further information on these sites, see my other guide *Brazil Up Close*, Hunter Publishing, 1997.)

Amphibians

Frogs

Bufo, pipa, spp.
SAPO (bufo); PIPA (pipa)
About 250-350 species of frogs inhabit the Amazon Basin. Near Manaus, the biologist Barbara Zimmerman identified 80 frog species within a few square kilometers of upland forest. It's not entirely understood why many of these frogs do not live in the water (perhaps a result of the high number of predatory fish); most live in the trees or atop floating meadows. The large **bufo frogs** are considered too ugly to eat and most northern Brazilians have no taste for those delectable species, which are actually bred in the South. The aquarium trade seeks out the **pipa frog**, which breeds easily in small ponds.

Water Life

Although the least documented group of vertebrates in the Amazon, freshwater fish claims its greatest diversity in the region. Only about 1,700 species have been identified, out of a possible 3,000. At present, scientists like Michael Goulding of the Rainforest Alliance are avidly studying the Amazon's fish population to track the effects of environmental damage. Fish habitats in the region change throughout the year according to water levels, which reflect the rainy and dry seasons. Once a year, most South American fish migrate to spawn in the upper regions of the main river or its tributaries. Unusual are the **migratory characin**, who make two migrations per year. They are easiest to observe during the low-water period because dolphins chase them, causing them to leap.

Pirarucu, red-fish

Arapaima gigas
PIRARUCU
The king of the river, the pirarucu is the largest of all freshwater fish, and has long been a delicacy in the Amazon, eaten by Portuguese colonists who substituted it for the traditional cod in their cuisine. There is a 100-year-old record of a pirarucu that was 15 feet long; Michael Goulding in his book *Floods of Fortune* shows a photo of a pirarucu half as long as his canoe. The pirarucu belong to a group of fish having primitive characteristics and ancient fossil records. They have a tail that appears unusually full and rounded because of the proximity of both dorsal and anal fins to the tail fin. The fish uses a primitive lung adapted from its swim bladder, which permits it limited air breathing. Dried scales are sold as fingernail files in many shops in Belém, Santarém and Manaus.

Piranha

Serrassalminae
PIRANHA
"Pira" means fish and "rana" means tooth – nasty, toothy little fish found throughout the rivers and lakes of the Amazon Basin. Their viciousness, though exaggerated, is not unfounded. Piranha only become dangerous when trapped in lagoons during dry season or when they smell blood. Seeing local people splash in infested waters is misleading; anyone foolish enough to wash meat or gut fish in a river ought to know that piranhas don't just take one bite, but nibble constantly. So sharp are their teeth that Indians use them as a cutting tool. Not all piranhas eat meat; some chow down on fruits and nuts of the flooded forest.

Dogfish

Rhapidon vulpinus
PEIXE CACHORRO
The dogfish is a kind of small shark of the families *Squalidae*, *Scyliorhinidae* and *Triakidae*. Schools of dogifsh are often a nuisance

as they damage fishing nets, but they are edible and are sometimes sold as food. Amazon fishermen catch these ancient predators, which reach a length of two feet, as they pursue migrating fish schools upstream during the dry season. Called *peixe cachorro* in Portuguese, this fish uses two enormous canine teeth to stab other fish (as large as itself), then swallows them whole, head first.

Peacock Bass

Cichla, soo.
TUCUNARE
Bass are not native to South America, but are today the predatory species most exploited by fishermen. Though they resemble their namesake, they are not actually bass, but belong to the *cichlid* family. Considered extraordinarily beautiful with a rich flavor, they are generally rated as a first-class market fish. Most commercial fish-catching takes place in several floodplain lakes near Manaus, the most utilized being Lago dos Reis on the island of Careiro near the confluence of the Rio Negro and the Amazon River. Peacock bass specialize in eating small fish.

River Dolphin

Inia geoffrensis
BOTO
The freshwater or long-snouted river dolphin is light gray when young, but takes on a pinkish hue as it grows older. Its very long snout is covered with strong hairs or bristles that are sensory in function. With 25-27 teeth on each side of the jaw, the river dolphin feeds on fish, which it eats whole. *Botos*, or *bufeos*, as they are called, are widespread in the Amazon and Orinoco basins; during times of flood, they even penetrate into the flooded forests, where they swim among the trees. They often turn on their backs to search for food on the river bottom, probably because their downward vision in an upright posture would be impaired by their bulbous cheeks. Because these rivers are usually filled with debris, dolphins in captivity prefer to have obstacles in their tank. Legends about dolphins turning into men and impregnating girls abound in the Amazon. Another tradition says that burning *bufeo* oil in lamps causes blindness, and that to carry a *bufeo* tooth means bad luck.

Sting Ray

The sting ray is one of more than 50 species of oceanic fish in the Amazon, which also include bull sharks, herrings, anchovies, soles, toadfish and puffers. The sting ray's flat body allows it to live on the bottom of the river with its lateral fins expanding to serve as rudders. It's a rather obnoxious fish, since it lies half-buried in the sand, unnoticed, until someone steps on its tail with a bare foot and is severely injured by one of its spines. Wounds due to these spines are ragged and ugly, and often subject the victim to the danger of blood poisoning; they are not, however, deadly. In many riverside medicine markets, the spines are sold for magical purposes.

BULL SHARK

A seven-foot bull shark, whose normal habitat is the sea, made a winding 1,860-mile journey up Brazil's Amazon River in 1994. Groggy and weakened by hunger, it was finally hooked by a startled fisherman; he sold it for $70 to a local merchant, who donated it to a research center. This was the second such case in 10 years.

Characins

Characiformes
PIABAS
Tetras are any of numerous attractively colored freshwater fish of the characin family. *Characidae*, which are often brought back to the States for aquarium use, are characteristically small, lively, hardy and unaggressive. They are egg-layers and breed by scattering their eggs among aquatic plants. The **neon tetra** is a slender fish most popular with aquarium owners. Its hind parts are a gleaming regrowth; on its side is a neon-like gleaming stripe. The **cardinal tetra** (*Cheirofon axelrodi*) is similar, but with more red on its body. The **glowlight tetra** (*Hemigrammus erythrozonus*) is a hardy fish that grows up to 1.75 inches and has a shining red stripe along each side of the body. A yearly festival is held in the city of Barcelos, which attracts collectors and fishermen from all over the world (for more information, see under the city section for Manaus, page 196).

Lungfish

This species exists today only in Amazônia and Australia – the first survivors of a prehistoric fish group that was once rich in different species over millions of years ago. Now only about five species in the world remain. During the summer when marshes are dry, lungfish safely rest in the mud. They burrow down to a depth of 18 inches, where they coil up in a flask-shaped chamber, with a hole in the cover through which they obtain air. As is often the case with hibernating animals, the fish live on fat stored up in the kidneys and other organs during the four or five months they remain underground. When the rainy season returns they wriggle out of their underground cells and breathe with gills again. Specimens of lungfish in their "cocoons" have been successfully shipped to various parts of the world, where they are revived and become active as soon as they are released in water.

Catfish

Pimelodidae,
BACU (doradid); DOURADA (dourada)
The most diverse catfish can be found in the Amazon. Until the last 25-30 years, Amazonians did not favor catfish, despite the delicious flavor of some species. But taboos against eating scaleless fish have dropped, the opening of highways (which encourags marketing) and the restaurant boom in Manaus has inspired exploitation of the species, now assuming enormously high prices. There are two types of migratory catfishes in the Amazon; the *pilomelodidae* are the most plentiful predators in river channels. As they migrate upstream during the low-water period, they prey on smaller fish and shrimp who are spawning, an act called tropic migration by scientists. Some of the largest catfish spawn in the western parts of the Amazon Basin. A species called **armored** eat fleshy fruits, leaves and mollusks found in the tidal forests.

A Fish You Wouldn't Wish On Your Worst Enemy

The *candirú açu*, a minute catfish found in the waterways of the Amazon, is one of the animals most feared by locals. Almost invisible, it swims with great energy against the stream and is known to force its way into the urethra of bathers, spreading its thorny spines outward, thus making it difficult and excruciatingly painful to extract. If the fish is not removed by surgery, it can cause death. As such, be cautious about swimming in unknown waters, avoid urinating in the river, and jump in only after your guide has done so.

Spiders

Spiders

Arachnida
ARANHA
Spiders abound in Amazônia, feeding on the ubiquitous insects on the ground, in the air, and among the foliage. Most are reclusive and select dark quarters as their residence. In seasonal climates they may be most abundant during wet periods when prey is available. Hearing is highly developed in many spiders and they also keep in touch by tugging and vibrating the web, through pheromones, and more rarely through vision. All spiders are obligate carnivores and possess venom used to subdue prey. **Tarantulas,** called *caranguejeiras* in Brazil, are feared for their size (a body length of five inches). While usually shy and retiring, they may become aggressive if threatened. Some neotropical specimens can produce a snake-like hiss by rubbing the surfaces of basal segments of the pedipals against the opposite surface of the first legs. Some spend their days in burrows, while others dwell in trees.

Insects

Entomologist Terry Erwin of the Smithsonian Institute claims that millions of yet-to-be-identified insects inhabit the Amazon. There are insects of every shape, size and color in the region, from hundreds of beetle variations to flies, mosquitoes, gnats, ants, and more. Depending on one's attitude, these wonders of nature can be fascinating, irritating or painful. As writer Alex Soumatoff said about the culex mosquito, "*all it takes is three in your room to leave you a sleepless wreck,*" due to the whine the female makes to attracts the male, a by-product of her wings beating together at 500 cycles per second. Repellent at dusk in all areas is a must.

Floating meadows prove to be among the most fertile habitats for insects, whose aquatic larvae burrow into submerged roots. Insects that bite are most plentiful along rivers rich in sediment, since they provide the nutrients for the larvae. Most insects are usually found where cattle have grazed due to the deposit of feces; since cattle and buffalo ranching have swelled in the region, disease-infested mosquitoes have also swelled in number along the Amazon River, particularly several African fly species. At the same time, other species of insects have been nearly eliminated due to disturbances of major biodiversity patterns as a result of deforestation.

In many Amazonian Indian tribes, insects have always been venerated religiously, playing a central role as deities or mythic figures. In Warao cosmology, the four guardians of the cardinal points are social insects – two wasps, a bee and a termite. Rituals also incorporate insects; for example, the giant hunting ants *(Dinoponera)* used in puberty ceremonies practiced by various Amazonian tribes. Similarly, among the Gorotire-Kayapó Indians, pain is endured from the stings of wasps, whose nests are purposely molested as part of a rite of passage. Metallic beetle parts are used in body ornamentation by Indians in all parts of the region. Insects, especially musical species (crickets and katydids), luminescent forms (headlight beetles), large beetles and orthopterans are kept as pets and curiosities. Many species are eaten by natives and locals, both for sustenance and as delicacies.

Ticks

Ixodoidea
CARRAPATOS
Ticks comprise an isolated and specialized group of mites. After molting, they wait on the tips of twigs or leaves, forelegs outstretched and ready to snag any passing animal. They anchor themselves onto the host's skin by a median holdfast organ with curved teeth called the hypostome. They do not drop off until they finish feeding, and if forcibly removed, the hypostome (erroneously thought to be the head by most people) may remain in the wound and fester. They feed primarily on the blood of mammals, birds, reptiles and amphibians. Some remain on their single host for a lifetime. Specimens may reach the size of a grape after 5-6 days of feeding.

Centipedes

Chilopoda
CETOPEIAS, LACRAIAS
Centipedes are slender, elongated and multi-segmented arthropods. They are distinguished by bodies with only one pair of legs per segment, and may have anywhere from 15 to 81 segments. They possess a single pair of long, very flexible antennae and mandibula, forward-projecting mouthparts. The majority are relatively small, but some extremely large ones have been known to bite humans, causing pain and great inflammation. It is probably a myth that they leave a wound with each leg as they crawl over bare skin; there is no evidence that the legs contain venom. Centipedes are most at home in warm, humid retreats, where they hide by day

under stones, beneath loose bark, in rotting wood, and in caves and similar niches.

Crickets

Gryllidae
GRILOS
Although many orthopterois produce highly audible and complex sounds, it is the cricket that is best known for its musical talent. Males can make a variety of notes, most characteristic are short, pulsed chips or continuous soft trilling, more melodious and less rasping than the katydid. The sound is produced by the vibration of membranous areas of the forewings. Most crickets are small, but have enlarged, muscled hind femora, making them good jumpers. In Caraguatatuba, Brazil, a black cricket is a signal of sickness, a gray one is a sign of money and a green one, hope. In Rio Grande do Sul, Brazil, killing a cricket is thought to bring rain.

Cockroaches

Blattodea
CUCHARACHAS
Cockroaches are one of the most primitive and ancient of winged insects, dating back 250 million years. Ecological niches occupied by tropical American cockroaches are extremely varied. They are associated casually with vegetation, usually seen sitting on the upper surfaces of leaves, or are disposed to feed on the fruit leaves, bark, roots and other parts of living plants of particular species; others consume the wood of rotting logs. A number live symbiotically with ants. Numerous cockroaches are capable of sound production, by rubbing the abdomen against the wings. Of the 3,500 known species in the world, about 30% are found in Latin America.

Termites

Isoptera
CUPIN
Termites are the analogues in tropical soil of earthworms in temperate regions. Their physical burrowing to construct nests and digestion of plant material (cellulose) add significantly to soil fertility and earn termites a place in nature as highly beneficial. They live in nests of their own making, either wholly subterranean or above ground, and form conspicuous edifices in the landscape. The building materials may be clay, soil, excrement or plant fragments mixed with saliva. Nests provide an inviting abode for other animals, including nesting birds. In the forest, away from sunlit

riverbanks, crocodiles find termite nests a convenient incubator for their eggs. Like bees, they are organized into a social caste, with a queen, attendant male, sterile workers and soldiers. The queen can grow to enormous proportions over a lifetime. In times past in Brazil, large, hard, termitaria have been hollowed out and used for ovens. The same nests were pulverized and used as a kind of cement to make concrete floors for early settlers.

Giant Hunting Ant

Formicidae
TOCANDIRA
The two best known and largest of the gigantic forest ants are the **smaller** and **larger Dinoponera**. The smaller version is fiercer and can subdue a healthy adult human with a venomous stab that is often described to feel like a blow from a hammer or bullet. Serious symptoms may follow that last a day or longer, such as prolonged, aching pain that rapidly spreads from the site of the wound, sometimes labored breathing, cardiac palpitations and fever. Death is rare. The larger ants are gentler and less apt to sting. These ants are employed in male initiation rites by Amazonian tribes. Large numbers are caught and tied to contrived wickerwork panels and applied to the initiate's bare skin. The maddened mass of ants sting repeatedly; only youths who can endure the excruciating experience without a word are deemed worthy of passage to manhood.

FIRE ANTS
Tell Me It's Not True

Texans know this quarter-inch nasty as the fire ant, scientifically labeled *Solenopsis saevissima*. In the fall of 1993, experts from the US Dept. of Agriculture were called in to save Envira, a town of 7,000 people on the Tarauca River, 12 days by river from Manaus. So many thousands were attacking the residents that they had to retreat to the concrete streets to sleep. One woman was bitten at least once every hour and residents became so desperate that they spread diesel oil on the flood stilts of their rickety wooden houses and set them afire to bar the ants' entry. Even with house stilts on fire, the ants found ways to drop down on people from the ceiling, especially when they were sleeping. The only way out of town was by small plane or boat, but since the average salary was less than $1,000 a year, most people couldn't afford to leave. The USDA's Agricultural Research Service, deterred by the residents' aversion to DDT, which inflicts harm indiscriminately on any animal it contacts, tried using Logic, which acted as a natural birth control. But the problem was not solved. **Traveler's warning:** During the rainy season, these clusters of ants from infected areas can float downstream unscathed and burst into a swarm at the very moment they hit something hard – like your canoe.

Flora

For the early explorers, such as Alfred Wallace Bates, and for many modern researchers like M. C. Meyer and Mark Plotkin, the Amazon jungle has yielded hundreds of thousands of plants for examination. Not only are they fine examples of nature's artistry, but their

Many flowering plants thrive in the Amazon

therapeutic value appears to be limitless – a wisdom long guarded by the secret traditions of Indian shamans. For more information on the healing powers of plants, see pages 65 through 72.)

Orchids

Among the most beautiful plants in the forest are the orchids, which perch like parasites on host trees. About 500 species of orchids can be found in the Amazon Basin, showing an impressive range of inflorescence, from minute single petals to profuse blooms. Pollination of orchid flowers by insects is a highly specialized art, often involving bizarre ecological behavior. Most orchid seeds are distributed by the wind, but a certain species of bee, called **orchid bee** (family *Euglissinae,*) is attracted to orchids, which mimic the scent of female bees. Among the many varieties are *Catasetum macrocarpum, Oleanesia amazonica, Rodriguesia lancelatta, Acacallis firmbriata* and *Gongora quinquenervis.*

Water Lilies

The largest water lilies are those that form the tropical South American genus *Victoria*, comprising two species of water lilies. The leaf margins of both the **Amazon** or **royal water lily** (*V. Amazônia*, formerly *V. Regia*) and the **Santa Cruz water lily** (*V. Cruziana*) have upturned edges, giving a thickly veined leaf the appearance of a large, shallow pan two to six feet across – a characteristic which accounts for its common name "water platter." The fragrant flowers of Victoria have 50 or more petals and are seven to 18 inches wide. They open white toward evening and shade to pink or reddish two days before they wither, to be replaced by a large berry-like fruit. They provide food for fish and wildlife, but sometimes cause drainage problems because of their rapid growth. Many varieties have been developed for ornamental use in garden pools.

Water Vines

It is extremely important that you are able to identify the plant *cipa d'agua*, or water vine, since it often provides drinking water for jungle travelers. Common to high, nonflooded ground, it is a large liana. To retrieve the water, hold a piece of the stem up and cut; a substantial quantity of clear, fresh water should run out. Water can also be drunk from the surface of a species of the cecropia, a common tree in Amazônia.

The **water hyacinth**, called *aguapé-purua*, sports a beautiful blossom that lasts only a day, wilting after sunset. It grows profusely, branching in all directions and sprouting plants on barely new tips. Within a few months, an entire tangled network of plants is established, which often proves hazardous to waterways, except in Amazônia, where the ecological balance keeps it under control.

Guaraná

Among one of the most important crops grown in the Amazon is guaraná (*Paulinia cupana var sorbilis*), from the *Sapindacae* family. It was first discovered in 1800 by the scientists Humboldt and Bonpland along the upper Rio Negro. When it remains in open ground, it grows as shrub; in the shade, it grows like a liana. It is used in the production of a popular soft drink by the same name and for various medicinal purposes.

Trees

There are thousands of tree varietes in the Amazon region. Here is a just a sampling that your guide might point out to you.

Samaúma/Kapok Ceiba

Ceiba pentandra (L.) Gaertn
BOMBACACEAE
As one of the forest giants, the famous kapok ceiba stands high above most other trees in the canopy, reaching well over 50 meters (165 feet). It casts enormous tabular roots called *sapopomebas*, and it grows on humid, unstable soils along waterways. These roots are used as huts by Indians and other forest dwellers. It's thick and irregular with an aculeate trunk and branches, a feature also found in adult trees. The trees bloom at the end of the fall season, and the digitate leaves are replaced each year. The capsule-like fruits appear soon after flowering and, when mature, break open to reveal numerous black seeds enveloped by white cotton. This cotton is used as a mattress, pillow and cushion stuffing, as well as in the manufacture of life jackets. The kapok ceiba wood is pinkish-white and opaque and is used to make rafts.

Pau-de-Tucano

Vochysiatucanorum Mart
VOCHYSIACEAE
The pau-de-tucano is one of the most brilliant trees of the rainforest with its yellow inflorescences, which, from a distance, resemble the beak of an exotic toucan bird. The taller trees reach six meters (20 feet) in height. In general, the verticillate leaves are grouped by fours on each node and have a leather-like texture and bright green color. The colorful yellow flowers emerge between December and March and stand erect, displaying the characteristic spores of their corollas. The small, dark fruit appears from September through to November. The wood is light and used for making crates, boards and paneling.

Rubber Tree

Hevea brasiliensis Muell. Arg.
SEREINGUEIRA
The first Portuguese to arrive in Brazil noticed Indians playing with heavy black balls made of the latex extracted from a local rubber tree. Native to the Amazon, the tree produces a yellowish latex with a strong odor, which provides the raw material for its first-class rubber. The tree has a rough, pale green, slightly wrinkled bark, and

can reach up to 40 meters in height (132 feet). Due to the tree's longevity (over 200 years), the latex can be extracted for a significant period of time. Leaves are formed by green folioles, which turn reddish or brown before they fall. Its yellowish-white flowers bloom from the beginning of July, and the fruits appear in October. The seed itself produces a thick yellow drying oil, adequate for the production of paint and varnish. Its light wood serves as raw material in the production of crates.

Sapucaia

Lecythispisonis Camb.
LECYTHIDACEAE
The Sapucaia tree attracts attention due to its enormous stature. Its natural habitat is the Amazon jungle and the Atlantic rainforests between the states of Ceará and Rio de Janeiro. It can reach up to 50 meters in height (165 feet). In the wintertime it loses all its leaves, which sprout again shortly before the flowers appear in the spring. The pale purple aromatic flowers attract bees, thus playing an essential role in the pollination process. Various Amazonian tribes consume the fruit, a large pyxidium containing 11-30 oily seeds. The tree's brownish-red, uniform wood has a smooth, resistant and somewhat opaque surface and is used in the housing and naval industries. Young monkeys eager for food will reach into the urn-like fruit. Unfortunatley, their hand has been known to get stuck there.

Mogno/Brazilian Mahogany

Swietenia macorphylla King
MELLIACEAE
The Brazilian mahogany tree, also known as *aguano*, is one of the best-known hardwood species in the world. The tree, first discovered in 1923 in South America, is now widespread throughout the Amazon jungle. It has a tall, upright trunk, with a narrow crown covered by dense, bright green foliage. It may reach 30-50 meters in height (100-165 feet), forming tabular roots. The tree blooms soon after the leaves are renewed, between August and September. The flowers are small, cream-colored and aromatic. The fruit is a dark brown capsule with woody valves. Its seeds are winged and easily dispersed. The color of the wood deepens over time from a reddish/yellowish-brown to a uniform reddish-brown shade with fine stripes. With its shiny golden surface, it is used to make luxury furnishings, light sailing vessels and rulers, among other items.

Capaiba/Balsam Copal

Copaifera langsdorfii Desf.
LEGUMINOSAE
The long-living balsam copal tree, a native of the *cerrado* and of tropical and subtropical forests, is easily recognized by its red bark. Its branches spread out in different directions, forming a wide and attractive crown. The leaves are characteristically compound, generally formed by six small folioles. In the summer its delicate pink flowers emanate an aroma very attractive to bees, which extract the nectar. In the fall its fruit becomes mature and releases dark seeds. Oil from this tree is popularly used in small doses as an antiblennorrhagic, a stimulant, and as medicine to treat bronchitis. The wood has a pale red duramen (heart) with dark grooves and is widely used in the naval industry and in luxury-cabinet making.

Chichá

Sterculia chica St. Hil.
STERCULIACAE
Parrots and apes can often be seen eating the fruits of the chichá tree. It grows along the ciliar forests and the rainforest, in the Northeast and in the states of Minas Gerais, Mato Grosso, São Paulo and Espirito Santo. In the forest it reaches about 30 meters in height (100 feet), with a trunk covered by smooth gray bark, featuring irregular grooves. It's supported by tabular roots, which provide a stable base. The large, duck-shaped leaves fall in the winter, leaving scars in the thick branches. The small flowers have no petals, but usually bloom from February-April, and sometimes continuously until June. Its capsule-like fruit is red and emerges between July and August, with a velvety texture and containing seven or eight black, oily, and edible seeds, similar to peanuts. Quite tasty, these seeds can be roasted or cooked for consumption.

Castaneira-do-Pará/Brazilian Nut

Bertholletia excelsa Humb. & Bonpl.
LECYTHIDACEAE
This exuberant tree reaches up to 50 meters (165 feet), way above the canopy of the forest. Its rich nut is considered one of the main food resources of the forest. Generally, the nuts are ripe from December-March. Its trunk is smooth and very long, with a wide spread-out crown, covered with simple, alternate leaves. Its white or white-ocra flowers have a rare and exotic beauty and emanate a pleasant aroma. This attracts bees, which extract nectar, helping the pollination process. The wood is used in housing and naval industries.

FUTURE OF THE FOREST

A Healing Pharmacy

---

by Professor M.C. Meyer

A passionate spokesman for the potential of Amazonian pharmacology, Professor Mario Christian Meyer provides a privileged look into the future potential of Amazonian plant life. Trained as a neuropsychiatrist at Université Paris VII, he is presently a guest professor at the University of Paris, as well as Deputy Governor and senior adviser to the Governor of Amazonas for international development of business. He is a senior expert of scientific, technological and industrial cooperation in biotechnology, as well as environmental sciences, to leading industrial groups around the world. As a liaison between medicine, science and business, the Brazilian-born Meyer represents a new kind of Amazonian advocate – dedicated to utilizing the resources of the planet in an Earth-supporting capacity for all involved.

Professor M.C. Meyer with Katrimara, his jaguar.

~

The Amazon posses nearly two-thirds of the world's living plant and animal species and, by consequence, two-thirds of our planet's genetic heritage. For thousands of years Amazonian Indians have been well aware of the active therapeutic properties found in the colossal arsenal of jungle plants. Even prehistoric man used medicinal plants. Researchers have detected pollen in medicinal levels of usage in bones dating as far back as 60,000 B.C. What we have come to discover is that prehistoric usage of medicinal plants have been related mainly to stimulants, diuretics and astringents. Aspirin, today one of the widest known and most consumed medicines in the world, was initially an extract of willow bark, from which the active principal 'salicine' was isolated, along with vitamins, glycosides, etc.

Since the beginning of the century, teams of the "Institut Pasteur" have traveled to Amazônia in order to extract natural substances from plants; these studies are becoming increasingly important today in the face of AIDS and other immunological catastrophes that are affecting our modern-day population. It was nearly 90 years ago that **Professor Charles Richet**, a French scientist, discovered in Amazônia a new vegetal toxin, the **crepitine**, an extract from the plant assaku, that allowed him to understand the basic functioning of the immunological mechanism of humans. Today, crepitine appears to be an important antivirus compound. In 1908 Richet brought back from Rio Purus (a tributary of the Amazon) the latex of this plant that the Indians used to 'poison' the river water to facilitate the capture of fish.

Biotech & Bio-industry

Plant-based medicines, once reserved mainly for shamans, folk medicinemen and herbalists, and at the beginning of the century, for artisanal biological-chemistry scientists (discovers of aspirin, for example), were later harnessed by pure chemists, who often replaced the plant-based molecules with synthetic molecules. Today, plant-based medicine moves away from pure chemists and synthetic transformation and onward to an original universe of high-tech production, based again upon biological models. From this movement has arisen the present-day advent of the BIO-industry, that is to say, any technology-oriented industry that uses biological systems, living organisms or derivatives to make or modify products or processes for specific use.

Given the rapid evolution in biotech research, one could conjecture that by the end of the century pharmaceutical labs will have even more useful techniques. This advanced technology would permit the selection of new natural molecules of Amazonian origin, and verification of the active principals in a considerable number of plants. These plants are prescribed in the treatment of 75% of the illnesses of the planet – diseases treated even today, in many cases, by an artisanal plant-based therapy (traditional natural folk medicine, over-the-counter herbistry, etc.).

Technological, Economic & Environmental Challenges

Due to high research and development costs, pharmaceutical giants find themselves today confronted with a slowdown in the number of chemical innovations in pharmacology, reducing the discovery, on average, to only one new and profitable molecule per year among 10,000 synthetic molecules tested. In contrast, 20 years ago, 20 new molecules were being discovered per year.

Pharmaceutical companies are now particularly interested in research alternatives that traditional medicine and its "living" molecules can offer. For example, a leading US pharmaceutical company, interested in identification and selection of plants having new therapeutic properties, recently passed special agreements with **INBIO**, a Costa Rican institute and the government of Costa Rica. In return for a $1 million investment of technical assistance on the part of the American company, the Costa Rican side agreed to furnish 100 plant extracts and microorganisms, together with an exclusivity on the pharmacological analysis for a period of two years.

As a result of our anthropological and biotechnological work, major French pharmaceutical laboratories have committed themselves along the same lines for plant research in the Amazon, precipitating a landmark Franco-Amazonian government commitment without precedent. This cooperation has great potential for the establishment of joint ventures, as well as significant positive social economic repercussions for the Amazon region. This kind of rational exploitation of the Amazonian biodiversity, through bio-tech, is, in my opinion, the only pragmatic and realistic way to deal with delicate and crucial environmental problems. Indeed, it could be said that natural molecules from Amazonian flora and fauna have, in themselves, a direct and indirect economic value.

They serve as indirect models for new synthetic molecules and are even more active, more specific, and provoking fewer side effects than classical chemical medicines.

High-tech vs. Savage Mind

The contribution of natural molecules raises a crucial question as the century comes to an end. It concerns access to genetic resources and the "royalties for nature's know-how." This was a key point in the **Convention of Biodiversity at the Summit** of Rio 1992, attended by 160 heads of state and numerous scientists, ecologists and activists.

In my opinion, the use of Amazonian Indian knowledge by First-World pharmaceutical companies requires some fundamental reflection. I have come to believe that there is an inherent cultural conflict between the American and Western scientists in their perceptions of their psychocultural identities.

In my own project, called the **Franco-Amazonian Project for Scientific Technological and Industrial Cooperation**, the cooperation between the Amerindians and high-tech scientists has demonstrated that we must give important consideration to the means and limits of their interaction to avoid a 'power struggle' between Indians and Western-thinking scientists. Indians who today come into contact with urban Amazonian centers, often enticed by money or too embarrassed to return to the tribe because of a failure at urbanization, are exploited as prostitutes, or fall under the influence of drug dealers or *garimpeiros* (gold miners), as well as being adversely affected by mercury pollution. Moreover, isolated native tribes that come into unsupervised conflict with outside influences are also at great psychological risks and have been known to suffer deeply from loss of roots, emotional orientation, intellectual dynamism, and even brain functions, resulting in a psycho-social form of schizophrenia. If those in the so-called 'civilized sector' continue to invade and exploit the forest without forethought to social, psychological and environmental consequences, tribal peoples, the true kings of the richest forest in the world, may easily become the "rubbish" of this cross-cultural conflict.

In the final analysis, the only way to safeguard tribal peoples from acculturation or even extermination is to respect their knowledge in a practical way by integrating their traditional technology and their "science of nature" into the development of modern society. The Indians, as scientists of nature, could be integrated into the labor force at a level where their skills and thousand-year-old traditions would be respected in a fairly balanced cooperation. Otherwise, the Amazonian Indian will become what they themselves fear most: an insignificant piece of a fossilized "wax museum" zoo.

Sacred & Secret 'New' Molecules

The ancient botanical knowledge of Indians, oftentimes characterized as sacred and secret, has from its initiation been associated with myths of longevity and youth through invoking the "gods of nature" or by cultivating the "magical" virtues of plants.

It is therefore not surprising that our analytical and structural chemical studies of these plants have shown the presence of powerful antioxidant and anti-free radicals in high concentration (such as various flavonoids of the rutaceaes family). Responsible for equalizing cellular metabolism, these plants contain important protective and regenerating properties for tissue; external tissue in the field of dermatology, by improving the quality of collagen and elastin, thereby acting against skin aging, as well as internal tissue; in the field of cardiology, where they have proven effective against rigidity of the arteries, as well as being highly beneficial to the vascular system. In the same Amazonian plant family, we have identified numerous plants, particularly rich in saponines, glycosides and terpenes – often associated with rare metals such as germanium, which according to unpublished Brazilian and Japanese studies, has strong reactions against cancerous tumors. Such is the case with a recently discovered molecule, hexacyclique nortriterpene, unknown until the present, which is reported to inhibit the growth of cancerous cells in vitro, according to 1986 research at Tokushima Bunri University in Japan.

Through the efforts of my collaboration with many Brazilian and French scientists, a large arsenal of vegetal hormones has recently been identified, which has proven effective in regulating the human metabolism, notably diminishing the cholesterol level in the blood and increasing the coronary circulation. Stigmasterol and sitosterol are principally responsible; the latter has the power, among others, to increase the level of estrogen in the organism in a balanced manner, as well as playing an essential role in the regulation of the cellular aging process.

As scientists delve deeper into the hidden aspects of forest potential, they are finding that native legends often provide "sacred" clues into the vast potential of a species. For instance, according to legend, the well-known Amazonian plant **guaraná** was given to the Indians as a gift by the thunder god Tupan to help them fight against the evils of the bad spirit Juruparo. The plant was rediscovered by Europeans in 1669 as a result of the mission work of Superior Betendorf, a Jesuit priest, among two Amazonian tribespeople, the Andiras and the Saterés-Mawés. Throughout the centuries guaraná has been used by jungle inhabitants as a psychostimulant tonic, appetite suppressant, and anti-cramping compound, as well as an aphrodisiac when associated with an energetic neuromuscular tonic (family *olacaceae*). Today, all strata of the population consume guaraná in many forms (bark, powder, and as an additive to a popular Brazilian soft drink, among other forms). In the future, untapped usage of guaraná may include weight control as well as anti-cellulite combat, but at the present the research results remain industrial secrets.

~

The entities involved in this research include the Universidade do Amazonas, Fundaçãi Oswaldo Cruz, INPA (Instituto Nacional de Pesquisa da Amazônia), EMBRAPA (Empresa Brasileira de Pesquisa Agropecuaria), and UTAM (Universidade Technologica do Amazonas, among others.

(Also see M.C. Meyer's other article starting on page 85, detailing his adventures with the Sateré-Mawé tribe.)

An Exotic Medicine Chest

by Professor M.C. Meyer

The richness of Amazonian biodiversity constitutes a double treasure for specialists of "natural medicine": first, the large variety of plants with therapeutic properties and second, the great diversity of mammals natural extracting healing substances from these plants.

In response to the pressing need to discover new superior medicines in plant life in the face of growing epidemics like AIDS and other social and environmental illnesses, a new, exotic specialist has thus been inspired to arise within the scientific arena – the **zoopharmacologist**. These specialists study plants used by animals to treat their own illnesses (such as antibiotics) or to regulate certain vital biological functions, such as contraception.

For instance, among the uncountable varieties of monkeys in the southern region of the Amazonian forest, we find the **muriqui**, the biggest monkey of the Americas. Apparent masters at controlling their own population, the females manage to reduce their fertility, thanks to the ingestion of certain leaves rich in isoflavoids , which have a physiological effect similar to that of estrogen. Inversely, the same females have been found to ingest '*orelha de macaco*' (monkey's ear) , a vegetable rich in a steroid that facilitates fertility. Scientists have discovered that these females often tend to chew on this plant during times of ovulation, suggesting that they may have the firm intention to be fertilized.

Medicinal Plants

COPAIBA. The copaiba can be found in large amounts in the Amazon's *terra firme* regions. Rich in beta-caryophylene and copaene, its therapeutic property is antivirus and antipsoriasis. Its oil is anti-inflammatory, antirheumatic, and has other numerous healing properties. It's also used in cases of chronic varicose ulcerations and pharyngitis.

CRAJIRU. This is a type of creeping plant used as an anti-inflammatory. The dry leaves contain tannins, quinonas and alkaloids. The plant, often served as a tea, is used to counteract intestinal colic and uterine inflammation. Other therapeutic properties are used as an astringent and as a powerful anticheloid (to heal rough scar tissue). In Amazonas, silkworms fed crajiru leaves (rich in flavonoid pigment) produce red thread.

URUCU. The seeds of this plant, which contain carotenoid-like beta carotene (pro-vitamin A), have properties capable of increasing the pigmentation of fatty tissue and thus making the skin resistant with natural coloration (it contains an excellent UVR filter, which acts as sunscreen). It is also a bio-insecticide, a cure and protection against insect bites. It can either be ingested as capsules or by cooking with it in powder form. For thousands of years Amerindians have used urucu for their body-painting rituals because of its bright color. They also mix the pulp, which surrounds the seeds, with the oil of Amazonian fish to make a cream that protects against the sun and insect bites.

The famous red dye "bixina" obtained from the fleshy red pulp inside the seed pods of "Urucu" (*Bix Orellana*), called annatto in English, is the principal sinew coloring used in most initiatory body paintings and is associated with such extraordinary uses as:

- Protective filter against the ultraviolet rays, which incisively strike the Indian skin exposed to the equatorial sun during the many hours spent fishing. Used internationally today in creams for tanning, solar products, and by the bigger multinationals for cosmetics.
- Powerful repellent and insecticide, utilized today by the majority of *selvicolas*, indigenous workers in the forest, who put the fresh red pulp directly on their face, hands, and arms and also apply it on various skin infections.
- Capillary treatment for the elasticity and brilliance of the hair.
- Food coloring for margarine, butter, cheese and other dairy products.
- Soft drink, when mixed with carbonated water.

VOICES FROM THE AMAZON

A Shaman's Apprentice Speaks Out

I had followed the old shaman through the jungle for three days and, over the course of our trek, we had developed an enigmatic relationship. The medicine man obviously resented my desire to learn the secrets of the forest plants that he knew and used for healing purposes. Still, he seemed pleased that I had come from so far away – he called me the pananakiri ("the alien") – to acquire the botanical wisdom that the children of the tribe had no interest in learning. I did not yet speak his language; an Indian from a neighboring tribe served as our translator. At the end of the third day, the shaman turned to the other Indian and said, "Tell the pananakiri that I have taught him all that I am going to teach him. Tomorrow I am going hunting." I had no objections; there were other shamans in the village with whom I wished to work, and I returned to my hut with the medicinal plants I had collected.

That night, I had a terrifying dream. An enormous jaguar strode into my hut and stared into my eyes, as if trying to divine my thoughts. Powerful muscles tensed in its back as it arched its body to spring.

So vivid was the apparition that I awoke with a scream. I sat upright in my hammock, trembling, my body soaked in a cold sweat. Carefully, I looked around the hut: I saw nothing – no footprints on the dirt floor, nothing disturbed or overturned, nothing to indicate the presence of an unwanted visitor. The only sound was the rustling of palm fronds as a gentle breeze blew through the village.

The next morning, just after sunrise, the young Indian who had served as our translator came to my hut. "Shall we go into the forest and look for more plants?" he asked. "Before we do," I said, "find the old shaman and tell him that last night I saw the jaguar." I gave no details and the Indian left. He returned a few minutes later. "Did you tell him?" I asked. "Yes." "What did he say?" I asked. "He broke into a big smile and said, 'That was me!'"

Reprinted from *Tales From A Shaman's Apprentice*, with permission of the author © Mark Plotkin.

~

The above narrative marks the beginning of the one of the most riveting books I have ever read about the Amazon: Mark Plotkin's *Tales from a Shaman's Apprentice* – a must-read for anyone planning to trek through the rainforest. Since the late 1970s, Plotkin, a Harvard-trained ethnobotanist, has been traveling through the Amazon to document how rainforest tribes are using plants for medicinal purposes, participating in their psychotropic rituals and sharing an intimacy with native cultures that few are ever afforded. As his mentor, the famed scientist Richard Evans Schultes writes in the book's introduction, Plotkin is indeed a member of the last generation of ethnobotanists who will be able to witness Amazonian Indians living the traditional life their ancestors lived for the last thousands of years. More importantly, Plotkin is part of a growing movement of visionary scientists who are determined to give back to the communities they research: first, by presenting to the tribes he has researched a book entailing their own vast shamanic wisdom, he has inspired future generations of natives to become shamanic apprentices within their own tribes. Moreover, he has also instituted various trust funds that recycle profits back to the tribes themselves. Based in Washington, DC, he heads what he calls "a new virtual rainforest," – **The Ethnobiology and Conversation Team**, which interacts with the best rainforest scientists in the world through fax, modem and e-mail. He has also been deeply involved in the work of Shaman Pharmaceuticals, a drug research company now on the verge of releasing cutting-edge medicine based on the tribal knowledge of tropical plants. For the following interview, I caught him on a rare day in his office just as he was leaving for Peru and

Dr. Mark Plotkin with Indian guide on the Brazil-Venezuela border.

Colombia to film a documentary on Amazônia for IMAX. Passionate, outspoken, and disarmingly candid, he shares what he has learned about interacting with native cultures, the uses and abuses of tropical hallucinogens such as ayahuasca, the secrets to avoiding malaria, and much much more.

~

Your book starts with this stunning jaguar dream episode (see the beginning of the article). As you pointed out, Amazonian shamans feel a tremendous connection to jaguars and much of their healing work is done on the dream level. Did you feel, then, this dream was an initiation, the turning point in your work?

Yes, I really did. Once that happened, the walls fell away and the tribe began to accept me. I believe many people have the wrong idea about indigenous cultures, and I have to confess I had the same ideas. I grew up on Tarzan films, which make you think all you have to do is show up in the place and say 'Take me to your leader' and you're in. But I personally see ethnobotany and the building of relationships as an interactive process – something that you keep working on and going back to. It's not like, all of a sudden you are my best friend and I trust you and will tell you everything . Rather, the more I know you, the more I might open up to you. Twelve to 14 years later I am still finding new shamans and new plants, which says to me it's about growing together and and working together and continuing to build that trust.

~

In your book you call this beautiful attitude 'cultural integrity.' But I was also impressed by the fact that the Indians had a somewhat ironical relationship with you. On the one hand, they saw you as a superior being, on the other, they were often making fun of you.

They saw that I really did understand that they were superior in their own ways, in the ways of the forest, in the ways of the plants, and that made a entirely different dynamic. When you drop that defense and you don't play the great white man or woman, or the great military man or the great missionary, or tell them what God to worship, it creates a much more human dynamic.

~

And yet one of the biggest things that impressed me about your book was the seemingly inordinate amount of trust you did exhibit toward your native guides, whom you really didn't know in the beginning and upon whom your very life depended. Did you ever feel – in retrospect – that you had been a little foolhardy?

On one hand, to do this work you have to have an open mind and an open heart. People make the mistake that Indians are just noble savages. They aren't. They are people like anybody else and they are wonderful, noble, generous people; there are greedy, treacherous Indians as well. To think that all Indians are trustworthy would be a mistake. I have lived with Indians and it's been a wonderful experience, but at another time I was in a gold mining town in Peru trying to get someone to take me to a shaman, and I just had a very strong feeling that as soon as we got around the bend they were going to stick a machete in my back and throw me in the river. So I said thanks, but no thanks. I believe that we all have to trust our instincts, but by the same token we shouldn't be foolhardy.

~

When you go back to these tribes today after so many trips, how are you treated ?

I have essentially grown up with these guys – for over 14 years. So it's not like I am an old friend that they see now and again when we get together. In some instances I have been in and out of their villages several times each year and it's like seeing a close relative who lives somewhere else.

~

You also had some travel habits I was really surprised by, such as taking drinking water from the river and putting it in your canteen. Did you leave out the part where you purified it?

There are creeks that come off the hills behind the village that are clean as water from a faucet because the rain comes right out of the sky and into the creeks. But anybody who drinks out of a creek that is downriver from a village is asking for trouble, since the village's waste always runs that way. That's just a basic public health trick that anybody should know. Only drink when there's nothing upstream.

~

Then there was that blood-curdling scene in your book where you got bitten by a vampire bat. It didn't seem that you had any anti-venom medicine with you.

The only thing you need to worry about with bats is rabies. But as I wrote, there was nothing to worry about because there was no rabies vaccine for hundreds of miles. There was no hospital, no roads, the only way out was a plane and it wasn't coming for another week. So I asked the Indians to take care of the wound and they said, "Okay, but there's no rabies. " I did get a little worried when they said later, "By the way, what's rabies?"

~

After so many trips to the forest over many years, have you also found that your navigational skills in the forest have improved?

Oh, yes, but they still stink. There is something more important than navigational skills. All my experiences in the forest have simply deepened and broadened my religious feelings. It has given me an incredible appreciation for nature, an understanding of the spirituality inherent in nature, a sense of spirituality and oneness that you don't get sitting in Hebrew school or Sunday school or church. When you live in an culture that is dependent on an ecosystem, it changes your perspective. I would say it has changed me in more profound ways than just my ability to navigate in the forest, which I can't, or whether I can find clean water better than I used to, which I indeed can.

The entire jaguar sequence shows me that there are other realities out there, and that this type of thing is as real to them as mortgages and lawyers are to us. When you stop having this attitude that the West knows everything, and that if it's not in Western culture then it's not worth knowing, having or worshipping, then all of a sudden you open yourself up to new universes, new worlds that are out there. When you read about Indians that can communicate telepathically through the use of ayahuasca (a hallucinogenic substance made from several Amazonian plants and used by shamans and tribal people for "journeying" to other worlds), and when you read about curses thrown over long distances, over hundreds of miles of jungle, you realize there are things we can't explain or understand, but it doesn't mean they are any less real.

~

In your book you write at length about the vast botanical wisdom held by Amazonian shamans which is now being lost. Is their metaphysical power – their deep psychic and spiritual knowledge of the curative properties of plants – also being lost, or have you been the recipient of this kind of wisdom, too?

I believe these powers are being lost in the sense that they are not being passed on. When the shaman has no apprentice, it's not just knowledge that's lost; it's a whole way of life, a whole way of thinking, a philosophy, a whole system of medicine, healing and curing and relating to the world. So I do think these powers are on the wane. I am just an apprentice. I am not a shaman. A colleague of mine works with the Huichols in Mexico and in his eight years of living with the Indians, there were four outsiders – all Westerners – who wanted to be shamans. Today three of them are dead and one is a shaman, but he is prone to epileptic seizures. These powers are not magically invested in these shamans; there is a collective unconscious out there, but the Indians seem to access it more readily than we do. I want to learn how to access them, how they discover plants, and put that work to the betterment of not only our own culture but theirs as well.

~

Have you yourself learned any rituals related to the ethnobotanical uses of plants?

I don't want to become a dabbler where you open these magazines and see my ad that says, "Pay me three thousand dollars for my workshop and I will turn you into a shaman in a weekend." People wouldn't buy it if I were giving out MDs in a weekend. The point is, I am interested in learning rituals only as a chance to access the sacred and participate in these things, but I am not the ultimate apprentice of these shamans. I want the youngsters of their tribes to carry on the tradition. Still, I have been very honored, very lucky, to participate, but I am not the ultimate repository of this knowledge. The people of their own tribe are.

~

What political obstacles (i.e., with the Brazilian government) have you found in working with indigenous populations?

Go back and read the about the voyage of the Beagle *and Darwin is complaining about the Brazilian bureaucracy and the natural resources of the country. It hasn't gotten any easier since then. So I have been careful to work with tribes outside of Brazil because it's just so damn complicated. The Brazilian government is forever changing, everything is always a mess. I love Brazil dearly but it's "O pais do futuro"(the country of the future) and it always will be. How many times have we heard about people who went to Brazil to do research and spent two years just waiting for the permit, which they eventually never got, and then had do their thesis somewhere else. I have heard this story a million times over. I don't have two years and I'd rather work in other countries where the flora is no different, and the people are the same.*

~

What health precautions – for the tribes – do you take upon visiting? We have heard of so many instances when contact from the outside has decimated whole communities because of a mere cold germ.

I am very careful about approaching Indian villages. I don't go into Indian villages with coughs or colds. And when I am working for Shaman Pharmaceuticals, which is several months a year now, I always have a physician with me, who is there specifically to provide treatment for introduced diseases that have not been introduced by me, but are there when I arrive. I was in Brazil a week and a half ago, and what is really killing the Yanomami right now is malaria from the gold miners, not to mention the water being poisoned by mercury. Anybody who has a romantic vision of what the settling of America was like hasn't been to a garimpeiro *(gold mining) camp. By the same token, the irony is that the* garimpeiros *are the friendliest, kindest people to visit in the forest if you stumble into their camp. They are the first to give you food and drink, but toward the Native American people their behavior is revolting.*

~

From your perspective, what do you see as a solution?

People need to control what is within their border. And human rights abuses should be of concern to all of us. I don't want to see garimpeiros *poisoning the waters that Yanomami children drink no more than I want to see US power companies pouring waste where poor little African American kids go fishing. So we all should be concerned about these global problems because it ends up affecting us. An example: I was a meeting at the Hotel Tropical in Manaus, and we are sitting there hearing about the mercury in the water, and what is everybody doing? Eating fish coming out of these very waters. Another time I was working in Minas Gerais (an interior state of Brazil) doing a primate survey and was reading a Time magazine article about how pesticides banned in the US were being shipped to Brazil and used on tomatoes. And there I was sitting there eating tomatoes. So, these things that are shipped to Brazil or Mexico and put on crops and then are sent back to us – well, who pays the price? We all do.*

~

Over your nearly 15 years in the forest, have you gone back to areas only to find it destroyed or burned?

I haven't personally, because I intentionally work in such incredibly remote areas that it isn't really a problem.

~

Are there other experiments being carried out presently on Amazonian plants that are on the verge of changing the face of Western medicine?

Shaman Pharmaceuticals is 100% devoted to finding new medicines for diseases we can't cure – cures based on indigenous knowledge. No one is going to spend $120 million to bring a new headache medicine to market because you aren't going to beat aspirin, but people will spend that kind of money to find new treatment for AIDS. Or for that matter, herpes, which is what Shaman's first drug focuses on. If things go according to plan, which they seem to be doing, we are about two years from market. The medicine is based on a plant from Peru, and although it has been in laboratories for years, Shaman Pharmaceuticals had the best chemist and the best shaman who showed how us to do it.

~

Is there something you personally discovered that is cutting edge?

The fellow whom I call the "poisoner" in my book turned out to be the paramount shaman. He spent 12 years not showing me a diabetes drug, but now it is in the lab and it shows itself to be a promising lead. Diabetes doesn't have much of a press agent, but it's a plague that kills more women in this country than breast cancer by a factor of four.

~

It seems as if this work has taken you into many realms that you could never have imagined.

That is the romance and adventure of it, really.

~

Reading about your extraordinary adventures, I sense you must feel a very strong connection to the early pioneer scientists.

I like to feel that I and all my colleagues in ethnobotany are following in their footsteps. We are all involved in the great trek to understand and explore. But there is one thing we have to be concerned about which they weren't, which is the cultural degradation and disappearance that we see all around us.

~

To avoid recreating this situation yourself, you have come up with a very interesting solution. Instead of exploiting tribal knowledge without fair exchange, you have been deeply involved with The Healing Conservancy Program developed by Shaman Pharmaceuticals, which allows the tribes to share in the profits of your research. If they are living such isolated lives, what do they use the money for, exactly?

It's not just a question of cutting a check. It's finding out what the people need. In some cases they need malaria medicine, which they can't make themselves because the quinine grows too far up in the Andes and it is a slow-growing tree. They want to enlarge their airstrip to allow planes to come in to take people out for medical emergencies. They need filters for water because the water has gotten crummy because the missionaries have settled too many people in one place at one time. So, it is way too simple to say we are going to help them, so let's just cut a check.

Another aspect is that you can't say, "When we get that to the lab and find something 10 years later, we will cut you a check," because these people have real needs now. In the case of the Tiriós, they have Indonesian loggers to the north of them, Brazilian garimpeiros to the south, they have real needs right now. I have taken a percentage of my book and have set up a trust fund for them, which we manage together, dealing with problems as they come up.

~

In your book you talk about developing a pro-active and holistic approach to the problems we face. Can you explain this?

It means not waiting till something burns down to save it. It means not waiting till there is one little tree left that has an anti-cancer compound to protect it. It means figuring out ways to use the enviroment and to engage people in environmental protection, to get the Republicans in Congress to realize how many strategic materials that we need for industry, and even the military, that are tied up not only in the rainforest but in indigenous people's knowledge. It means not to run around and butt heads and make enemies, but rather to work together and realize common ground, our commonality, and then move forward. At the same time environmentalists shouldn't be afraid to kick ass when necessary.

~

Do you think ecotourism is helpful or an obstacle?

Ecotourism is potentially the most valuable non-timber forest product out there. But I see few examples of it being done well. Ecotourism is pariculary difficult with indigenous people. First and foremost, ecotourism should focus on protecting national parks and forests where indigenous people are not living. If indigenous people want to get involved, they should be welcome to do so. But the idea of showing up in somebody's village and taking pictures is a potential cause of a lot of unhappiness and anguish and a definite cause for backlash.

~

What's the biggest mistake of tourists and scientists who travel to the Amazon?

They don't bring enough to read – I'm not joking. That's number one – mainly because we operate at a different pace. We live in a different society. Thanks to MTV, commercials, fax machines, computers, most people don't know what to do when the bus breaks down, when the plane shows up a hour late, when there is a hole in the canoe and your guide has to spend a day patching the canoe. Instead, if you have a rucksack of books, which I travel with, you sit down, pop open your book and make great use of that time. But people who end up on a riverbank or a bus stop outside Lima or Quito and don't have anything to do just can't handle it. Once I waited on an airstrip for seven days for a plane. I had a box full of books and I was just fine. I read lots of biographies.

One of the secrets of ethnobotany is that you have to spend a lot of time doing nothing. We have this linear approach to science and life – you want to get there, you want get the formula, you learn how to prepare. If you show up at a village and want to approach things that way, you're screwed. You gotta be down there, you gotta go hunting with the guys, fishing, watch the women grate cassava, and then you say, "Oh, by the way there's this disease we have in our country, I don't know if you guys get it here, it looks like this, do you have a plant, for it? Uh-huh, you do? Well tomorrow let's go hunting and I'd really like to get a nice walking stick and see that plant and maybe put it in my plant book." I learned this from the great Schultes himself, and through my own experience.

What I'm saying is that if you try to take an American can-do approach in the Amazon, they will throw you right out, as well they should. When I have meetings in my office in Washington and I say three o'clock I expect them to be there at three o'clock, and when I am in another country and sometimes three o'clock means five o'clock or maybe today, maybe tomorrow, or maybe next year, you just gotta go with the flow.

~

What's the second worst mistake travelers make?
In 1980 I was in a cheap hotel in Peru and a night watchman turned the TV on overdrive, which seems to be the preferred way to listen to TV in many of these countries. I kept waking up and asking him to turn it down, which he did and then I would go back up and he would turn it back up and go to sleep. So, simply put: No one should ever go to Latin America without earplugs. It's advice I follow religiously. For all of us who can't endure a constant drone of noise in the background, which is most gringos, that's very useful advice.

~

Are you still a proponent of wearing tennis shoes (rather than hiking boots) in the forest?
Absolutely. And long-sleeved shirts. I started wearing Ex Officio clothing – that's the label. The reason I love it dearly is that it dries incredibly fast, and it's super light and tough. I work in my clothes all day, then I jump into the river and wash them, and then I have to put my clothes back on the next day, so I can't have them cold and wet. You wash these and the next day they are dry.

~

What do you do to get in shape physically for your trips?
I find as I get older I have to make a concerted effort to stay in shape. When I was 25 I could just pick up my backpack and head out. The heat, the physical exertion and the humidity wouldn't bother me – after all, I grew up in New Orleans before there was air conditioning. But now I am 41 and going to the gym isn't just something to impress people at a single's bar, but to be in shape for the work I do.

~

What about malaria pills, do you take them?
Anybody who has a macho idea about malaria should have their head examined. I almost lost two Indian guides to malaria, and let me tell you, it is an ugly disease. You want to know how people get malaria? They go out and pee at night. They go out from their hammock, out from under their mosquito net, they don't have any clothes on, and they figure they will just pee quickly and nobody will notice. Well, guess what? The mosquito bites

them in the ass and they get malaria. So if you are in an area with bad
malaria, if you are a guy, you should have a little bottle next to your
hammock and you should pee without getting out from under the mosquito
net. And if you are a woman, put your clothes on before you go out there
and take a leak (and make sure you are doused thoroughly with repellent).

~

Speaking of women, are there any female botanists who are
working with women shamans?
There are, but not enough. We need more of them.

~

You are very vocal about the unhealthy polarization in the West
regarding traditional medicine and alternative healing methods that
use so-called natural compounds.
I keep running into people when I give talks and they say to me, "I read
your book and we obviously feel the same way. I would never go to a doctor."
And I tell them I hope they don't get appendicitis because if they don't go
to a doctor they are going to die. Today it's Western medicine or shamanist
medicine or Ayurvedic medicine. I would much prefer to see a
complementary approach. If the dermatologist can't cure my fungal
infections, which he can't, then the medicine man or woman can. I envision
an approach of combining the best of all systems so health care can become
more accessible and more affordable and more effective for all.

~

What are your latest projects in the forest?
The Shaman's Apprentice Program has taken off like a rocket. We have
a whole generation of shaman's apprentices and a new generation of
apprentice's apprentices. The guys who were in their late teens or twenties
when I started doing my work have kids now, and not only are they into
this, but so are their kids. So when we go into the forest now, the old
shamans have a newfound status and so do the apprentices and the
apprentice's kids. It's been particularly successful with the southwestern
Tiriós in Suriname, where most of the book takes place, and we've
introduced it to the southeastern Tiriós in Suriname and the Inganos in the
Colombian Amazon and now successfully with Indians in western
Panama. We are even being approached by other indigenous people who
want to try it in their own culture.

~

And the federal governments in these areas are in favor of the
work, or have they given you opposition?

Neither. This is too obscure for them. Anyway, the participation of federal governments isn't needed if things can be done successfully and correctly at the local level.

~

What do you as the most pressing need related to the forest?

To increase the awareness of the past, present and future value of these forests and to create more awareness of the need to protect both the forests and the cultures that inhabit them.

~

Any last words of advice for would-be shamans traveling to the Amazon?

I like to see shamanic ritual done the right way, I am not into quickie rituals, the quick and dirty version of ayahuasca – it's quite dangerous. You don't know what you are putting in your body; these things are very powerful chemicals; and if you're not under the care of a professional shaman you are playing Russian roulette. I have been fortunate because I have been able to work with great healers and great shamans. I can't say if you go to such and such ecotourism outfit they are going to give you a real ayahuasca experience. I saw a fellow poisoned by the stuff, the last time I was in Peru. We had to call in a shaman to resuscitate him. He was so full of toxins he couldn't get out of bed.

I was working with the Mazatecs in Oaxaca in January and the first night the shaman gave me a very small dose of mushrooms and afterwards I asked her about it. She told me that you never know what people are made of and how stable they really are. And before she gives anyone a larger dose, she has to get a sense first of who you are. You can really sort of crumble psychologically with powerful hallucinogens. So don't be foolhardy.

~

Out Of The Forest & Into The Lab: Amerindian Initiation Into Sacred Science

by Professor M.C. Meyer
(Translated and edited from the original Brazilian Portuguese by Pamela Bloom)

The following article is a rare and compelling account of a Brazilian scientist's first contact with an isolated Amazonian tribe, the initiation they gave him, and their subsequent commitment to work together not only for the survival of the tribe, but also their forest and the forest wisdom they possess. As an indefatigable liaison between Amerindian tribes and growing Western markets (both cosmetic and medicinal), Prof. Meyer feels the precious onslaught of time as he jets around the world today, negotiating with cosmetic companies, drug manufacturers and bureaucrats from various countries on behalf of different Brazilian tribes, including the Sateré-Mawés, a tribe of which he is now an "official" member – the result of a rather shocking ritual, which is described in this article. As Meyer passionately states, *"In order to survive into the 21st century, this tribe must find a way to sustain itself financially."* To that end, he is creating scientific, technological, industrial and commercial structures to valorize their products, i.e., their natural resources and know-how. He is restoring an old mansion in Manaus to house and publicly display Indian artifacts that he has collected throughout his many expeditions into the jungle.

~

In 1981, I began my odyssey through the "Green Paradise" of the Amazon forest when for the first time I traced the minute shadow of our biplane as it hovered over the vast jungle floor. In the next moment, with a curious boldness, my boots touched the ground of this last great utopia and my life irrevocably changed. The magnetism of that first step, one which I would only later comprehend, marked the beginning of a passion for Amerindian knowledge that, little by little, transformed itself into a reason for living. Little did I realize, then, that the quest to understand the healing potential of the forest would also lead me into a fabulous journey of self-discovery.

In truth, the immense profusion of vegetal, animal and human life – as represented by Amazônia's vast biological diversity – exerts an irresistible fascination over everyone who has had the privilege to know it and to live with its indigenous population. Aided by my Western medical training, I have been able to verify and document, through traditional empirical research, the therapeutic properties of plants utilized for thousands of years by our native Indians: the so-called "sacred and secret molecules," which are empowered and legitimized in the eyes of the Indians by their magical, ritualistic dance – a psycho-physiological combination, I believe, which is quite equal to (or at least parallel to) a Western medical prescription. (Compare this to the traditional Western relationship between doctor and patient, and the similar ritualistic dispensation of medicine – the pharmacist's so-called "sacred and secret molecules," which are empowered and legitimized in the patient's eyes at the moment the physician takes up the prescription pad and puts pen to paper.)

New Languages Of Healing

For years I had sought to acquire a more profound knowledge of Amerindian traditions as much on the physical as the spiritual plane, but my first official mission began when UNESCO in 1983 contacted me to write a report, and afterwards a book, which would have the honor of being prefaced by the prestigious College of France. The project's objective was to analyze different neurobiological, psycholinguistic and psychocultural data to facilitate the learning of written language in autochthonous, socially disfavored populations. (On this particular occasion, UNESCO was trying to address the needs of certain populations from Africa, Latin America and the Orient, which had for a time been "literate," but were now returning to a state of illiteracy). For me, the UNESCO opportunity was perfect, since I had been seeking to collect through field research the linguistic heritage of Amazonian Indians. In this first initiative, I had the privilege of being able to document the immense richness of indigenous Amerindian graphic systems, which, in their own way, constitute a type of natural, though highly unconventional alphabet. But I also made a startling discovery: what might be called traditionally "illiteracy" had, in many of the tribes I visited, evolved into a ritualistic use of "body paintings" of such depth and detail that they might literally be considered masterpieces of contemporary plastic art. Essentially, what I discovered was that the Indians, using their bodies as canvases, manage to transform themselves into a painting or pages from a book containing the quintessence of their history, the human body becoming a living diary, a veritable surface to record a millennia of their cultural values. What was being played out before my eyes was a rich storehouse of psycho-spiritual treasures replete with its own mysteries.

It was natural, then, that my fascination with the Indians' "ambulatory" works of art extended to the prodigious choreography of their ritual dances, which constitutes an authentic *linguagem corporal* (body language, possessing a perfect signifier-signified relationship, structured like our alphabet) – a language categorized in my UNESCO book as "mimo-posturo-gestual" (mime-postural gesture); the term refers to the richness, precision and the meaning of their gestures. Over the 30 days of my first trip, as I visited over 10 different tribes (including the Kayapó, the Waimiri-Atroari, the Sateré-Mawé and others), I continually marveled at the wealth of this artistic tribal expression, more natural and vital, more artfully dramatic than the masks of the Carnival of Venice, or the Peking Opera or the Japanese Noh Theatre. Transfixed by the rich palette of color and the intricate designs, I felt like a child, eyes goggling, as if I were listening to a grandmother recount magical tales of fairies and witches, full of electrifying suspense that left goosebumps on my skin. It was as if the Indians were "writing" in another way besides their body painting (this time, through their gestures in the air and their steps on the soil) a genuine legend, a story or history – as if we, the observers, were reading a book. Even more than the ancient Greek rites, these dance rituals documented the Indians' daily agenda, as they went about celebrating birth, baptism, marriage, combat, harvesting, hunting, fishing, etc. – all the rites of passage that cement an Indian's familial relationship to his/her tribe. Confronted with such richness, my curiosity was voracious, at first provoking a certain timidity in the Indians, but in a short time my enchantment with their creations was felt by them as proof of my genuine interest in their costumes and traditions. And in this way a beautiful story of trans-cultural communication was born, founded on the deepest of mutual respect.

Scientifically speaking, the Indians' magnificent body painting, employing the natural pigments offered by forest plants, also deeply aroused my medical instincts and led me to inquire about the origin and nature of the colorant and therapeutic active principles they employed. How did they select these varieties of plants among the multitude of possibilities so generously afforded by nature? What criteria did they employ to avoid unpleasant surprises? For example, besides life-supporting medicinal plants, the lush Amazonian rainforest harbors powerful substances whose application on the skin can provoke irritation, or worse, can penetrate the bloodstream.

As I further discuss in another chapter of this book, this native art of botanical selection based on thousands of years of empirical knowledge surprised me with the abundance of hard-to-find information, not only because of the variety of colors and fixative principles, but also, and above all, because of the multitude of associated therapeutic principles. Such a rich patrimony of active principles available from the storehouse of the Indians' collective wisdom, along with their generous cooperation, convinced me to dedicate myself to the protection of this culture so at risk of extinction. To that end, it has become my mission to help them find a way to develop a project that would valorize these natural resources before it is too late.

The Forest As Sensual Art

To arrive at the home of the 1,000-member Sateré-Mawé tribe, which is situated in the center of the largest forest on the planet – about 400 kilometers from Manaus (the capital of the state of Amazonas) – we took a small bi-motor plane to the picturesque little city of Maués, where we spent the night after an interview with the local radio station. The next day, we embarked in a regional boat made of Amazonian hardwood, partially covered by a roof of woven palm leaves from the piaçaba (*Barcella odorata* – a common Amazonian palm tree from which brooms and *ocas*, indigenous Indian houses, are made) in order to protect us from the powerful, but brief equatorial rains. In truth, the weather was a glorious festival of sun and rain, punctuated by sumptuous rainbows, where the palette of colors appeared like concentric fragments, independent yet juxtaposed, just like the designs of the Indian's body painting. In fact, the tail end of the rainbow seemed to dive right in front of the prow of our boat, leaving us with the distinct impression that a celestial artist had just dipped his paintbrush full of color into the waters below, then brushed it luxuriously across the sky's canvas. In a few minutes, the sky passed from gray-black to oceanic blue to turquoise, reflecting the powerful "emerald forest" overhead as a feeling of strength and radiant peace came over us. Rejuvenated both physically and spiritually, I finally began to understand more profoundly the psychological theory of the effects of color on the human psyche.

Navigating the Rio Marau, which is only a sub-tributary of the great Amazon River, we often had the impression of crossing a broad sea, since we could not see the banks on the other side. The night, calm and serene, made navigating turns more difficult as we approached the confluence of the two rivers, such was the volume of the waters and the confusion of currents from the equalization process. Even our boatman, despite having a great knowledge of the rivers, was confused by the various trajectories. And he had good reason to be, since the magnetic force of the region – so abundant in rich minerals – disoriented the artisanal needle of our compass, turning the boats in circular spirals, just like the spiral of Archimedes. Despite hugging the banks whenever we could so as not to lose direction, we found ourselves at dawn practically in the same place as we had been hours before.

It was in this dizzying fluidity, however, that the innate sensuality of the forest – what, I believe, the Indians experience as a "spirituality of the senses" – revealed itself to me. The rising sun, the setting sun, the moon itself, in their natural quest to radiate light through the canopy, crafted mysterious shadows against the panoply of ferns, branches and leaves, making the voluptuous patterns difficult to discern and at the same time providing steamy fodder for hungry imaginations; even a jacaré-açu (*Melanosuchus niger*, family of alligators restricted to the Amazon), its little red eyes glowing in the darkness, leapt out at us as if arrived from a different world, returning finally to the bank with a ferocious whip of its tail. Lost, as the old song goes, in the "sweet solitude" of so much life, I suddenly saw in my mind's eye, behind the savage shadows projected by the silvery moon, dozens of painted Indians in ceremonies dedicated to the cult of sacred nature. I believe that it was in this moment that I began to comprehend in vivo yet another aspect of the Indian's pantheistic naturalism.

After a short night spent resting in native hammocks, we began the second day of our navigation with a wakeup call from a flock of brilliantly colored birds. Perhaps the presence of our boat set off their deafening but cheerful symphony. From the distance came the long, melodious cry of the inambu (*Crypturus cinereus*), a song both plaintive and mysterious. As we took up our canoes again, other exotic birds presented themselves, such as the coquettish uiramembi, whose voluminously arranged topknot made it look as if it had just come from the hairdresser. At times we seemed lost in a labyrinthine of *igarapés*, the arms of the river (named "way of the canoes" by the Tupis), which go deeply into the forest. It was here that we caught sight of marvelous acrobatic fish, who make heroic leaps up toward the tree branches in the naturally inundated forest, snatch a piece of fruit, then plunge dramatically back into the water with Olympic-style grace.

At the end of the afternoon, we arrived at the symbolic "harbor" of the tribe, a clearing of devirginized tropical forest, where we beheld a magnificent *maloca*, an indigenous habitation surrounded by many primitive huts.

First Impressions

Despite knowing that my companions were friends of the Indians, I felt a certain apprehension, mixed with joy, to come so close to this tribe for the first time, principally because this time our trip was not about impersonally analyzing their modes of expression, but rather about establishing a real relationship of cooperation between them and the so-called "civilized world."

When we landed the boat on the shore, we saw high on the hill a group of children that looked, according to their movements, quite excited to see us. (We could only imagine the stories they were inventing about us.) In contrast, the adults appeared more remote, keeping back approximately 100 meters (330 feet) above the hill while they tried to judge our intentions by our first gestures, unsure whether we were to be respected as guests or feared as conquerors. This is a beautiful illustration of "proxemics," the science that studies different kinds of approaches between human beings. In general, the Indians are usually mistrustful in relation to white people; their devastating past, ruled by *garimpeiros* (gold miners) and some forest product companies, certainly justifies their mistrust.

At the moment we arrived, however, a very delicate problem arose, but it had a very lucky, even auspicious ending that finally favored our communications.

At first, the group appeared completely spontaneous, but as soon as we started walking toward them, they ran away like lightning into the jungle. (Never had I seen such speed and flexibility!) So odd they looked, running so quickly, yet simultaneously looking backwards so they would not lose the least of our gestures. In one of those coming and goings, climbing up some vines, one of the children, a very young girl hardly three years old, who was always looking backwards at us, tripped and started falling in my direction, headfirst, into a huge hole that probably was at least 13 feet deep. Without even a pause to think, I threw away my package, leaped up and caught her in mid-air – *in extremis* – by one of her legs. The group, even more surprised than we were, burst into applause.

I cannot adequately describe how this single moment of response has deeply changed my life. Even today, I marvel about what would have happened if I had not been able to reach one of her legs; she would have severely hurt herself and perhaps fatally so. Further conversations with the Saterés made me realize that such a circumstance as this could have been viewed as a test (from the jungle gods?) to test my true disposition to help them. What risk would have I been willing to run for them? What sacrifice would I have made? The Indians never talked to me directly about this; I learned about it only through indirect comments.

The only thing certain was that the little Ceci never again left me alone, except when we left for the "inside" of the jungle, when she remained with the adult Indians. Otherwise, she was always silently present. Each time I would look over my shoulder, her black and brilliant eyes were fixed on me, sometimes wide-eyed with curiosity, other times serene, but always full of love, with a contagious smile, even somewhat complicitous (maybe even genuinely so), her black hair reflecting the brilliance of the sun. In ways I cannot even put into words, her bronzed skin, her charm and her childlike primitive beauty became indelible. She even wanted to live with us on the boat – a fact that her elders met with surprised amusement.

Even today, after so many years when I am writing these lines, I have this sensation that if I were to turn my head, I would see her beautiful black eyes.

From The Forest To Paris And Back

After the introductions were made by the interpreter Moises, following some Indian rites, many doubts arose in my mind regarding my attempts to communicate, since I was always trying to avoid any type of behavior that could be wrongly seen by the Indians. Even the gifts that one person normally gives another upon visiting presented a problem. What could I give in order not to contaminate such a pure natural environment? Not to give anything would also be impolite because they would certainly give us handmade presents, in addition to their gracious reception and food, when we completed our stay with them. What a dilemma! Finally, thinking over the objective of this trip, I decided to offer them the French perfumes that I had taken with me as a gift for my friends in the capital city of Manaus because they were made with Amazonian products. As a matter of fact, one aim of our encounter was to make the Indians aware of their roles as guardians of this rich forest, the future rational exploitation of which could secure for them and their ancestral culture a survival with dignity. Perfumes such as Shalimar from the house of Guerlain and Coco from Chanel are excellent examples of that creative richness because the Amazon is considered a paradise of *lauraceaces*, a family of plants that is extremely aromatic and already a source of essential oils famous all over the world. Another classic example of this is Pau rosa (*aniba roseadora variedade Ducke* and *parviflora Mez*), from whose tree we can obtain the famous linalol, one of the natural products most utilized in the perfume industry for more than a century.

Besides aromatics, the Indians use this product as an antiseptic and an astringent, as well as to relieve dental pain, eczema and lice. (At the present time, we are studying flavonoids from the leaves of this tree that apparently have a particular property to combat cellular degeneration, a common problem today.) What a beautiful contrast between the indigenous naturalism and Parisian sophistication. Besides an aromatic for Havana cigars, the Indians use cumaru or muirapagé as a powerful anti-spasmodic, breath and heart moderator, hypothermic and in the fight against pneumonia.

Of course, since none of our Indians had ever seen "fragrance" in the form of perfume packaged in such a sophisticated manner, they examined it as if the gift were an extraterrestrial object. When I showed them how to open the delicate bottles, they thought the system to be very amusing. The Judge Almeida and Senhor Michelis, who already well knew their usual reactions, were very much entertained by the scene. The person most perplexed was I, who had not the capacity to anticipate their behavior. These sympathetic beings, isolated from the consumer world, loved to laugh. Indeed, everything new was a reason for an outburst of giggles, which followed a brief moment of perplexity and introspection. Their emotions lay very close to the surface, and when they finally opened the packages, I could literally feel their emotions on my skin. Certainly it was this affable and enchanting temperament that inspired Ronsard, Montaigne and Rabelais, well before Rousseau, to write beautiful passages celebrating the myth of the "Bon Sauvage (Noble Savage)".

And yet cultural exchange in every age has its own special irony. When the natives smelled the contents of the perfume I had given them, they made grimaces, as if overwhelmed by the intensity of the perfume or as if they had seen a strange spirit coming out of the bottle, like the genie rising from Aladdin's Lamp. I now believe that if it had not been me who had given them the present, they would have thrown out the contents; when in reality the formula of the perfumes was a product of the Amazon. Such an strange twist of fate!

And yet, some days later, the Sateré women had fully adopted the Parisian perfumes, making a real ceremony of cosmetic application! Bejeweled in body paintings and surrendering to exotic dance movement, they seemed to me to be invoking the spirit of the fragrance to be released on their skin.

From Serious Business To The Laws Of Nature

After this moment of relaxed geniality, as we began our more serious conversations about medicinal plants, our hosts listened a lot, without talking much. I tried to find meaning in their native silence. Finally, the *cacique* (chief), Tuchaua Evaristo, after calm consultation with the other authorities of the tribe, decided that it would be interesting to organize for the next day a meeting of the Tribal Council so that I could present all my propositions.

Finally, after long discussions and much hesitation, the *cacique*, the *pagé* (medicine man) and the other Indians accepted the proposition to analyze together different medicinal plants utilized by the tribe as a joint project with shared renumeration to create medicines of the future. It was also decided that at sunrise we would leave for the interior of the forest to collect plant samples. The explorative mission would turn out to be particularly exotic: certain plants were collected uniquely when the drops of the morning dew were suspended on the medicinal leaves; others, when the sunshine caressed the petals of their narcotic flowers; others when the fruit fell on the ground giving access to its miraculous beans; others only when the sun is setting and the ground is very dry, giving access to its aphrodisiacal roots. As explained to me, these practical directions were given to the Indians by the forest gods. (Scientific analysis would say that empirical native wisdom "oriented" the gods.) In reality, the Indians themselves felt the necessity to legitimize their knowledge acquired through real experience with "divine guidance."

In truth, it was the Indians' humility and respect before the great mysteries of nature that made such a great impression on me. Contrast this to the Western approach, which feels the arrogant necessity to dominate nature – such as with the ancient myth of Prometheus, who stole the fire from the gods of Olympus to offer it to humans, or that of Doctor Frankenstein in the last century, who in wanting to create artificial life succeeded only in making a monster that takes back life. These stories teach us that whenever the ambitious try to betray mother nature, they are invariably punished: in the first case by Zeus who had Prometheus chained to a rock on the summit of the Cacusus, and in the second case, by Doctor Frankenstein's own monster which he himself had created. Simply, the Indian doesn't accept the pact that Faust made with the devil because he knows viscerally the power of nature and the beneficence that it contains. And for the so-called civilized world, where the results of excessive technological development have been often catastrophic, there is a great lesson to be learned here. We need only begin to list the "perversions" of our lifestyle: the nuclear leaks of Chernobyl or the proliferation of infectious diseases; the epidemic intoxications ensuing from technological manipulations of the foodchain, such as the ongoing drama of the Mad Cow Disease (*Bovine Spongiform Encephalopathy*); the nutritional emptiness of our modern diet created by the excess of synthetic and artificial food products. What few in our civilized world are aware of is the vast range of natural alternatives that the native culture has already developed that speak to the needs and conditions of modern man. For the sake of our planet, their contribution should not be ignored.

Otherwise, nature will ask her price!

The Hidden Forest

An expedition into the forest with members of the Sateré-Mawé tribe showed beautifully what nature, aided by native knowledge, can offer us in terms of natural alternatives. For example, when we began our exploration, we left without any provisions for food. After several hours of walking, the first signs of fatigue and hunger showed. Not wanting to interrupt the walk, the Indians had a solution for both symptoms: two seeds per person of guaraná (*Paulinia cupana var. sorbilis Ducke*). Baptized the "fountain of youth" by the Sateré, this plant, now used in many modern products (including a Brazilian soft drink) has important psychotonic and cardiovascular effects, promoting prolonged energy, thanks to the high dose of guaranina, guaranatina, guaranic acid and caffeine. (Another added benefit: guaraná also acts as a powerful appetite reducer.) Hours later, our Indian guide asked us, via the interpreter, if we were thirsty. With a fine dexterity, he leaped like a Tarzan to pluck a compact cipo, about six inches in diameter, which he cut into two pieces. (The cipo, commonly known as liana, is a luxuriantly growing woody tropical vine that roots in the ground and climbs around tree trunks.) From that one piece of cipo poured forth into our mouths about one liter of cold, crystalline water, rich in healthy mineral compounds, even though the outside temperature was about 35°C (95°F).

In the beginning of the afternoon, feeling our exhaustion, our native guide proposed a new elixir from the forest: the *leite do amapa*, a sap originating from a flowery tree called Amapa doce (*Brosimum potabile Ducke*), which made an potent tonic. My attention was called to the agility with which our guide cut a zig-zag route in the enormous trunk for the sap to run out. As the "tap" started, my native companions fashioned a "cup" in a matter of seconds by folding a large leaf picked from a nearby tree, as if nature itself was providing the most efficient tableside service – sufficient enough, in fact, to reach out and serve oneself. I could almost hear live music in the happy orchestra of birds, Papageno's leitmotif, perhaps, from *The Magic Flute* of Mozart.

After a long and tiring day of collecting medicinal plants recommended by the *pagé*, many kilometers from the tribe, it was impressive that none of us were really hungry. Despite having said that, at the end of the afternoon before the long return, our guide decided to give us more agreeable surprise: he stopped before a splendid tree, the Massaranduba (*Mimusops amazônica Hub*). Also called in some regions *arvore de leite*, it is the real queen of the forest. Rich in tannin, its abundant latex was as tasty as cow's milk, but thicker and richer in flavor. With the same agile grace as before, our guide served us up this nectar of the gods, which satisfied us till the next day. Besides being nutritious, the Indians combine the latex mixture with honey to make a respiratory tonic, in doses of 60-80 grams twice a day, which serves to expand their lung capacity for those long walks, principally during the hunt, that demand nonstop physical energy. Modern phytotherapy utilizes this mixture in the treatment of tuberculosis and as a plaster, a pasty preparation spread on cloth, which is applied to the body as a cure for bronchial-pulmonary diseases.

On our return, we crossed *igarapés* in a 100-foot canoe made entirely from one trunk, called *uba*. Majestically piloted by the Indians, it skimmed elegantly and silently though the inundated trees, where the leafy branches made bridges and voluptuous tunnels overhead. For moments, the only sound we heard was the ping of waterdrops as they fell from the oar. One of the surrealistic images that really struck me was a monkey who, swinging by its tail from a flexible branch, launched itself in one long impulse over the river with one hand, filled a *cuia de macaco* with water, then returned to its branch, from where it stared at us with intense curiosity as it drank its water. The *cuia de macaco* is made of the knot of wood that contains the chestnut of a well-known tree called Sapucaiauassu. When hard, the nuts fall from the shell, which is used by the monkeys as a dish. The Indians use the bark and shell as diuretics, and to fight jaundice and albinumin diabetes.

The Indians joke with these animals as if they are their friends and playmates, as if they had between them a kind of complicity based on a very special humor which escaped our comprehension. Truly, there existed between them an inherent harmony and a great familial solidarity.

A Passage Of Fire

After many diverse and long expeditions into the forest to collect medicinal plants, the *cacique* and the *pagé* of the tribe summoned me to say how satisfied they were with the possibility of establishing an equitable relationship to protect the future of their descendants – this, in the face of the "white invaders" who were coming closer and closer each time to their land – the inevitable march of progress.

To demonstrate their acceptance of our relationship, the tribe proposed my initiation into the ritual of the *Dança da Tocandira* called in Sateré-Mawé Waty ama. As a male rite of passage, this impressive, if terrifying ritual usually has the objective to initiate the Indian youth at about 10 years old (equal to our 18 years) into adulthood and its virtues of courage and harmony with nature. In order to prove his bravery before the tribe, the boy has to stick his arm, from fingertip to shoulder, into a handwoven cylinder containing an anthill of large, voracious, bitterly stinging ants (the tucandeiras are actually gigantic, about an inch in length). Tears run down the initiant's young face and he is permitted to cry out – not as an absence of courage, but in respect to the forces of nature which are considered superior to man. What is not permitted is screaming, nor any retreat from the challenge, since that would display disrespect to the tribe and would essentially bar the initiant from participating in certain ceremonies of hunting, fishing of certain fish, collecting medicinal plants, etc.

In my case the ritual was being given to offer me the title of "Patente de Capitão," a kind of decoration equivalent in the West to an honorary citizen, who had been deemed acceptable to pursue beneficial work on the behalf of the tribe (something akin to receiving the keys of the city, but much more serious, because of the implications, responsibilities and confidence agreements). Certainly it was to be considered a ritual that conferred on me the confidence of the Sateré, in thanks to the Supreme Being, called Tupana, whom they believed was the god of nature represented by the force of thunder.

Whereas usually one's father, godfather and *pagé* accompany the initiant into the forest to meditate and invoke the spirits, the *cacique* and the *pagé* took me into the jungle, where during a walk we first ate a tasty *inga-açu* (*Inga edulis M.*), a sweet pulpy fruit that is also used for mouthwashes and gargles to fight thrush, laryngitis and bronchitis. As the interpreter had been given no directive to accompany us, I couldn't ask the reason for the ingestion; perhaps it was to purify the buccal cavity and the vocal cords, since later we had to sing exotic chants to invoke the spirits of the forest and ask for their blessing. This was done on foot under the powerful sumauma tree (*Ceiba pentandra Gaertn*), about 80 meters high (260 feet) and whose trunk, at its base, was so huge that it required the arms of 15 men to encircle it. (The Indians use its sap against conjunctivitis, and on this occasion we made a ritual face and eye washing from the excellent fresh water obtained by cutting one of its enormous emerging roots. Then, as if we could now turn our purified eyes toward heaven, we began the invocations of protection to the nature deities who guarded the initiation ceremonies. Cautiously, I tried to repeat it, without comprehending, but soon I felt an immense sensation of peace which, little by little, transformed into a real jubilation. A sense of magical protection encircled me, giving me the impression that nothing bad would ever happen to me. Then I was prepared for the ritual, which consisted of a dance that lasted for hours.

The day before, the Indians had gone into the forest to look for ants. In order to fill up the glove with ants, they stunned hundreds of tucandeiras with the sap of an anesthetic plant, whose name I do not want to divulge since it would be a sacrilege for persons other than the Saterés to use it in a commercial context. (In fact, the glove is woven with the anesthetized ants inside in order not to hurt them while putting them inside.) The following day the ants wake up from the anesthesia and remain inside the glove for two more days at which time (the time of the ceremony), they have become hungry and furious. The glove to be used in the ceremony was made with very fine and resistant fibers from a special palm tree called tucuma, which is already used in the making of hammocks, and whose nuts are rich in oils and fatty essential acids for good digestion. The fibers of the glove are specially colored with forest plants by a weaver, who creates an artistic motif especially for the initiant. In my case, they evidently used a symbolic number of ants since they knew well that "city whites" couldn't maintain the same resistance to the powerful toxins of the virgin forest as they could.

Some days before, the Indians submitted me to two ant bites – with an interval of five days in between – to see if I would have an allergic reaction; the interval between the two bites showed that the Indians already possessed a secular empirical knowledge of anaphylaxis, which consists of an extreme allergic reaction that could result in death if the toxin is injected a second time into an individual allergic to such a toxin. (Evidently, the quantity of toxin I was given was kept to a minimum to avoid any problem.)

The irony of fate: anafilazia was only discovered by Western medicine in 1910 by the famous French researcher Professor Charles Richet, of the Pasteur Institute. Incredible as it seems, the discovery was made from a toxin, crepitina, isolated from an Amazonian plant called assaçu (*Hura crepitans*), which the Indians used in fishing to stun the fish and whose properties are described under *An Exotic Phamacy*, above). Thanks to this discovery, Professor Richet received one of the First Nobel Prizes of Medicine in 1912.

Dancing Into Eternity

For the unusual event of my initiation, the Sateré invited members of the neighboring tribes, who unintentionally performed an improvisatory ballet of *ubas* (canoes) on the river Maraú before mooring on the Sateré quay. Just a moment before, in this bucolic twilight scene, the horizon burst forth in a multicolored display.

We were directed to a central maloca, where the women of the tribe served us the famous *açaí* wine (*Eutepe oleracea Mart*). The round fruit of this palm tree, when mature, is treated with hot water and left to ferment with other ingredients: the result is an aromatic drink of dark violet color which, at the sound of the drums, whistles, panpipes and other exotic musical instruments, took us deep into the merry festival atmosphere. At my side always were the *cacique* and the *pagé*, the tender Ceci always close by. All together, we began to dance with arms entwined, forming a linear chain, which circled about on its own axis. My first steps were hesitant, but rapidly the melody and the ecstatic rhythms marked the duple beat and my steps fell into perfect harmony with the group. (In fact, back in Paris, whenever I listened to a cassette recording made of this occasion, I would find myself immediately transported to this supernatural moment of synchronicity, peace and communion.) Indeed, in this moment I felt myself to be truly and completely Indian.

After an hour of dancing (perhaps two or three – the notion of time disappeared completely), they ceremoniously placed the famous Tucandeira glove on me. Immediately, there were many sharp incisive bites, and my head twisted in agony from the thunderous fire through my body – pain beyond words. The music, the dances and the singing continued to encourage me and give me nerve. Some time passed – I don't know how long since it seemed like an eternity – and finally, the *pagé* took off the glove. The Indians came close with choreographed footsteps, holding a basin with a macerated mixture of medicinal analgesic plants, whose names they showed me in sign language. Then they bathed my arm delicately with this mixture, and the pain progressively subsided. On the following day I practically had no swelling or edema, and two days later absolutely no hematomas, though at least light scars without infection.

At the end of the ceremony, after a discourse with the *cacique* whose contents only he can reveal, I was dispatched to receive the famous "Patente de Capitão." In response, I offered a few emotional words, to honor what they had bestowed on me and to acknowledge the highly privileged moment of their ancestral traditions. I felt a tremendous emotion and a certain shyness, much much greater than I felt in my first degrees at the College of France, in the conference I gave at the Sorbonne and in all the international congresses. Moved by the touching expression of affection from my new friends and comrades, I offered to the *cacique*, in a confraternal gesture, my shirt sweaty from the inebriating dance and the tumble of emotions provoked by the tucandeiras. It was as if I were offering to him, the respected chief of my tribe, the sweat from his own brow.

On the following day I rested a little from the fateful event and I felt like a new man.

In the final ceremony of the initiation, one normally has one's shoulders scratched with the teeth of a paca so that they should become large, the buttocks well toned and the chest strong and muscular. I don't believe that in my case they had expected that my shoulders, buttocks and chest would have been particularly developed to confront the challenges of nature. Certainly they had considered that since I had already long passed the age of puberty, they should spare me this heroic epilogue.

~

Note: The primary contact I had with the Sateré-Mawés, was established thanks to two personalities of the region: The Deputy Darcy Michelis, whose father during the middle of this century had already succeeded in establishing the first peaceful relationship with the Sateré and who, himself, was as much a naturalist explorer as he was a politician. (Her father actually abandoned his political career and left the capital of the state to dedicate himself to a more natural life among the Indians.)

Judge of Justice Alvarina Miranda de Almeida of Manaus, who for many years has been dedicated to the protection of this indigenous community, with important programs especially directed toward the Sateré-Mawé women, and with whom I am organizing an international symposium on Amerindian literacy and the economic development of Brazil's Amazônia. The objective of this symposium is to create a system of written communication adapted to an indigenous people which would permit them to safeguard their previous cultural patrimony and to document their knowledge of medicinal plants, so that in the future they could establish equitable relationships with interested industries of forest products, based on the respect for the Indians' "sacred molecules" previously deemed secret and thus inviolable to materialistic gain.

Where Are The Fruit Trees?

By Trish Shanley

The following article by scientist and sociologist Trish Shanley records an incredible epoch in the life of one forest village in their quest to use, but not abuse, the resources of their primeval backyard. Shanley's own work is itself an inspiring example of how Western scientists are now giving back to the communities they research. Though not outlined in this article, Shanley has been instrumental in assisting rural communities to generate and exchange ecological and economic information necessary to conserve forest resources. Based on five years of

The epitome of a caboclo: *tough, independent and dressed for success. This old lady lives alone in the jungle.*

participatory research on the ecology, use and management of local species (fruit, fiber, game and medicinal), Shanley's team of forest residents has generated data demonstrating the subsistence value of nontimber forest products, experimented adding value to these products and created community forest reserves to protect fruit and medicinal oil trees. What Shanley is discovering through interfacing with *caboclos* (rural peasant farmers of mixed descent) is that creatively designed educational and intercultural exchanges can have profoundly beneficial and long-ranging results, not only for the local populations, but for the preservation of the forest as well. Among other projects her team has developed traveling troupes, populated by locals, who disseminate essential information to their nonliterate neighbors through drama and nonverbal pictorial manuals. In order to give my readers a more intimate look at Amazonian life, I have chosen the following article of Shanley's to show in minute detail the day-to-day struggle of forest dwellers.

~

Deep in the Amazon forest, 230 miles south of Belém, Clemente, (a 35-year-old forest dweller who has never traveled further than 130 km. from his village) leans against a corner support beam on the porch of a neighbor's sagging, gray hut.

"Patricia," he calls to me through the night air. "I cannot bring the fruits to market tomorrow. My wife is sick. I am here to ask Beca to go, but he refuses."

In a dark corner Beca, a large, strong man, now looks suddenly small, his posture obstinate and unwilling. I stand silent, stunned. Clement's nonchalant voice belies the consequence of his statement. For this is not the sale of just any fruits – it is an experiment. It is the first sale of forest fruits in the history of this small Amazonian village.

Clemente is a good teller of tale, so I am not sure what to believe. We decide to check in on his wife. The moon in its first quarter is a mere cuticle. Through the blackness, Clemente moves sure-footed through the muddy pig path to his house, leading me up a leaning wooden plank into his one-room home, where eight, faded, threadbare hammocks stetch at odd angles between four walls. Cocoon-like, the center of each hammock sags, holding the small, curled bodies of sleeping children. We duck under cord after cord to reach the ninth hammock where his wife, Branca, is lying, stomach down, groaning and spitting towards the floor into a wrinkled aluminum basin. We call Ambrosia, the local midwife, who arrives quickly. A widow with black sunken eyes, she inspects Branca and informs us it is time.

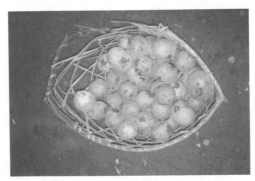

A bowl of piquiá *fruit*
© *T. Shanley*

Fruit-bearing Treasures

It is also time for another type of ripening. In the darkness, between the homes of Clemente, Beca and Ambrosia, sit eight large wooden boxes crudely secured with forest bark and rusty nails. Within lie fruit that have been gathered over the last two days from primary forest fruit trees, the brown spherical *piquiá*, its bright yellow oily pulp eaten after boiling in salted water; the green, egg-shaped *cho*, its thick layer of grainy flesh eaten raw and in juices, and the *bacuri*, its sweet white pulp a favorite not only in its natural state but also in jams, potato chips and ice cream.

For centuries, these fruits have been appreciated by both human and animal populations throughout the Amazon Basin. In the last few decades they have begun to appear in Amazonian fruit and vegetable markets, in supermarkets, even in airport gift shops. Products of these fruits are atop ice cream cones, spread on toast as jelly, used as filling in fancy pastries and in soaps. For poor, rural villages like Clemente's, the sale of forest fruits could be a source of much-needed cash. The fruit sale planned by Clemente and the villagers is an applied outcome of two years of ecological research that we (the Capim River communities, the Rural Workers Union of Paragominas and The Woods Hole Research Center) have conducted together.

The question all of us have pondered is: Might the sale of forest fruits offer more than the sale of trees?

Obstacles Natural & Man-made

But fruits from Clemente's village have never reached a market. What is not eaten by humans from the hundreds of fruit trees scattered throughout the 3,000-hectare community-held forest are eaten by paca, deer, armadillo, squirrels or ants. Most of the fruit, however, remains on the forest floor to rot.

Even more salient to the problem is the lack of accessible transportation. Travel to town, and thus sale of forest products, is rare. Located on a tributary of the Amazon, the village has historically been reachable only by canoe. Many folk never set foot on the "street," as they call the nearest town, during their lifetimes.

However, a remarkable turnabout in land ownership through the Brazilian Amazon has brought an onrush of new neighbors to this wooded river region. In merely the last 10 years, the scene looking out across the river from Clemente's home has changed. To the north and to the south forests have been removed. In the place of thousands of trees stand a few head of cattle.

You Can't Eat Just One

A bacuri plant in the arms of a child
© *T. Shanley*

When Clemente was a kid, he regularly swiped a canoe from a neighbor, paddled across the river, and scrambled over the opposite bank to reach the famed forest of *bacuri,* where he and his buddies downed hundreds of bacuri and toted even more home. (As with potato chips, few folks can eat only one *bacuri;* without even leaving the shade of a tree's crown, individual gatherers regularly down 10-15 fruit a pop.) Today, in this former forest, badly shaved, burnt and oddly bald, not a single *bacuri* tree remains. Beyond the blackened stumps extend rough-hewn logging trails, which cleave open the remaining forest. These roads haphazardly wind their way to one of the nearest city's 137 sawmills.

Ironically, however, such roads offer new means to markets. A few days before Clemente's wife begins labor, the heeding ears of his nephew detect the sound of a truck crossing the river. Curious, he swipes a canoe from a neighbor and paddles upstream. There, he discovers that the truck at the ranch will return to town in a few days. There is room for people and products. And it is smack in the middle of the rainy winter, the season of forest fruits.

Global Synchronicity

Unbeknownst to Clemente, discussion of the marketing of forest fruits has been surfacing in distance offices of policy makers the world over. Research results from tropical forests had demonstrated that the potential income from the sale of select non-wooded forest resources could, in certain cases, well outstrip income from the sale of timber. Among conservationists, the notion has caught fire, offering an avenue for local people to glean income from forests while leaving them standing. For a number of nimble industries, the gathering and sale of non-timber forest products (NTFPs) became more than a concept. Juices, candies, ice creams and body oils featuring exotic ingredients from places only dreamed of, have swiftly reached the shelves of corner grocery stores all over the world.

Unaware of marketing trends and policy discourses, Clemente and the villagers continued to harvest and utilize the vines, plant remedies, fruits and game their forest offered. Although they had never sold any forest products other than timber, they began to look for new ways to generate income from their forests. After five successive timber sales over the last decade, the number and diversity of trees and game within their land was diminishing. Therefore, to assist the villagers, the local rural workers' union began seeking technical assistance to determine if the forests of the river basin had any species holding market potential for non-wood forest products.

A New Kind Of Western Invasion

Two years ago, our team of researchers entered the river communities to explore the commercial and subsistence value of the area's non-wood forest products and the ecological sustainability of their harvest. By the time the villagers began to consider selling forest products, we had two years of market and forest research results and knew that, of all their products, the fruits of uchi (*Endopleura uchi*), bacuri (*Platonia insignis*), and piquiá (*Caryocar villosum*), held both ecologically sustainable and economically compensatory potential.

When the truck arrived at the ranch during the harvest season, the community plunged headfirst into their first concerted effort at marketing NTFPs. The humble marketing attempts that followed exploded into a myriad of lessons in commercialization, lessons unseen and unreckoned from the desks of distant policy makers.

First Dilemmas

Because villagers are accustomed to gathering fruit for only their own consumption, the number of trees kept in a family's sphere is small, perhaps 10 or fewer. When considering selling fruits, however, a village must collect a greater abundance of product. While some villagers, especially hunters, are well aware of the exact location of many forest fruit trees, others are not. The morning after the truck arrives, as the pink sun rose over the brown river, Clemente entered my hut with a question, "So where are the fruit trees?"

Most large trees no longer stand near the village. Most have been swept into the river by logging companies that make their profit from the valuable hardwoods. Others have been harvested to build canoes or logged and burnt to make room for small agricultural fields. Therefore, Clemente and his neighbors must walk a distance of three to five kilometers (3.1 miles) past quilt-like patches of low secondary growth to find these high forest species. When located, skidder trails and logging activity have not infrequently dumped crowns of trees on top of others. Clemente, with his two friends, Beca and Branco, must climb underneath the branches of felled trees, searching for hidden fruit.

Beating The Odds

On their first collecting day they work swiftly, hopefully inspecting one *piquiá* after another. In the forest, the practical consequences of biodiversity signify that one must walk one's pants off to find similar trees. In two hours, Clemente and Branco pass 12 enormous *piquiá* trees, but only three have fruit, for a total fruit count of just seven. At 10 cents per fruit, this was not a huge haul. When asked about whether a particular tree will fruit and what its possible production could be in any one year, *caboclos* remain silent; it's a crap shoot on which few are willing to bet. Variable fruiting patterns of rainforest species signify that the odds of any one tree giving fruit in any particular year may not be good. Enormous inter- and intraspecific variation exists.

Beneath *piquiá* number 20, however, they spy close to 100 brown fruit, the size of softballs. Tan with a slight green underpaint, they lie randomly scattered 100-130 feet below the massive winding branches from which they have fallen. They spill over an area larger than the size of a baseball infield. Clemente opens one that has crash-landed onto a log, smashing its thick exocarp. The pulp inside is bright yellow and he sniffs it: yes, sweet. He and Branco quickly gather the night's fruit fall, 79 *piquiá*. All those which have opened upon landing are separated and taken home for consumption.

In this fruiting season (1993), the *piquiá* and *bacuri* trees giving a good deal of fruit happen to be found at the limits of the community forest. But paca, armadillos, ants and locally abundant rodents have beaten Clemente and Branco to these remote trees. *Uchi*, being a food of forest squirrels and bearing fine skin, needs quick pick-up. During a recent harvest season, close to 80% of the total production of 24 uchi trees was eaten by game or insects. Fortunately, *bacuri* and *piquiá*, with their thick skins, stand up well for days on the forest floor. In the shade of the wet forest, mosquitoes, whose populations rise with winter rains, bite at the arms and legs of Branco and Clemente as they pause to gather fruit. The fruit are thrown quickly into large woven plastic sacks and slung over their backs, each holding approximately 80 kilos. The *piquiá* and the *bacuri*, bruised by pressure of their weighty neighbors, begin oozing, causing stains to clothes and irritation to skin where the heavy sacks rub backs and arms. Thus, Clemente and Branco begin their riverward journey.

Carrying The Booty Back Home

It is a circuitous walk of five kilometers (3.1 miles) that the men must traverse to reach the river. Vegetation, spurred on by winter rains, suffocates former trails. Clemente's shinbones are lost in muddy streams as his thighs break trail against leaves, twigs and vines. He must not move with speed by caution. The rain brings a disparate medley of snakes which endure in trails, puddles, brush. Some, as he fortuitously discerned when collecting, dwell frozen, camouflaged beside ripe fruit.

Back in the village, Clemente and Branco drop the fruit onto the dusty ground outside their homes. A pack of hungry kids scoop up the open yellow fruit thrown and rush off to drop them into a pot of river water to boil and eat. The remaining fruit are packed tightly into sacks and knotted with vine. With his thumb and middle finger, Clemente unearths a nub of charcoal from the damp earth and slowly marks his initial C on each bag.

Having heard of fruit loss due to transport in sacks, Clemente and Branco decide to package some fruit in boxes. They collect thick slabs of forest trees which have been cut for home construction and jerry-rig these together using nails resurrected from soil and neighbors. With the butt of a machete, Clemente pounds rusty nails into hard damp wood, dumps fruit wholesale into the box, conjures a lid out of remaining wood scraps and seals everything with thick forest twine. Stars and a slip of a moon cast faint light onto the boxes.

Under this same moon Clement's wife begins labor, and under this moon an alternative seller of fruits must be found. Clemente begins to scout. He decides to awaken Neginho because Neginho is known for his understanding nature and interest in the fruit sale. As his family sleeps in hammocks behind him Neginho, looking troubled, stands silent and immobile, wanting to respond favorably, but obviously still pondering. Walking away, Clemente is hit with the realization that Neginho does not know numbers well. In villages along the river, illiteracy can reach over 70%. This and the general lack of market experience cancels out many candidates. Clement returns to Beca, who has collected the largest chunk of fruits. Clemente warns him that his profits from the sale may be in jeopardy if he does not go. Beca consents.

At pre-dawn, the blackened silhouette of Beca and the fruit gatherers bend beneath unwieldly boxes. They lack flashlights. In the black of night, their leathery, ragged feet instinctively feel their way down a fire-ant infested trail along the steep bank. The coffin-like boxes, weighty with wilting fruit, are dropped precariously in small gray canoes. Hoping for a profit from the sale of fruits, Beca's wife, Lucia, president of the village mother's club, descends the slippery bank, removes a worn flipflop and scoops up excess water from one canoe. Along the river bank, bags and boxes of fruit sink the weighty canoes deep into the river. Scant room exists for the human occupants. The river's winter width is fully three times that of its summer girth. Consequently, its current is strong. The destination is the truck, five kilometers (3.1 miles) upstream. Three hours later, with the help of seven men, the fruit is loaded. Now, 122 kilometers (134 miles) of uncertain logging roads lies before them. The winter has brought not only rain and falling fruit, but collapsed bridges, overturned logging trucks and lost lives.

This day, however, the journey goes well, and the party reaches town within only four hours of departure. Pulling up to the muddy, rambunctious marketplace, Beca, Nego and Branco glance about. Milling around the marketplace are hundreds of strong poor, hopeful farmers, some with more sales experience and some with less. Some bear *farinha*, others fish, still others fruit. It is past midday, the sun is high, and trade began six hours earlier when light first touched the vegetables, dust and dogs.

Quantity Or Quality?

All of Clemente's village have experience in making and selling *farinha*, a product of manioc, the main agricultural crop of the region. It is their principal staple and market commodity. Unlike durable *farinha*, which travels well, fruits are likely to bruise, break open, spoil or rot. In the commotion of this spanking new activity, quantity of fruit, not quality, had been paramount. The fruits had not been washed, dried, selected or carefully packaged. Thus, more than half bit the dust.

In addition to rotting fruit, competition for cramped marketing space is high. Living within 3,000 hectares of spacious forest, Beca and his comrades have little practice brandishing sharp elbows. Their non-aggressive natures and heavy loads of fruit combine to settle them at a fair distance from the front row of buyers' traffic. Pilferers, posing as taste-testing customers, visit only to fill their stomachs with fruit samples and run. Nonetheless, true customers do appear. A wizened former farmer, accustomed to the taste of uchi on her lips each winter, approaches the stand, happily requesting 60 fruit. Sixty? What do we put them in? While Beca stands guard over their products, Neginho and Branco run between makeshift stalls, kicking up dust as they go. With scant change that they scrape up between them, they purchase 25 thin plastic sacks. Christened, they return to await more trade.

The Commerce Of Empty Stomachs

Uncertain of prices and numbers, Nego is unable to help at the booth. He is large, young and hungry. Beca lets him go. He scouts work and finds some. For eight hours daily he runs hunched over carrying 60-kg. sacks of *farinha* from truck to market. With his earning he is able to eat a meal of rice and beans with a sliver of meat and *farinha*. At dawn, he catches a ride atop a logging truck through the forest. Waves of dusty clay paint his sweaty body and throw fine yellow particles into his dark brown eyes. Under the equatorial sun, hatless and penniless he walks the remaining 22 kilometers home.

For Beca and Branco, a day, a night and another day pass. Nightly, they drag their unsold fruit to a deposit area. From there they enter a cement-walled room, where they dodge layer upon layer of occupied hammocks to find space for theirs. Latecomers, they must hang their hammocks close to the latrine. Mosquitoes orbit their sweaty heads and the smell of rotting vegetables and urine surrounds them. Exhausted, they throw their bodies into their hammocks. Soon, it is dawn. They rise, scramble to the deposit area and drag the remaining fruit to their stand. Lowering the price to liquidate what will soon rot, they sell the last of the edible 2,408 fruit and throw the rest into the gutter. What is their net gain? It is hard to know. Their own cost of eating, and of a few nights drinking cachaça, have dug into Beca's take. By the time he makes it back to the village aboard a rancher's truck, it is a full five days after his departure. Some collectors receive a take of the profits, and others, none.

A Taste Of Success

Three generations of Clemente's ancestors had lived along the river and yet this was the first time in the history of this forest that its fruits had made the journey to a market for sale. After this first sale, the rural telephone, swifter than any electronic network, spread word fast about the small, easy "fortune," that might be gained from fruits. Jeering or jealous, many remained skeptical and continued working steadily in the manioc fields and sweating in the production of farinha.

Inspired by the men's success, however, Theodora and women from a neighboring village enter the forest together to scout fruits. They are beginning a mother's club, and are hopeful that with small fruit earning they might buy used clothes and lye to make soap. Three months into the season, trees have already released the bulk of their harvest. If they are not been eaten by parrots, armadillos or ants, the skins open and rot, leaving a thick brown muddy fruit spread atop the forest floor. Barefoot, the women carefully pick their way around the red ants and putrescent fruit. Putting together their joint knowledge of the forest, they recall which trees bear late in the season, and scout these, rescuing the last of the year's fruit. Antoninho, a relative and natural entrepreneur, agrees to accompany them to market.

Tallying Learned Wisdoms

Fortunately, lessons had been learned from the men's first sale. This time fruits are selected, washed and left to dry. Small boxes of thin wood with cushioning leaves are used to transport the fruit. The women and Antonino leave the village at night, arriving in the city pre-dawn. They fight their way to the front of the sales area. Since there are no other farmers selling fresh fruits, they can now set the price, doubling it from the first sale. Taste-testers who have no intention to buy are shunned. An ice cream shop owner buys all of Theodora's *bacuri* and promises he will buy any more that she brings. They sell all 268 fruits, go shopping for exactly what they had planned and return to the community the next day.

One month later: Proudly wearing used clothes purchased with fruit money, two members of the mothers' club visit another river community to speak of the forest fruit sale and the practical benefits they have gained. They speak of saved income, health, nutrition and goods. One sack of fruit has brought 10 times the value of a sack of farinha for less than a tenth of the time or effort. The sale of only seven *bacuri* equals the same value that the logger offered for an entire tree. It was also found that three hunters glean 77 kgs. of goods under fruit trees in one month, while the vitamin contents of fruits are cited as chasing away flus and sicknesses that might otherwise be treated by costly remedies. The community also calculates the value of the fruit that certain families have eaten. (Such subsistence utilization, while not directly placing money in villagers' pockets, offers a substantial hidden income.) Laughter rings out as Mangueira, a full-bellied fellow, figures that he and his family ate over $200 of forest fruit in one month.

A Mother's Counsel

Lastly, now in darkness, Theodora rises to speak. A small oil lamp shines light upon her blue and white lace skirt. Unaccustomed to attention from a crowd, she talks quietly, timidly. She begins by relating what the sale gave to the mothers' club, she tells of the gathering of the fruit, of laughter and singing under their trees. She tells of the lack of any gain from timber sales, of continual impoverishment, of sweating day after day after year in the production of farinha only to sell the product for a pittance. She tells of the small earning from the fruit which went towards purchasing clothes and lye for soap making. She speaks of their gain from their forest. And they have not been cheated. They have not sweat only to be robbed.

The crowd of men and women remain standing, quiet. Their hands, hanging at their sides, laying in their laps, are worn, tired, cut, bruised. Then suddenly, in the darkness, their palms meet and applause breaks out. No, they will not all take fruits to market. They will not all have the time, the transport, the means. They will not all wear fruit clothes. But as long as the forest stands they will all collect vines, hunt game, eat fruits and apply medicinal oils. The forest will continue to offer what in the city they could find only in supermarkets, pharmacies, hardware stores and construction outlets, markets presently out of their reach. However, to shop in the forest, their pockets need not be full. They know that they may freely roam and harvest in the forest, where there exists a veritable fortune, and (at least for the time being) no cash register.

~

CULTURE

Cuisine

Since Brazil has been a country populated primarily through immigration, its various delicious cuisines reflect an enormous variety of ethnic influences. From the German delicacies in the South to the heavy Portuguese fare in the interior, Brazilian cuisine at its best has incorporated old-world traditions along with native products to create a heady blend of taste and textures. By necessity, cuisine in the Amazon is highly original and regional, combining exotic tropical fruits, vegetables and fish with cooking techniques that often come straight from Native Indian traditions.

Dishes of Pará

The state of Pará, which includes the cities of Belém and Santarém, has over generations developed specific dishes that are not to be missed. Among them are:

Pato ao Tucupi (Duck in Tucupi Sauce)

This is one of the most tantalizing dishes in the Amazon. The *tucupi*, a yellow liquid extracted from the manioc and cassava root, contributes to the intense flavor. Long hours of cooking and blending are required, primarily because the manioc root is poisonous in its raw state. After the duck is roasted, it is cut into pieces and left to simmer in the tucupi sauce, to which has been added garlic, basil and chicory. *Jambu*, a sharp-tasting plant, is boiled in salt water, drained, then placed over the *tucupi*-based duck. The dish is best served with fluffy white rice, *farinha d'agua* (a starchy flour made of fermented manioc that is eaten as habitually as bread), and *pimenta-de-cheiro* (hot pepper).

Desfiado de Pirarucu (Shredded Pirarucu Fish)

Dried slices of *pirarucu* are soaked to remove the excess salt, then boiled and shredded. The mixture is then sautéed with a common Brazilian seasoning of crushed garlic, olive oil, onion, *cheiro-verde* (green herbs) and tomatoes. A more substantial dish called *mexido* is made by adding eggs. (For more information on the fish *pirarucu*, see the *Flora & Fauna* section, page 52.)

Pirarucu Grelhado or "Na Brasa" (Grilled Pirarucu Fish)

After soaking to eliminate excess salt, pieces of fried, salted *pirarucu* are grilled or cooked over a brazier until golden. The traditional side dish is *farinha d'água* (manioc flour), which is eaten often with *feijão manteiguinha-de-Santarém* (butter bean) salad. A delicious variation is to serve the sliced fish sprinkled with olive oil and topped with onion rings.

Pirarucu no Leite de Coco (Pirarucu Fish in Coconut Milk)

The dried, salted fish of the *pirarucu* is first soaked overnight, then simmered in a delicious tropical coconut milk, which is not coconut water, but juice extracted from the coconut meat through a long process of grating and pressing. At times, chefs make a tantalizing substitution with the milk of *castanha do Pará* (Brazil nut).

Pirarucu na Chapa Quente (Pirarucu on Hot Plate)

This is a huge freshwater crayfish served sizzling on a hot plate.

Peixada (Fish Stew)

This steamy broth is usually made with only one type of fish, preferably *filhote, pescada amarela* or *tucunaré*. The fish steaks or slices are first marinated with lemon salt and garlic. Separately, a stock is made with the fish head and seasoned with *cheiro verde* (green herbs, such as parsley, coriander, and onions, along with salt and crushed garlic). When the heads are cooked, they are removed, and potato halves and fish slices are added to the stock and simmered. The accompaniments include hard-boiled eggs, *farinha seca* (dry manioc flour that tastes a little like sawdust) and *pirão de farinha d'agua*, a flawlessly smooth, gelatinous gravy of manioc flour, made using the same fish stock. *Pimenta de cheiro* (hot pepper) puts a tang to the flavor.

Caldeirada (Caldron of Fish Stew of Chowder)

The huge kettle in which fishermen cook their freshly caught fish is called a *caldeirada*. Similar to *peixada* in style of cooking and seasoning, the dish *"caldeirada"* involves a potpourri of fish and vegetables. It's excellent as a light nutritious meal. Served alongside are usually boiled eggs and *farinha seca* (dry manioc flour) or *farinha d'água* (manioc flour with the same stew liquid).

Vatapá paraense (Shrimp Pará-style)

This glutinous shrimp entrée, with the texture of a thick gravy or mush, requires two days for preparation. It's delicious, though not visually appealing. Dried salted shrimps are soaked in cold water, then sautéed with palm oil (*dendê*), onions, tomatoes and chives. Coconut milk is added and the mixture is left to simmer. Rice, flour, cornstarch or breadcrumbs are used to thicken it. Garnishes are made with cooked *jambu* leaves (sharp-tasting) and shrimp.

Tamuatá no Tucupi (Tamuatá Fish in Tucupi Sauce)

This typical Amazonian fish, also known as *cascudo*, has a hard shell and a yellowish meat. It's seasoned traditionally with chicory or endive and basil. The topping is the ubiquitous *jambu*, a plant with a sharp tang.

Maniçoba (Stew of Maniva and Mears)

Appreciate this dish fully since its takes one week to make. Shoots of the *maniva* species of manioc are ground, then cooked no less than four days. Then an array of products reminiscent of the Brazilian *feiojoada* is added: jerked beef, calves' feet, bacon, smoked pork, blood sausages, pig's feet and ears. The difference is that *maniva* shoots are used instead of black beans.

Caranguejo Tic-Toc (Whole Crabs)

"Tic-toc" is the noise made when cracking open crustaceans. Freshly caught crabs are boiled in water spiced with salt, lemon and garlic. Diners are given a little wooden mallet to break the shell and are expected to eat the crabmeat without the use of a fork.

Unha de Caranguejo (Crab Claws)

After the crab claws are boiled in salt, garlic and lemon, the part with meat is wrapped in a mixture of potatoes, shredded crab meat, egg and corn meal, then deep fried. *Pimenta-de-cheiro* (hot pepper) is sometimes added for spike.

Casquinho de Carangejo (Stuffed Crabs)

After the crabs are boiled in water and salt, the meat is removed and sautéed with olive oil, various herbs and the little yellow pepper indigenous to Pará. The mixture is served in the crab shell and covered with *farinha d'agua* (manioc flour toasted in butter with olive oil and sometimes mixed with eggs).

Caruru Paraense (Dry Shrimp Pará-style)

Shelled dry shrimp is the staple of this dish, sautéed with palm oil, onion, garlic, scallions, green peppers and black pepper. Everything is boiled in water, then thickened with sifted *farinha seca* (manioc flour). Okra cut crosswise to resemble little wheels (the amount used is subject to the chef's whim) is added while the mixture boils. The finished dish is often garnished with cooked *jambu* leaves and dry shrimp.

Tacacá (Shrimp Soup in a Gourd)

You'll find lots of urban Amazonians sipping this soup on the street. Traditionally, it's drunk from a small bowl made from a gourd, called a *cuia*. It is sold by *tacacazeiras*, generally in the late afternoon on the principal street corners in such cities as Belém. Various ingredients are mixed into the *cuia* after you order one, such as *tucupi* (a preparation of manioc liquid spiced with onions, *jambu* leaves, etc.), cooked tapioca and dried shrimps. If you want added spice, ask for pimenta.

Farinha d'agua (Flour sidedish)

One of the numerous varieties of *farinha* (flours) that are made from manioc, this dish is a ubiquitous companion to most Parense dishes. The finest quality comes from the colonies (small truck farmers). The flour itself can be purchased in the local outdoor markets, but it must always be toasted. Other types of flour made from manioc include tapioca and seca.

Jambu (A condiment)

This sharp-tasting narcotic plant is an inseparable companion of the *tucupi* sauce, and is also essential to other dishes native to Pará, like *tacacá* and *pato no tucupí*. If you chew the leaves, you will experience a small quivering of the lips; as such, it is sometimes referred to as an aphrodisiac. It must be boiled rapidly in water with a little salt before it can be added to dishes.

Pimenta-de-Cheiro (Fragrant Hot Pepper)

Among the enormous varieties of regional plants, this little round hot pepper, an indelible mark of Parense cooking, is remarkable for its unusual and aromatic perfume, as well as its brilliant yellow or red color.

Tucupi (Manioc sauce)

As explained above, *tucupi* sauce is the yellow liquid extracted from the manioc root. Its preparation has never wavered from the original Indian technique, which incorporated an elongated woven straw called an *espremedor* as a squeezer. Since it is poisonous the juice must be cooked for a very long time before it can be added to dishes. Its addition to dishes like *tacacá*, *leitão* (suckling pig), and all forms of game and fish is indispensable.

Amazonas Dishes

Many of the above dishes can be found in the state of Amazonas as well, with some local variations in cooking style and spice. As in Pará, local fish remain the mainstay of the Amazonas diet, which is cooked with some Portuguese, African and French influences. Among the principal fish that are eaten in this region is the *tambaqui*, which is typically served baked or in a chowder. The *pirarucu*, known as the codfish of the region, is preserved for eating through a salt process. *Tucunaré*, with its milder taste, is often used in chowders. The *jaraqui*, a local favorite in Amazonas, is served with manioc flour and hot sauce.

Amazonian Fruits

Do not even think about leaving the Amazon without tasting at least one of the literally hundreds of tropical fruits found on the riverbanks and on *terra firme*. They come in all shapes and sizes, and are eaten in a variety of forms – from the raw fruit itself, to fruit juices, jellies, compotes and unbelievably delicious ice creams. Among some of the most favored are:

Açai

A staple of the Amazonian diet, the *açai* fruit is made into a popular local drink, taken cold and mixed with sugar and *farinha* made from manioc. It comes from the small fruit of the **açazeiro palm**. Tupi Indians called it the palm yai, or "the tree that cries." Rope-like tassels of fruit (almost black round seeds the size of the end of a human finger) hang from the thin palm, which reaches up to 30 meters (100 feet). To make *acai*, the berries are soaked in water to soften the fine covering, then squashed in a clay vessel (or modern equipment) and strained. The condensed purple liquid has a flavor similar to grape juice, aromatic and substantial. It can be found in ice cream, mousses, liqueurs and strong red wine.

Bacaba

The Tupi Indians discovered this palm fruit, giving it the name of *wa'kawwa*, meaning "it produces soil." The 12-meter (40-foot) palm has crinkled leaves that resemble fans. Its fruit is similar to the *açai* and is often described as a horse's tail, hanging with dozens of seed kernels. The process by which the dark-gray liquid is obtained is the same as that of *açai*. A refreshing drink for the hot tropical clime, it is also served with sugar or manioc flour, *farinha de tapioca* or *farinha d'agua*. It's extremely popular as ice cream.

Cupuaçu

One of the most popular fruits in the Amazon, the sour-tasting *cupuaçu* is an elliptical-shaped fruit, about eight inches long, five inches in diameter, rounded on the ends, and weighing about two kilos. It has a strong smell and a brown, egg-shaped shell with a velvet aspect. Inside the shell are 50 seeds surrounded by a thick, white pulp with a strong rose-like perfume. Honey from the *cupuaçu* flower is considered an aphrodisiac. Related to the coca plant, the fruit produces a kind of chocolate made from the toasted seeds. A beverage known as *cupuaçu* **wine** is made from the pulp and is quite popular in Pará. Omnipresent are jellies, puddings, pies, creams, candy, liqueurs, fruit preserves, fillings, mousses and innumerable desserts made from *cupuaçu*. The ice cream is particularly delicious.

Castanha do Pará (Brazil nut)

Pará's principal export, the tasty Brazil nut, comes from an impressive tree 50 meters high (165 feet). Equally impressive are the large globular capsules about the size of a man's head and weighing between 700 and 1,500 grams. The hard shell shelters anywhere from 11 to 22 tightly packed, triangular, oily nuts, which are themselves covered with fine shells. The flavorful nuts are rich in protein and can be eaten raw or roasted. They are excellent for making sweetmeats, fillings, pies, cake icings and other desserts. Also, a variety of indigenous fish recipes makes use of this nut.

Bacuri

The fruit of the *bacurizeiro*, a magnificent tree 20-35 meters high (66-115 feet) with rose-colored flowers, is a little larger than an orange. Its thick yellow rind must be removed with caution as the resin it secretes can irritate the skin. Inside are two or three large seeds covered by a salty white, perfumed pulp with a bittersweet taste. Between the seeds are *filhos*, pieces of pulp with no kernel that are used for making beverages, ice creams, liqueurs, jellies, marmalades, pies, creams, cakes, mousse, candies and other delicacies.

Pupunha

Rich in vitamin A and oil, the *pupunha* is harvested from a tall palm whose trunk is completely covered with thorns. This makes collecting the fruit, which gathers in red and orange clusters, difficult. About the size of a plum, the oval fruit is flat in the upper part where it is attached to the cluster. Before eating, *pupunha* must be cooked in salt and water to remove the skin. The yellow pulp is fibrous, mealy-like and delicious. In the middle is a small coconut (*coquinho*), which is, in fact, the pip. It can be eaten as is, or with syrup or butter as an excellent complement to coffee or tea. It's also quite tasty when caramelized or made into fruit preserve.

Tucumã

The *tucumanzeiro*, a palm tree about 10 feet tall, produces numerous greenish yellow, egg-shaped fruit in bunches. The yellow fibrous pulp is edible.

Muruci

Muruci is the fruit of a small tree of the same name, that bears yellow flowers. Similar to plums, the fruit is generally round, flat on the bottoms and approximately half an inch in diameter. Inside the yellow skin is a pulp of the same color, which envelopes a small round seed. The pulp, considered the sweetest in northern Brazil, and literally melts in one's mouth. It has an agreeable perfume unlike any other fruit. The sour-sweet *mucuri* makes an excellent beverage as well as ice cream and an infinite number of other desserts.

Piquiá

This round fruit above the size of an orange comes from the tree of the same name. It has a grayish-brown coloring with a thick and fleshy outer covering that protects four kidney-shaped segments of yellow pulp surrounding one woody stone. The stone itself contains a wonderfully flavored kernel. The pulp must be cooked in water and salt before it's edible.

Taperebá

The enormous *taperebazeiro* tree bears a cylindrical fruit, rounded on the ends, about the size of a small plum. Inside the thick skin are three millimeters of dense pulp clinging to a pit, which is the major part of the fruit. *Taperebá* is a dark yellow, perfumed fruit, tart but of a sweetish flavor. It is quite popular as a beverage, ice cream and liqueur.

Graviola

Extremely strong tasting, *graviola* (custard apple) has a sweeter aroma than *cupuaçu*. Its pulp is used to make juice, custard and ice cream.

Buriti

This is one of the largest palms in the Amazon; its fruit is rich in oil. It's often made into yellow wine, which has a very strong taste.

Other fruits native to the Amazon include: mango, *abricó* (apricot), *taperebá do sertão*, *goiaba* (guava), *jaca* (jackfruit), *tamarindo, sapoti, sapodilla, caramabolo* (Chinese gooseberry), *mari-mari, abacaxi,* (pineapple) and *burubá.*

Whenever a river boat stops at port, crowds gather to buy and sell fruits.

Dainty Morsels & Sweets

Besides the above-mentioned ice creams, beverages, puddings, pies, creams, liqueurs, fruit preserves, mousses and candies you will also encounter homemade confections such as *beijo-de-moça* (literally "girl's kiss"), *munguzá* or *mingau de milho* (corn kernels cooked in syrup and sometimes in milk or coconut milk).

Festivals

The rich mixture of Portuguese and Northeastern Brazilian culture, which itself is a study in multiple ethnic groups, have produced a remarkably colorful and even indigenous Amazonian folklore. A deep-rooted mysticism and a profound connection to nature runs through all its traditions. Throughout the year popular folklore celebrations, from the spiritual to the secular, occur in Manaus as well as in other cities in the interior. In June in Manaus and Paratins, a huge festival celebrating the legend of the mystical *bumbas* (bulls) takes place, with open-air markets selling regional foods, processions and impressive dance performances. In Manaus, the Amazonas Cultural Center accommodates thousands of people. In the city of Paratins, the last three days of June draw over 35,000 people to cheer the two great *bumbas* – Garantido and Caprichoso.

This highly competitive folklore festival called **bumba-meu-boi** tells the legends and indigenous mythology of the Lower Amazonas regions. You can recognize the bull Garantido by its red and white colors, and Caprichoso by its blue and white. During this celebration, Paratins is petitioned off with colorful banners. In a rivalry almost tantamount to that of soccer, family members sometimes fight over the loyalties they feel to their chosen bull; participants in the festivities actually dress up as bulls. Animating the festival is the music of the *toada* (folk song), which gives the beat to a variety of dances with ancient Indian roots. Beating drums propel the odd assortment of characters who fill the streets as cowboys, Indian chiefs, medicine men, ghosts of the forest, wild animals and satirical characters, such as Pai Francisco and Mae Catirina.

Handicrafts

As with the festivals, the local handicrafts emerge out of a strong connection to roots, utilizing the natural resources drawn from the forest. Handicrafts produced by riverside dwellers most always use Indian techniques, even if the artists are not native. **Pottery** is partcularly fine, especially in the city of Belém, where there are two major traditions. (For more information, see the section under *Belém*.) Artisan products made from the paste of the *guaraná* plant are an explosion of Parense ingenuity, but many feel that these handicrafts stem from the Sateré-Mawé tribal culture. The most characteristic objets d'art are miniatures of typical Amazonian riverboats filled with regional products, such as fish, manioc flour or fruit.

Fine **basketware** from the Upper Negro Region is made by the Tucano, Baniwa and Dessana tribes, among others. In the Upper Solimões region, the Tkuna are recognized as the only specialized sculptors in the state, rendering wood carvings representing human and animal figures; they also are inventive with masks and clothing made from tree bark. The Hixkaryana are masters of the art of feather adornment. Among the peoples of the Javari Valley, a region on the Brazil-Peru frontier, the Marubo tribe craft adornments from shells (freshwater mollusks); the Matis are known for their fine **seed**

necklaces, shell earrings and **nasal ornaments** made from wild boar teeth.

(For more information on local products, see *Shopping* in the various city guides.)

OPTIONS FOR TRAVEL

In all honesty, it takes a certain kind of traveler to enjoy a jungle adventure. Sometimes, however, humans can vastly surprise themselves. I, who was nearly sent home in tears from Girl Scout camp, immensely enjoyed my Amazonian treks, but they were not always easy, nor was I left with an overriding desire to return for the unbeaten tracks. (The beaten tracks were plenty exciting.) On your first trip to the jungle, I would not suggest braving it alone or with unreliable guides; believe me, you will want to feel there is someone looking after your welfare. Good guides (usually those officially trained) know the trails where you are least likely to meet poisonous snakes, voracious ants, man-eating piranha and malaria-infested pools, not to mention mudslides and other debacles of nature. As for travel options, there is such a variety of possibilities that anyone from senior citizens to responsible children (nine and older) can make the grade. My suggestion is to plan a number of different treks that will give you a multi-dimensional perspective of Amazonian life. Among the possibilities:

- □ Packaged boat tours (or special charters) through the *igarapés* (streams) shooting off from the Amazon near Belém, Manaus or Santarém.
  Advantage: Good for those with limited schedule. Trips usually last between four and 28 hours. Can include fishing, jungle walks and overnight stays in the forest. The best trip is out of Belém, with Amazon Star Turismo (see *Hands-On Belém*). Travelers seeking air-conditioned cabins should investigate the 22-passenger *Tuna* or the eight-passenger *Hawk*, which conduct three-day and six-day cruises out of Manaus. For most information contact Brazil Nuts, ☎ *(203) 259-7900* in the US.
- □ Two- to three-day stays at lodges built inside the jungle, mostly accessible by boat from Manaus.
  Advantage: Secure accommodations with adequate-good food, bath, and organized excursions day and night.

A typical river boat in the Amazon.

- ☐ Two- to three-day trips down the Amazon on public river boats (the region's buses), such as the Cisne Branco, which goes between Santarém and Manaus.
  Advantage: Slow, relaxing, requires no effort and gives you a chance to hobnob with locals. Best for those who speak Portuguese and for those amenable to less than luxurious accommodations.
- ☐ Sidetrip excursions to river beach sites, such as Alter de Chão near Santarém, and Marajó Island, near Belém.
- ☐ Luxury resorts, such as Floresta Amazônica in Alta Floresta, Mato Grosso, where you can sleep in comfort and take expeditions into the forest, down the river, to neighboring farms and even to gold mines.
  Advantage: Offers the greatest options of adventures and the largest perspective of Amazonian lifestyles. Good for those who don't like sleeping on boats.
- ☐ Ocean-going cruisers, which dock in Amazonian ports. (See *Specialty Tours* in the back of the book.)

Fly-Fishing

John C. Jones has fished the fly rod from Africa's Zambezi for the fighting Tigerfish, in the Amazon for the Peacock Bass, the Andes of Argentina for their famed trout, and the remote bonefish flats of Central America. From his home in Cisco, Texas, he sits in his office decorated with various specimen trophies, including a record black piranha taken from the Amazon jungle on the fly. A promoter for various travel groups for fly-fishing and exotic travel worldwide, he also conducts customized tours on request and has written a brochure called *Rod and Fly-Fishing in the Amazon*. Below, he shares his adventures and recommendations for successful fly-fishing in the Amazon.

~

I am on the Juma River just beyond the Amazon Lodge about 4½ hours outside of Manaus. There it is before me! The earth's largest river system – so magnificent in beauty that I lose myself in the gaze, forgetting the humidity and the tropical heat. The 120° sun reflects from the river, making deep crows' feet in the corner of my eyes; the sweat rolls as the peacock bass on the end of my line fights for his very life. As the dugout canoe tosses dangerously off balance, I remember what keeps bringing me back to the ends of this earth – the thrill of feeling I've got a freight train on my hook. The 3/0 hook of the large, very fully tied, Mickey Finn bucktail fly (red & yellow) is being tested to its limit. The reel is well into backing now, gasping and groaning in protest! An incredible weight struggles for freedom at the end of my line, sending the spinning wheel out of control. As I try to slow the monster by palming the reel, the reel handle hits my thumb at such speed that the blood squirts out from busted flesh.

Twice I get him up to the boat, but he doesn't like what he sees, showers me with water and makes another run. Each run is shorter than the last, and after 15 minutes of hard fight, I see his thick sides and deep-yellow-gold sides, guessing he must weigh in around 20 pounds. He looks tired and depressed. My muscles are tired, and my hands are still shaking. For the first time now I feel the pain from my bleeding thumb. I let the pilot take the necessary photographs, as I ease the fish back into the water, looking into his tired eyes. I wink and salute him in honor of his good fight. Now he is ready for another battle with another fisherman.

Hours on the river have become like lover's hours – fast disappearing in the wake of such concentrated involvement. Looking up finally, I notice the haystack of deep purple storm clouds to the east and hope the possible showers will cool the heat of the jungle. Disappointed, we endure the merciless increase of heat through the day. As the sun sets, we make our way to the little hut where we have asked permission of gracious *caboclos* (jungle dwellers) to hang our hammocks for the night. To think that we just walked up the river embankment to this hut and asked strangers to allow us to spend the night in one of the two rooms of their house! On other trips, we have simply pulled our float plane up to the hut, announced that we wanted to fish the area that evening and spend the night in their two-room hut on the river bank, the next morning asking if they would mind rowing us out in the dugout canoe for a reasonable fee. It is work they are always glad to do, especially for the companionship, since most might meet less than 50 new people in their lifetime. As night falls, we welcome the cooler air and fold our hammock around us so the vampire bats won't bite our toes, spraying down with our ever-present Deep Woods Off. Warding off the bites of more than 250 species of mosquitoes, we drift into memories of another great day in the mysterious Amazon jungle.

John C. Jones with his trophy peacock bass.

The next morning we fly back over the "green hell" to the city of Manaus. Once into the air it looks as if the entire world is on fire from the sun's rays hitting the cool humidity of the night and producing steam that rises "world without end." By mid-morning the steam has vanished, the sun shining across a cloudless sky, and flying low we look down upon the winding river, the multi-shades-of-green jungle forest that often gives way to long stretches of white sand beaches along the bank. As we near Manaus, the blue skies are filled with smoke from fires that are burning away at the forest so "civilization can expand."

The jungle vanishes behind me as Bennie de Merchant, one of the world's finest jungle pilots, drops us down into the muddy water of the Amazon River at the edge of Manaus, and we taxi into the floating hangar. Back in America, I think of the more than 30 trips I have made into this jungle from the headquarters of Manaus. All of these alone with only my Orvis duffel bags, fly rods, reels, backpacks and power energy bars (the last, very important for endurance in the jungle).

~

Fishermen as famous as George Bush have been hitting the Amazon for fly-fishing, a sport that has taken flight in the region for several reasons. The most exploited species, peacock bass, grow at exponential rates. Their attack is explosive, and their access is doubled by the fact that they are both fly and topwater oriented. And the peak fishing period – October to March – comes at a time when many fishermen are frozen in and are looking for a getaway.

According to John C. Jones, a 15-year veteran of the scene, exact locations for the best fishing cannot be given in an annual guidebook, since prime sites and access change weekly with water drainage and flooding and dryness. Even pilots' maps, which John tries to make use of, do not apply after a few months and perhaps not again for several years. Believe him or not – Jones says, "*No one except possibly less than 100 fly-fishermen (like myself) in the world should attempt to go out 'on their own' if they want any type of success and enjoyment.*" Facing the average traveler without such guidance will be language problems, as well as those ever-changing fishing conditions, made worse by universally changing weather patterns, not to even mention general transportation problems.

Tips For Great Fishing

☐ Get the best guide you can afford.
☐ Never use a company until you have checked out some previous clients. Don't hesitate to ask for referrals. Use the Internet.
☐ Take extreme care in choosing equipment – never go with less than the best. A good company can provide

you with a pack list, according to brands, sizes, etc.
Don't hesitate to phone them as often as it takes to
assure yourself that you have enough of the right equipment.

☐ Be careful not to overpack; excess weight is a problem
on small planes and boats.

☐ Bring a good survival kit. Research articles in fly-fishing
magazines and sports books. Compile the information
and make a specialized list just for your trip.

☐ If you have special dietary needs or medical conditions,
be sure to bring a statement from your doctor as to your
needs in case of emergency. Inform your guide/travel
service in advance of these needs or conditions.

☐ Regarding photos: A good rule of thumb is to allow two
rolls of 36 exposures per day; 100-200 ASA for most
conditions. Jones likes to take two of the self-focus
cameras in case one falls into the water. (I would add
that you should load each camera with a different ASA,
since the overly bright sunlight on the river requires
different settings from the sunlight filtering through the
canopy.

☐ Carry a small notepad in ZipLock bag to write down
memories for future trips, etc.

John C. Jones' Recommendations

Varig Brazilian Airlines	☎ 522-2084/1084
Rod & Gun Guides	☎ (512) 556-8233
. . . .	☎ (800) 211-4753
Fax.	(516) 556-2367
Ron Speed's S & W, Inc.	☎ (903) 489-1656
Fax.	☎ (903) 489-2854
Frontiers	☎ (800) 245-1950
Fax.	☎ (412) 935-5388
Rod & Reel Adventures	
Worldwide Angling	☎ (800) 356-6952

Jones also recommends the **Amazon Lodge**, stating that the "food
is wonderful and there's excellent fishing in the surrounding waters
of a two-mile radius." (See further listing under *Manaus* section,
page 202.)

Equipment

- ☐ #9 Rod, heavy-duty reel of Orvis or Able quality with 300 yds of line backing.
- ☐ 10-25 lb. Saltwater leader 10 ft.
- ☐ #9 sinking tip line and one slow sinking line on separate spool.
- ☐ Take lots of leaders, at least two of each of the above lines, 10 heavily tied Mickey Finn type bucktails – with some sparkle sparsely tied inside – per fishing day (red and yellow are best), and some tarpon poppers. Also, a pair of Able fishing pliers, deluxe Swiss Army knife, hook sharpener, Orvis line clippers, plus the usual tropics pack list.
- ☐ Sting-Eze is a must for insect bites. Plus, all suntan lotion should be "waterproof" to keep it from getting in the fisherman's eyes.

Jones adds that only a quality reel will work well with peacock bass and bonefish reef fishing. If you don't use the ones suggested or alternatives of equal quality, you can end up with a burned-out reel and a huge disappointment. Ditto for rods: *"A rod that can't cast the the heavy fly is useless."*

Top-of-the-Line Outfitters & Suppliers

Orvis	☎ (800) 541-3541
Kauffman Streamborn	☎ (800) 442-4359
Bob Marriott's Fly-Fishing	☎ (800) 535-6633

Tours

John C. Jones also customizes adventurous trips on a limited basis, and is presently forming a trip to the Amazon. His brochure on fly-fishing the Amazon can be obtained for $6.95 (P.O. Box 269, Cisco, TX 76437). He can be reached through **World Wide Consulting**, Fax *(817) 442-2673*, ☎ *(817) 442-2145*, or E-mail: GruShaman @aol.com

THE AMAZON SURVIVAL KIT

In Preparation

Be in good physical shape; even though the terrain is more or less flat, hiking through a high-humidity jungle can be exhausting. (In contrast, river trips border on the soporific.) Time your vaccinations over the month before you leave; you can't take them all at the same time. To ward off mosquitoes, many people swear by taking daily dozes of Vitamin B two weeks to a month before the trip (and during). Some professionals even believe that foregoing sugar helps. If you are particularly allergic to bees, make sure you travel with your own remedies (emergency medical assistance will probably be miles away). And above all, break in your new boots before leaving.

What To Wear

Light cotton clothing. Although native people walk through the rainforest barefoot and in shorts, I don't suggest it for foreigners, whose immune systems are unaccustomed to jungle life. Wearing jeans (tucked into boots) and light cotton long-sleeved shirts (with roll-up sleeves) will cut down on scratches and snake and bug bites. In both wet and dry season you'll need sturdy tennis shoes an/or waterproof hiking boots (I loved my lightweight, waterproof Merrell boots made with GorTex). Heavily treaded soles are needed to help you balance on tree logs. On any river trip you'll need a sunhat and good sunglasses with a strap to keep them from falling off. Kerchiefs are excellent for wiping sweaty brows. In rainy season, take a lightweight hooded rain poncho and an extra pair of clothes for when you get soaking wet. A swimsuit will come in handy, but pack a coverup. Some agencies supply rain gear (rubber boots and ponchos) when necessary.

What To Pack

Swiss Army knife, canteen, or plastic water bottle, thermos (with cup big enough to eat from), compass, binoculars, journal, pens, small backpack, and collapsible fishing gear. Pack water purification pills (but use in emergencies only – it's better to drink bottled water). If you plan to take river trips on the public boats, a hammock is advisable, even if you secure a private cabin. Mosquito nets are not generally needed, unless you venture out into the jungle on your own. (See *Health Kit* in the back of the book). Take plenty of bug repellent and reapply it often, especially at dusk and before going to sleep. A fellow traveler in the Pantanal swore by Avon Skin-So-Soft bath oil as a natural repellent (available through Avon Products). Suntan lotion with a high SPF is an absolute must; the sun at the equator is the hottest in the world; and the river water will reflect even more intensely. You should wear sunblock even in the tree-shaded jungle. Pack extras of all personal medicines, contact lenses and eyeglasses, etc. If you're taking a two-to three-day cruise down the Amazon, a juicy paperback will be deeply appreciated after a few hours.

Photographic Equipment

I went down the Amazon River with a professional German photographer who didn't give a hoot about humidity rot, bugs, or human carelessness – until I nearly knocked his equipment overboard. Truth is, bugs and infinitesimal-sized ticks are rampant on these boats and fungus abounds; the spray from the river alone is enough to render delicate mechanisms defunct. To avoid ruined film, keep rolls tightly secured in waterproof baggies and store all equipment with a small packet of silica gel. At least once a week, expose lenses and camera to direct sunlight (minus the film!). Also, remember to develop film promptly (Manaus has some good 24-hour processing shops), and if your camera allows for exposure adjustments, underexpose a ¼ f-stop.

Mosquitoes & Bugs

Almost all lodges near Manaus were chosen for their mosquito-free locations. Even so, independent-party mosquitoes always managed to find me, especially on my boat cruise from Santarém to Manaus. Off-the-beaten trekkers must be careful; some areas of the Amazon are so ridden with mosquitoes that few human beings even venture there. In his book *The Amazon* (Time Life), Tom Sterling recalls how he had to wear a bathing cap to protect his bald head in the notorious Jari Region.

Yellow fever, transmitted by mosquitoes, is considered endemic in Brazil, except around the coastal shores. Health authorities advise that the most infected areas are Acre, Amazonas, Goiás, Maranhão, Mato Grosso, Mato Grosso do Sul, Pará, Rondônia, and the territories of Amapá and Roraima. Vaccinations are good for 10 years and are essential if you are traveling either to the Amazon or the Pantanal. You may be required to show proof of vaccination when entering the country from Venezula, Colombia, Ecuador, or Bolivia. It's best always to travel with it. (For more information, see the *Health Kit* at the back of the book.)

Malaria

To take malaria pills or not to take – that is the question that doctors north and south of the equator are still debating. On the con side: prophylactics tend to mask symptoms of malaria, and, once the illness is diagnosed, they make it more difficult to treat. Also, new species of mosquitoes (from which malaria is contracted) are always developing and the latest medicines are not usually up to date. On the pro-side: pills give you some peace of mind. What's best is to wear strong repellent and avoid commonly known breeding grounds, such as stagnant water.

Vaccinations

Frankly, I took every form of vaccination possible before heading to Brazil and the jungle, including yellow fever (required), tetanus, and gamma globulin (for Hepatitis B), as well as a complete round of malaria pills before, during, and after my trip to the jungle. For the latest official advisories, contact the **Centers for Disease Control**, Atlanta, GA 30333 (Parasitic Division, Center for Infectious Diseases). Also see *Health Kit* in the back of the book.

What You Should Worry About

Snakes are an Amazon reality, but poisonous snakes are rare in the forest where official tours go. The most feared, however, is the *surucu* (bushmaster), the largest snake in Brazil, which measures up to 10 feet. Also common is the *sucuri* (anaconda), the largest snake in the world, though not poisonous. Silvery-green in color, it's a member of the boa family, meaning it kills its prey by constriction and suffocation, feeding on fish, birds, mammals, and alligators. Don't worry.

Do beware, however, that some rainforest plants and animals mimic each other in order to hide from predators or sneak up on prey. Snakes, in particular, love to look like vines. For protection, wear ankle-high boots and tuck in your pants.

An Amazonian lass nonchalantly holds a baby alligator

Piranhas: *Pira* means fish and *rana* means tooth – nasty, toothy little fish found throughout the rivers and lakes of the Amazon basin. Their viciousness, though exaggerated, is not exactly unfounded. Piranha only become dangerous when trapped in lagoons during dry season or when they smell blood. Waters in the Rio Negro around Manaus are harmless, but in general avoid swimming with open sores.

Squeamish tourists should enter the water only after their guide dives in first. More feared than piranha is the *candirú açu*, a minute catfish that forces its way into the urethra of the bather, making itself difficult to extract. Don't worry.

WHERE TO
GO IN
AMAZÔNIA

SANTARÉM

Located near the western border of the state of **Pará**, Santarém is the major city in the **Tapajós River Basin** – an enchanting, near magical region distinct from other Amazon terrains. Also called the Lower Amazon, this area is a verdant, almost continuous plain, rarely exceeding 1,000 feet high and overlaid with lakes, tributaries, island rivers and narrow streams, called *igarapés*. During low tide (July-Dec.), vast stretches of fine white sand and green water graced by pink porpoises turn the Tapajós into an Amazonian resort.

The most ecologically sound transportation in the world.

Though there are roads in the region, they are dangerous during rainy season, so most people travel by way of the *estradas líquidas* (liquid highways). Travelers can pick from every kind of water transport – from flat-bottomed barges to diesel-powered canoes to *barcos de linha* (water buses) where everyone, from teens to salesmen to old ladies with grandchildren, hang up their hammocks and settle in for the two- to three-day journeys. (For more information, see *Excursions* in the Belém chapter, page 169.)

Santarém is situated on the exact point where the Tapajós River pours its greenish waters into the brown waters of the Amazon. Ecologically, Santarém is fascinating because it represents an unusual microcosm of the Amazon, where all three types of jungle systems – *várzea* (flood plain), *terra firme* (flat forest ground), and *igapó* (stream) – can be fully experienced. Numerous cruise lines use Santarém as a stopover, not only because of the varied ecosystem, but because the city itself is a lovely Amazonian port to visit. Along the Avenida Tapajós, you'll see hundreds of boats loaded with goods that are sold to villagers within moments of arrival. There's also a colorful wharfside market, a few imposing colonial houses and several sleepy baroque plazas. Although you can browse through this Rip Van Winkle town easily on foot, the best way to see it is by hiring a cow-drawn cart and rambling down the dusty, cobblestone streets.

Cruiseliners also tend to stop at the nearby primitive community of Alter de Chão, known for its folklore and its "illusory" lakeside beach (some cruises leave their passengers off in Santarém and pick them up in Alter de Chão). Extra excursions can be made to Alenquer, a former Indian village, where an impressive assembly of hieroglyphics point to the remains of an ancient civilization. Also, a few hours away by boat is the community of Monte Alegre, a region ripe with rock paintings as well as amethyst mines and an unusual ecosystem: its meadows, part of the Great Lake, boast semi-submerged forests and an enormous variety of fish.

UP   CLOSE   TIP: *Typical of the region are enormous water lilies that look like saucers right out of* Alice in Wonderland. *Called Vitória Régia, this lily has bright green leaves that measure almost 6½ feet in diameter and a one-foot flower, making it the largest in the Americas.*

Huge lily pads are straight out of Alice in Wonderland.

History

Prior to the European discovery, the Lower Amazon was inhabited by several indigenous groups, including the **Tupaius,** from which the Tapajós River got its name. In 1661, an Indian mission was founded, and in 1758 the name of the burgeoning settlement was changed to Santarém, after the town in Portugal. If you come across a few locals with last names like Vaughon, Jennings, Hennington,

Wallace, and Riker, that's because two years after the American Civil War, one hundred Confederates immigrated to the region straight from the southern United States. (Unfortunately, hardly any of their descendants speak English today.)

Between 1821 and 1912, nearly half a million people from the Northeast migrated to the region in a desperate bid to flee a ravaging drought, helping the region become the world's prime producer of **natural rubber**. See page 14 for the full story on **Henry Ford's Fordilândia**.

In 1958, the Lower Amazon was shaken by another explosion when an enormous vein of gold was discovered in the Upper Tapajós River Valley, from Itaituba northwards. In 1969 the Santarém-Cuiabá Highway was opened, enabling makeshift towns and villages to multiply as thousands hurried to the river and its tributaries to bamburrar, or get-rich-quick.

Unfortunately, little money from the gold rush returned to Santarém, and many rivers were contaminated with mercury as a result of the rampant prospecting. In the last several years, however, Santarém has made a tremendous comeback. A new local government has stimulated substantial growth in tourism and agriculture, adding to the industrial economy based on extraction of gold, wood, Brazil nuts, rubber, and jute, as well as textile, cattle farming, and fishing industries. Qualification programs for hotel and restaurant employees, guides, and taxi and bus drivers have been developed, and school children are being educated about the historical and cultural aspects of the region. Impressed by the potential of the mineral-rich várzea, the World Bank is now investing time and research into extensive harvesting without insecticides or fertilizers. Even the Japanese government is investing in a recuperation program of the most devastated ecological regions.

A Bird's-Eye View

To get a pleasant picturesque view of Santarém, walk down Avenida Tapajós – past the river boats, chicken coops, and floating gas station – to where you can view the meeting of the Amazon and Tapajós rivers. From July to Jan., the beach in front of the avenue is full of sand and lined with mango trees. A night tour to scope out alligators can be taken to **Ilha de Ponta Negra**, an area known for its cattle and huge water lily lake. Early morning trips are best for birdwatchers. Beaches near Santarém are exquisite. Located about three hours away by boat, the **Arapiuns River** is reputed to have the most beautiful beach in the area, with 130 feet of white sand and dark rocks and excellent resources for fishing in unpolluted waters. Three or four km. (1.8-2.5 miles) into the forest, you'll discover a stunning waterfall. Four km. (2.5 miles) from Santarém is **Maracanã Beach**, which local people frequent. Among the chic beaches is **Pajussara**, about 30 minutes by boat from the city, full of lovely summer homes and palm-lined white sands. You must take your own food.

Sights

Santarém is a cinch to see on foot; just be careful about the heat, or the rain (during the rainy season). If you want to tour the city in a cow-drawn cart, contact **Lago Verde Turismo**, ☎ *522-7577.*

On Foot

Marketplace

Start at the marketplace along the wharf near Praça do Relógio, where between 6-10 a.m. you'll find the picture-postcard version of an outdoor third-world marketplace. Nearby is the indoor market called Mercado Modelo; between the two you'll find everything from live chickens to tropical fruits to hammocks.

A young Amazonian boy sells the lush produce of Brazil.

Nossa Senhora da Conceição

Walk up Rua Siqueira Campos to the cathedral. The original structure was built in 1711 by French architects, but had to be rebuilt 20 years later when it collapsed. The fully clothed model of Jesus holding the Cross in the front right vestibule is paraded during the Círio Festival on the second Sun. in Oct. In front of the church is the Praça da Matriz, where, about 60 years ago, a band used to perform.

Rua Siqueira Campos

Walking down the main shopping avenue you'll pass two record stores with good discount bins as well as recordings by regional musicians, such as Ray Brito and Tinho. Even if you're not heading out on a river trip, an interesting stop is the supermarket on this street called **Formigão** (Big Ant). You can stock up on beer, cookies, crackers, and especially Tang (the American orange drink mix, which is good for dehydration).

On the next block you'll find the **Varig** office, Rua Siqueiro Campos, 277, open 7-11:30 a.m. and 2-5:30 p.m. Closed Sun.

Pastelândia

Across the street is this clean and airy snack bar specializing in *pasteis* (dough pastries filled with meat or cheese), baked right before your eyes. Camera and film stores are next door. Along Rua Siqueira Campos are several drugstores that may exchange dollars; talk to the owners.

Turn left on Rua Senador Lameira Beiftencourt, also called Rua 15 de Novembro, past more shops, then right on Rua do Comércio, a pedestrian mall full of sportswear stores.

Mascote Bar

On the right is this good lunch stop. Nearby, at Rua Sen. Lam Bittencourt, 31 (the street running into Rua Comércio) is one of the best artisan stores (for more information, see *Shopping*, below).

Rua Francisco Correa

Turning left from Rua do Comércio onto Rua Francisco Correa, walk up the steep hill for a wonderful view of the Meeting of the Waters; you'll see the blue of the Tapajós River and the brown of the Amazon. Fortunately, there's also a cool breeze here, perhaps the only one in the city. The odd illusion is that you'll feel as if you are looking out onto the ocean; the water is so clear because the river is full of plankton (plants) and, therefore, does not allow for the penetration of light. Walk back to Rua Siqueira Campos and turn left, passing the only banana stand in the city.

Centro Cultural João Fona

Rua do Imperador.

Also called the Museu de Santarém, this fine museum was formerly the city hall, parliament, court and prison. Today it holds a famous collection of Tupaiu Indian crafts (there's also a good view of the Meeting of the Waters from here). Anthropologists and archaeologists have been studying the Tupaius' pottery (*ceramica tapajônica*) and have concluded that these were the most culturally advanced Indians in the Amazon; some of their pieces date back almost 10,000 years. Ana Roosevelt, granddaughter of the American president, has led research teams in the area and may be producing a book soon about this tribe, considered to be the most ancient civilization in South America.

To end this walking tour, walk back along the wharf. The best place to watch the sun set is at Mascotinho, an open-air café where you can indulge in pizza and cold beer. You'll also find an ice cream parlor where you can stock up on sweets and pastries, a good idea if you're planning a boat trip. Along the wharf you'll see cows tied to carts, still used for transporting goods and people.

By Car

Aparecida Hammock Factory

Av. Borges Leal, 2561; ☎ *522-1187. 7:30-11:30 a.m., 1:30-6 p.m.*

Thousands of *redes* (or hammocks) are handmade daily at this factory, where you can watch artisans work (until 3 p.m.) on looms imported from southern England. Excellent quality is assured here, and you're sure to find all varieties and colors (if you're looking for cheap, better go to the Mercado Modelo). All profits here go to support social welfare programs. If you're making any jungle trips – by land or water – a hammock helps beat the heat. Do practice slowly getting in and out of your hammock; many a gringo has fallen flat on his or her face, to the enormous amusement of locals, who do it so gracefully. (One hint: The safest way is to lie down slowly down diagonally.) Before you invest, note that a hammock takes up considerable bulk.

Herb Farm

For the past 15 years, Farmâcia Viva, a dirt-road community of 3,000, has supported this herb cooperative famous for its medicinal remedies. The village, about 10 minutes from the Tropical Hotel, is full of ethereal-looking children with curly, bright-golden hair that no one can explain. The old ladies who tend the garden seem like the salt of the earth; they'll love to show you their patches of patchouli, *capim santo* and other herbs whose aromas fill the air. And they'll be even more delighted if you buy some of their homemade tonics. The *banho capilar* is reported to grow hair on a bald head, and there's even a plant called "Vick" that is good for headaches. Since the route to the plantation often confuses even locals, you will need a guide to get there, but be careful about getting stuck in the mud (though the whole community will turn out to help you if you do).

❖ **GETTING HERE:** *Take the road to Cuiabám turn left on Av. Moaçara, right on Trav. Rouxinol and Rua Maravilha. Keep asking for directions.*

National Forest

Thirty-nine miles (62 km.) by good road from Santarém is the Floresta Nacional de Tapajós, a virgin forest where you can see a variety of animals, including groups of wild pigs, monkeys, and tropical birds. Ornithologists often come to research South American landbirds, which appear in quantity early in the morning. To visit the park, call IBAMA ☎ 522-3032, and speak to Rionaldo Almeida, director of the National Forest. You must provide your own transportation (boat, plane, or jeep) and translator, but you are also required to be officially accompanied by one of their guides. Lago Verde Turismo, the local travel agency, also offers a five-hour walking tour of this forest.

Excursions

Alter de Chão

Eighteen miles (30 km.) from Santarém lies Alter de Chão, Santarém's weekend resort. It's an outgrowth of a village of the Borari Indians, a place of magical leisure because of the still-native community and unusual beaches that spread over the bay of the Tapajós River. Some cruises that anchor in Santarém often leave passengers at port, where they can take a bus to Alter de Chão (the ship, via regional boats, retrieves them later in the day). Some cruises drop anchor directly at Alter de Chão, requiring passengers to reach shore through tenders. The trip to Alter de Chão from Santarém by car was once rough and rugged, but the road is now paved. (Lago Verde Turismo can arrange passage to the island.)

Muiraquitãs Lake

Alongside the village, this lake's clear water changes daily from deep blue to green. It provides the area's folklore, especially by the celebration of Festa da Sairé in the beginning of July. Slowly the village has been surrendering to modernism. Today, most of the locals, who used to fish and hunt, live mainly off tourism and their clay homes are now being squeezed in between more modern summer homes. During high season the city is so crowded you can barely walk through the dusty streets; at other times it looks deserted. One concession to modern life is that the beachside avenue is now paved. The city's "garbage collectors" can be seen flying over the city – huge black vultures or *urubus*. (They're also called turkey vultures because their heads look like those of turkeys.)

Praça de Nossa Senhora da Saúde

The main square is fronted by a native church and shaded by big, leafy jambeiro trees, whose fruits are quite tasty. Here, you'll also find local women selling *tacacá*, a native dish usually served in coconut shells. On the far side of the plaza, down Travessa dos Mártires (a side street from the beach), is an area of rubber trees. At 4 p.m. every day, the seeds blow up and explode, sounding just like a revolution breaking out. Don't miss this pinch of excitement.

Between Jan. and June, an island in the bay appears out of nowhere with 132 feet of sand, becoming the makeshift summer residence for about 1,000 *caboclos*. For about a dollar each way, little boys will ferry you in rickety canoes across to the island; there you'll find *barracas* for drinks, snacks, and barbecued fish and chicken.

> **UP CLOSE TIP:** *Avoid swimming on the river side (south); instead head for the north side of the island, where trees are growing out of the lake and the water is cooler and cleaner. Windsurfing is excellent (though you must have your own equipment) and kayaking is superb (rentals available). A very healthy hike can be taken up Morro do Cruzeiro, the mountain with a cross on top (about 45 min. one way). At the peak, you'll get an impressive view of Piranha Lake, Tapajós River, and Green Lake.*

Center for the Preservation of Indigenous Art & Culture
Rua Dom Macedo Costa

This beautiful museum in Alter de Chão has one of the finest collections of Indian tribal art in the Amazon River, with over 75 tribes represented. Visitors say there is no other place like this in the Amazon. Fee is about $3 per person.

Instituto de Pesquisa Amazônica

Buffalo fanatics can head for the *fazenda* of Will Ernestro Leal, Wil Ernesto Leal, whose 2,470-acre farm also houses the most famous research institute in the area. The land is primarily savannah, a vegetation uncommon to the Amazon, comprised of thin tall trees, around which scamper monkeys, capybaras and exotic birds. For more information contact **Lago Verde Tourism**, ☎ *(91) 522-7577.*

Hotels, Restaurants & Shopping

If you stay overnight in Alter de Chão during high season, you'll have to reserve a hotel in advance. Only primitive *pousadas* are available.

Pousada Alter do Chão

Av. Lauro Sodré; ☎ *522-3411.*

This is the best spot for location and food. Under Tia Deney's care you can find probably a room for less than $10 a person, including breakfast served on the veranda facing Lago Verde. Bathroom, but no air conditioning. *12 apts. Inexpensive. All cards.*

Lago Verde restaurant

7 a.m.-6 p.m., weekends, open at 6 a.m.

This is another good restaurant lakeside. Try the regional *tucunaré* (a family of black bass) or the *bolinho de pirarucú* (an extremely tender fish wrapped in a crispy fried crust).

Arte Grupo Lago Verde

This handicraft store features an interesting snack called *beijo de moço* (kisses of a young girl), a kind of tapioca flour baked into crispy crackers. Also stock up on jars of *doce de cupuaçu* or *licor de cajú*, sweets and liqueurs made out of regional fruits. Native crafts include hand-painted logs and twigs found in the forest – a little kitschy for my taste, since the local style is to paint over the natural bark with artificial colors.

River Cruises

The oldest and still most common mode of travel in the region is boat, as witnessed by the 7,000 vessels operating in the municipality, from small wooden diesel-powered crafts to large catamaran passenger ships owned by the ENASA Company. Luxury liners from the States and Europe are becoming a more frequent sight.

Larger boats and ships dock at the deep-water pier (Docas do Pará) at the far northern end of the Santarém-Cuiabá Highway. Most other boats leave from the area between the Market Place and the Praça do Pescador (Fisherman's Square). Though they are not always safe, two-decker *gaiolas* are the most popular way to journey downriver. Some have been known to sink from being overloaded with chickens, pigs, and produce, but better precautions are taken these days to avoid the kind of tragedy that befell the *Cisne Branco* about eight years ago. (On a New Year's cruise the ship sank, drowning everyone aboard when all the passengers moved to the right side at the same time to see the approaching port of Manaus. I must add, however, in 1991 I risked everything (for the sake of a previous edition of this book!) and took a cruise on the newly resurrected *Cisne Branco*, obviously happily surviving. And I liked it! For reservations on any river cruises, contact **Lago Verde Turismo** or **ENASA** directly.

Most boats headed for Manaus or Belém offer a limited number of private cabins, and should be reserved as early as possible. The cabins in *gaiolas* are extremely small, but their virtue is privacy; if you rent one, you may also want to hang a hammock in the main galley to lounge during the hot days. Usually, there is an upper deck with a snack bar where you can sit and watch the banks pass by. More often than not, the price of the ticket includes meals, but do take a pile of bananas, oranges, and cashews because the food may not be up to your personal standards of cleanliness.

ENASA Boats have been one of the most popular tourist excursions between Belém and Manaus (with stops in Santarém). Made for touring, the boats boast air-conditioned cabins with private bathroom, restaurant, telephone, video lounge, bar, sun-deck, and swimming pool. The trip from Belém to Santarém runs three days; Santarém to Manaus two days. Schedules in the past have run once a month. In Santarém, contact **Representante ENASA**, Tr. Francisco Correa, 34; ☎ *(91) 522-1934;* in Belém, Av. Presidente Vargas, 41; ☎ *(91) 223-3011;* in Manaus, Rua Mal. Deodoro, 61; ☎ *(92) 232-4280.*

A favorite stop for cruises is about three hours by vessel from Santarém – the point where the Amazon River meets the Cruá-Una River. This tributary of the Amazon is singular in that its banks host the greatest amount of native wildlife to be found in the entire Amazon's *terra firme* (primary forest that never floods). Upriver is Pacoval, an original village settled by fleeing black slaves and native Indians.

Romantic Cruises

River Curuana

An excellent three-day/two-night package that could serve as an exotic honeymoon starts from Santarém's airport, where you transfer to a 10-person boat and head up the river. Here, a canoe with outboard motor will be awaiting you for navigation through the numerous *igarapés* (streams) full of water lilies, pink dolphins, alligators, and birds. The region is known for having more native trees than any other, and as the river meets the Amazon, *várzea* (flood plain) appears, which is good for piranha fishing

After lunch you return to the regional boat and go upriver to visit **Pacoval**, a village founded by runaway black slaves originally from Guyana. At dusk (5:30-6:30 p.m.), small canoes are taken out for alligator hunting. Afterwards, a special candlelit dinner is served in the middle of the forest. The next morning you visit the outdoor and indoor labs of SUDAM, a research center for reforesting projects. Then you cruise downriver to **Alter de Chão**, arriving at dawn and breakfasting on the island. After eating you are invited to climb the mountain; successful trekkers are rewarded with ice cream and champagne. The rest of the day is spent at Alter de Chão (on the beach or in canoes); then you may either head for the airport in the evening or spend the night in a hotel. Groups of 8 to 10 people pay $300 per person. A private package for two people runs about $1,900. **Lago Verde Turismo**, Rua Galdino Veloso, 384; ☎ *(91) 522-7577; fax 522-2118*, one of the most reliable and creative agencies, offers this trip.

Monte Alegre

Heading down the Amazonas River between Santarém and Belém is the town of Monte Alegre (10 hours from Santarém). Etched into the Ererê and Paituna mountain ranges are caves, rock formations, and primitive designs and paintings belonging to prehistoric Amazônia. Six hundred and sixty feet from the port is one of the largest egret rookeries in the region. At dawn and dusk, millions of birds can be seen flapping their wings in a magnificent display. Another attraction is the **thermal springs**, where pools of sulfurous water are used to treat skin diseases. For more information contact the **Secretaria da Cultura e Turismo/Prefeitura Municipal de Monte Alegre**, Av. Presidente Vargas; ☎ *(91) 533-1147*, Santarém, PA.

Alenquer

Nicknamed the "City of the Gods," Alenquer can be found upstream on the Amazon River between Santarém and the border of Pará (six hours from Alenquer). About an hour from the town are lakes and streams with giant water lilies. A family of rock pedestals with smaller stones in identifiable shapes can be found in **Morada dos Deuses**. There is also a tall cliff in a valley that forms a canyon with a waterfall. The folklore event **Festa do Marambiré** is held every June.

Lago Verde Turismo also offers excursions to both Monte Alegre and Alenquer on a three-day package. (For contact information, see *Travel Agencies* under *Hands-On* section.)

Lodge Expeditions

Tapajós-Amazon Lodge Hotel Ecológico

Av. Alvaro Adolfo, 1232; ☎ *(91) 522-2330, fax 522-5866.*

Tucked on the left bank of the Tapajós River (two hours by boat from Santarém), this new and extraordinary lodge is the only one in the Amazon to offer a beach of white sand and crystal water for swimming. Built into 370 acres of natural wildlife (320 of which is untouched tropical forest), the palm-roofed lodge's 18 wooden bungalows (with bathrooms) actually sit on stilts in a lake, offering terrific views. A footbridge links the rooms to the restaurant, which is known for its fresh fish. Two-day/one-night packages run about $80 per person, including transfer, jungle walk, fishing, and cruise down the river. Contact directly or through **Lago Verde Turismo** in Santarém, ☎ *(91) 522-7577; fax 522-2118.*

Where To Stay

In Santarém there is the Tropical Hotel and then there are the others – a gap of about three stars. If you're rugged enough to spend a few days in the jungle, you may be perfectly happy with low-star accommodations in the city, but there's nothing like coming back to clean sheets, civilized service, and reliable air conditioning. See page v, at the beginning of this book, for price chart.

Tropical Hotel Santarém

Av. Mendoça Furtado, 4120; ☎ *522-1533, fax 522-2631.*

Not as elegant as the Tropical in Manaus, but it is the best hotel here. It's also owned by Varig, so you'll find an airline office in the lobby. Rooms are tiled to accommodate jungle trekkers, and every effort is made to maintain high standards of cleanliness. *122 apts. Expensive. All cards.*

Santarém Palace Hotel

Av. Rui Barbosa, 726; ☎ *522-5688, 522-5993.*

The best of the budgets offers rooms that are spacious to a fault, with painted corridors and carpeted floors. All rooms are air conditioned and come with color TV, telephone, and mini-bar; even the lobby is air conditioned. Local tours are offered in the lobby. *Inexpensive. No cards.*

Brasil Grande Hotel

Trav.15 de Agosto, 213; ☎ *522-5660.*

Nearly a dive, but at least it's clean and efficiently run. In fact, in 1994 it was the cleanest hotel downtown, according to the government quality control. The fan-cooled restaurant with MTV is a favorite among locals. Across the street is Mascote Ice Cream Parlor, with exotic popsicles. Standards come with fan, color TV, and mini-bar; suites with air conditioning, color TV, and mini-bar. Rooms with only fan and collective bathroom are cheapest. *Inexpensive. No cards.*

New City

Trav. Francisco Corrés, 200/212; ☎ *522-4719.*

Funky on the verge of sleazy, but at least this hotel is cheap. Splurge on a suite, since it's air conditioned, with a double and single bed, color TV, and mini-bar. Because rooms vary in size, however, check what's available when you arrive. The apartments on the second floor are the quietest and the best ventilated. The lobby is dominated by a color TV, dirty plastic plants and a grungy aquarium. Laundry service available. *Inexpensive. No cards.*

Where To Eat

See page v, at the beginning of this book, for price chart.

Mascote Restaurante

Praça do Pescador, 10, ☎ *522-5997. 11 a.m.-midnight.*

Santarém is not the culinary king of the Amazon, but a good value meal can be had here. Pizzas are tasty, as is the *peixe de tucunaré,* a fish similar to black bass that arrives in light soup. The service is not fast, but you can spend the wait gazing out the window at the *gaiolas* (boats) loading up.

Canto do Sabiá

Est. Santarém/Curuá-Una, 6 km. 10 a.m.-2 p.m., 5 p.m.-1 a.m.

Set outdoors in the middle of a forest about 10 km. (six miles) from the city, this is a great place to see the Amazon's moon and stars. During the day you can swim in a natural pool made from *igarapé* or cool off at the big canopied tables. Local families crowd in on the weekend to feast on great barbecued chicken and beer. *Inexpensive. No cards.*

Mascontinho

Riverside.

Perched on the bank, this "little" version of Mascote, is perfect for pizza, sandwiches and dock-watching. Sunsets are spectacular from here. *Inexpensive. No cards.*

Lumi

Av. Cuiabé, 1683. ☎ 522-2174. 11 a.m.-2 p.m., 6-11 p.m.

Authentic Japanese cuisine made by the descendants of immigrants who arrived during the rubber boom. *Moderate. No cards.*

Peixaria Canta Galo

Trav. Silva Jardim, 820; ☎ 522-1174. Noon-5 p.m., 6 p.m.-1 a.m.

Specialty is regional fish cooked Parense-style. Browse through the aquarium of local species.

Tupaiu (Tropical Hotel)

Av. Mendoça Furtado, 4412-; ☎ 522-1533. Noon-3 p.m., 7-10 p.m.

Air conditioning is high on the list of assets here, along with a decent array of international cuisine. *Moderate. All cards.*

Mutunui

Tr. Turiano Meira, 1680; ☎ 522-7909.

Traditional *churrascaria* specializing in *galetinhos* – little chickens. *Inexpensive. No cards.*

> **UP CLOSE TIP:** *Bolo de Macacheira (macacheira cake) is a delicious, sweet, heavy cake made of shredded macacheira root (the non-poisonous variety of cassava root), sugar, eggs, coconut, and butter. You're not likely to find this on any menu, so stop by Dona Antonia's Lanchonete Quero Mais, Av. Rui Barbosa, 23, for a taste treat.*

Nightlife

A few years back, locals liked to confess that Santarém was no stranger to boredom at nights. But with the recent influx of capital, there are now several cafés offering regional and Brazilian music, as well as nightclubs for dancing. Ask someone in the know for details on who's playing where. Live music can be found at the **Mascote Restaurant** during dinner on Fri. and the **Mascotinho Café** on Fri. and Sat. (see *Where To Eat*).

Denis Bar
Av. Mendonça Furtado (corner with Irv. Barjonas de Miranda).
Live music on Fri. and foods typical of the Northeast of Brazil.

Babilônia
Av. Menonça Furtado, 2940; ☎ *522-7122. 5 p.m.-last customer.*
Shows are held in this 3,000-seat theater on Sat., Sun., and holidays. Top Brazilian musicians. Check the newspaper.

Bom Paladar
Av. São Sebastião, 309; ☎ *522-3891.*
Live music Tues.-Sun., with a capacity of 600.

Signus Club
Av. Borges Leal, 2712.
Live music on Sat. and Sun. only.

Boite Tropical (Tropical Hotel)
Av. Menonça Furtado, 4120; ☎ *522-1533.*
The nightclub at the city's nicest hotel features live music only on Fri.

Boite Ancora
(at the yacht club) Av. 24 de Outobro.
This nightclub for 500 features live music on Fri.

> **UP CLOSE TIP:** *Ask about Sebastião Tapajós, a fantastic local guitarist who's become well known in France and Switzerland for Amazon folk music.*

Shopping

Santarém is just finding itself, touristically speaking, so the likelihood of finding serviceable souvenirs at the marketplace is negligible. Normal goods, such as sandals, can run at outlandishly high prices here. The following stores offer some unique crafts made by local artisans. Also, check record stores on Rua Siqueira Campos for regional music.

Cerâmica Art Sousa

Av. Gonçalves Dias, 747.

Pottery specialists José Aniceto and his son Joel sell mainly to arts and crafts shops throughout the Amazon region, but they welcome visitors. Joel was an exchange student/professor at the University of Missouri-Rolla in 1981.

Loja Regional Muiraquitã

Rua Senador Lameira Bittencourt, 131; ☎ *522-7164.*

João Mileo's store has the most complete assortment of regional handicrafts and souvenirs in town, including Indian arts. Take the time to browse. *All cards.*

Artesanato Dica Frazão

Rua Floriano Peixoto, 281.

The most famous business in town, Dona Dica has been creating her own cottage industry since 1949, crafting natural bark, root, and vine fibers gathered by Indians on the Upper Tapajós River into dresses, tunics, purses, and fans. Some of her handmade arts are in the Vatican at the Pope's table and Queen Beatrice of Belgium bought one of her dresses.

Galeria dos Artistas Rock Lima

Av. Alvaro Adolfo, 492.

This father and his sons produce the most famous carved wood furniture in town.

Artesanato e Souvenirs

Rua Senador Lameira Bittencourt, 69-B.

You'll find a wide assortment of arts and crafts from the region here.

Livraria e Papelaria Atica

Trav. 15 de Novembro, 193; ☎ *522-2745.*

Stationery, fine gifts, and books by regional authors, such as Benedito Monteiro, João Santos, and Wilde da Fonseca.

Prönatus

Rua Galdino Veloso, 278. Mon.-Sat. 8 a.m.-noon, 2-6 p.m.

Across the street from the Brasil Grande Hotel, this store sells natural products from the Amazon, such as herbal soap, shampoo, and various herb capsules for impotency, urinary problems, etc.

Cabana

Travessa 15 de Agosto, 211. Mon.-Fri. 8 a.m.-noon, 2-6 p.m., Sat. 8 a.m.-noon.

An endlessly fascinating store that sells umbanda and candomblé paraphernalia, including statues of Christian and African saints, incense, candles, and all types of potions. (I once spied a very serious middle-aged man buying a potion to attract love.)

Manipulação

Trav. Francisco Correa, 168, ☎ *522-1303.*

A homeopathic store selling brown rice, homeopathic medicines, and anti-diabetic teas.

Hands-On Santarém

Arrivals

By Air

Flights are available from Belém, Campo Grande, Cuiabá, Alta Floresta, Manaus, Rio Branco, Rio, Recife, Fortaleza, Salvador, São Paulo and a few other cities.

The airport is 13 km. (eight miles) from town. Taxis to downtown are readily available at the airport: the Tropical Hotel provides complimentary shuttle bus service for its guests.

Airlines Serving Santarém

Varig/Cruzeiro
Rua Siqueira Campos, 227 . . . .   ☎ 522-2084/1084
VASP
Av. Rui Barbosa, 786 . . . .   ☎ 522-1680

By Boat

See *River Cruises*, above.

By Bus

The *rodoviária* (bus station), ☎ 522-1342, is on the Santarém-Cuiabá Highway. Conditions permitting, bus service is available to Belém (through connections) and other points.

Car Rentals

Localiza/National
Av. Mendonça Furtado, 1603 .... ☎ 522-1130

City Transportation

Aquila
(air and land taxis) .... ☎ 522-1848
(at the airport) .... ☎ 522-2596

Climate

Tropical temperatures range from 68-92°F in Jan. and 69-90°F in July. The dry season runs July-Dec.; the rainy season from July to Jan., when it precipitates copiously. Mar. receives the most rain and, therefore, is the coolest month. The annual alternation of low and high tide that occurs every six months makes for exuberant ecological contrasts. From July-Dec., the meadows become excellent pastures for cattle and buffalo; between Jan. and July, wildlife must swim through swamps or be transported to terra firme.

Medical Emergencies

José Garcia, M.D., ☎ 522-1044, specializes in tropical diseases and speaks English and Spanish. **João Otaviano de Matos**, M.D., ☎ 522-5276, specializes in internal medicine and cardiology.

Money Exchange

No one officially changes money in Santarém (it's best to arrive with a sufficient pile of *cruzeiros*), but in emergencies, drugstores along Rua Siqueira Campos may comply; inquire of the owners.

Post Office

Correio, Av. Rui Barbosa, 1169.

Private Guide

A favored licensed guide these days is **Paulo Henrique Melchior,** who is fluent in both German and English, and particularly experienced in ecological tours. Contact him through **Lago Verde Turismo,** ☎ *522-7577* or privately at ☎ *522-6951.*

Telephone

Local and international phone calls may be made at **TELEPAR,** Av. São Sebastião, 913.

Time

Santarém is one hour earlier than Belém – a fact that sometimes confuses even airline officials.

Tourist Information

Tourist brochures and information can be obtained at **Divisão Municipal de Turismo,** Centro Cultural João Fona, Rua da Imperador, no number; ☎ *523-2434.*

Travel Agencies

Lago Verde Turismo Ltda.

Rua Galdino Veloso, 384; ☎ *(91) 522-7577; fax 522-2118.*

One of the premier agencies in Santarém, Lago Verde offers personalized packages to all groups. Good English-speaking management and guides are available for fishing, trekking, scientific expeditions, photographic projects, and nature studies.

Agências Tropicais de Turismo/Hotel Tropical

Av. Mendonça Furtado, 4120, ☎ *522-1533.*

This agency provides transfers from the airport to the hotel for its guests, as well as a variety of group tours, including half-day city tours and trips to Alter de Chão, Meeting of the Waters, Belterra, piranha fishing, and nighttime alligator hunts.

Amazon Turismo Ltda.

Trav. Turiano Meira, 1084; ☎ *522-2620, fax 522-1098.*

This company offers overnight trips to Monte Alegre in a jeep, and Alenquer in a wooden riverboat, as well as day trips to Fordlândia and the national park.

When To Go

From Aug.-Jan. the flowers become increasingly more profuse and there's more sand on the beach. Jan. is peak time, and **New Year's Day** is celebrated with big bashes. **Festa do Sairé** occurs the first week in July. On June 29, a procession of bumba-meu-boi, a regional dance with costumes and music, takes place during the **São Pedro Festival**. In Sept. there is the **International Tucunaré Fishing Championship**.

BELÉM

The city of Belém effectively entered the 20th century in 1961, when Juscelino Kubitschek's highway from Brasília reached its final destination. For centuries prior, however, the city, strategically placed on the Amazon estuary close to the mouth of the Rio Tocantins, had served nobly as a natural port for the steady stream of products extracted from the Amazon. Dating back to 1621, the city of Belém, which is also the capital of the state of **Pará**, was christened on the feast day of St. Mary of Bethlehem, and at times is still referred to by its long nomenclature: Nossa Senhora do Belém do Grão-Pará or, at least, Belém do Pará. The state, which is larger than most European countries, is the wealthiest in Brazil in regards to ore; even Indian tribes, such as the Kayapó, are sitting on some of the richest mahogany and gold reserves in the country.

History

The native population in the region of Belém was not always so lucky. Shortly after its discovery, the city became a slave port for Indian trade, as well as a market for cacao and other jungle spices. So decimated did the native population become that the Portuguese Crown had to offer incentives to white colonists who married Indian women: their booty included "one axe, two scissors, some cloth, clothes, two cows and two bushels of seeds." In the late 18th century the city was further threatened by local Mundurukú tribes.

Following the abdication of Pedro I, between January 1835 and May 1836, one of the country's bloodiest rebellions shook the region, as bands of mixed-blood settlers and Indians revolted against the white owners of sugar mills and *fazendas*, After several days of violence, the *cabanos* (so-called because they lived in cabana huts on the floodplains and riverbanks near Belém) took control of the city, killing numeous landlords and inspiring the complicity of impoverished locals. Without a clear political program, however, the rebels could not sustain their goal to secede from the Brazil and chaos reigned. The **British Navy** inadvertently became involved when one of its ships arrived loaded with arms for the former authorities, and were decimated. Five months later, an English naval force demanded retribution, succeeding in creating a blockade while troops eventually invaded the area, beginning a relentless drive that, over the next several years, eventually wiped out over 30,000 people.

It was the 19th-century **rubber boom** that transformed this natty little port into a graceful, Victorian city of fin de siècle arches and Italianate palazzos. What makes Belém truly beautiful are its avenues and plazas, shaded with magnificent *mangueiras* (mango trees) that cool the cobblestones when temperatures soar. Today, the historic quarter, which retains much of its art nouveau and neoclassical structures, is a pleasure to stroll through, butted on all sides by a thriving market. One need only step inside the famed Teatro da Paz, the city's all-purpose theater, to appreciate the ingenuity of the rubber barons who longed to recreate European culture in the middle of the Ver-o-Peso market, facing the waterfront, which outclasses any other outdoor marketplace in Brazil, and perhaps in South America. Crammed, chaotic, and totally confusing to the uninitiated, the Ver-o-Peso market is a veritable lion's den of exotic sights and smells that could take days to exhaust.

Although most jungle-destined tourists have traditionally headed for Manaus, Belém shouldn't be missed. Not only is the city more navigable by foot, but the jungle expeditions I experienced here are some of the best in the region. Like Manaus, Belém is hot and humid, but the locals here have developed a sense of humor: They refer to themselves as fish because they feel they breathe more water than air.

A Bird's-Eye View

Belém is situated 120 kilometers from the Atlantic Ocean, where the Rio Guamá veers northward, becoming the Baía do Guarajá. As the biggest port in the Amazon, Belém serves as a jumping-off point for most river excursions. The city is ruled by the activity along **Avenida President Vargas**, which stretches from the bay to the Teatro da Paz in the Praça da Republica. Several shopping centers sequestered on narrow streets are west of Avenida Presidente Vargas, including **Rua João Alfredo** with its hammocks and inexpensive gear. Also nearby is the **Cidade Velho** (Old Town), full of colonial-style buildings. To the right is the city's market and the waterfront.

Sights

On Foot

Belém is a perfect city to stroll through. The following is a walking tour, which is completely safe to follow on your own during the day.

Hilton Hotel

Start your walking tour in front of the Hilton. (If you're not staying there, you might take a peek at the lush breakfast buffet, open to the public but free for guests.)

Praça da República

The park is directly across the street from the Hilton. Once dense with tropical forest, the site was cleared in the 17th century to make way for Belém's first cemetery; later it became the city's principal park. There's even a coreto, an iron-grilled pagoda where brass bands used to perform.

Teatro da Paz

Mon.-Fri. 8 a.m.-noon, 2-6 p.m.

Dominating the square is the city's pride and joy, the theater, an unabashedly neoclassical opera house surrounded by Greek columns and adorned at its entrance with the four busts of the Muses. Inaugurated in 1878, the plush theater, with its bronze staircases and fabulous tiled floors was fueled by the ostentatious passions of the rubber barons who continually looked to Europe for style. Consequently, the foyer's crystal mirrors are Italian, the massive chandelier in the lobby German, the pastel, fluted light fixtures Art Deco. The theater's ceiling is a finely orchestrated marriage of Italianate painting and grillwork from which is suspended an eight-tiered, 1½-ton crystal chandelier. The adjacent Salão Nobre is absolutely charming, once a salon for the elite balls and now the stage for chamber concerts and voice recitals. Note that the salon's ceiling painting is not from the original construction, but was designed in 1960 by São Paulo artist Armando Balloni to reflect the abundance of Amazonian animals. Walk out to the balcony and look up to see the four Muses: from right to left, Comedy, Poetry, Music, and Drama. In 1986 the building, after laboring under a blue facade for many years, was restored to its original pink color. Backstage, you'll see plaques honoring performances by the great ballerina Anna Pavlova in 1918 and the great Brazilian soprano Bidu Sayão. If you have the opportunity to catch a performance of theater or music, grab it; ask your concierge or check the daily newspapers for listings. Free tours are given continuously throughout the day, though only in Portuguese.

Bar do Parque

This outdoor café, on the side of the theater near the Hilton, is where the city's artists, singers, and streetwalkers gather until the wee hours of morning. Nearby is a kiosk that sells bread and coffee in the morning and beer and *caipirinhas* in the afternoon.

Teatro Experimental Walder Henrique

Rua Pres. Vargas, 645; ☎ *222-4762.*

Walking down Rua Presidente Vargas, you'll come upon this theater. Started in 1979, this experimental theater is a showcase for avant-garde music, plays, and dance, with preference given to non-professional artists. Due to their tight budget, shows are not given daily; they start around 9 p.m. when they do happen. Seats go for about $1.50.

Rua Santo Antônio

Walk down Av. Presidente Vargas to the right of the theater, passing a travel agency, the Varig office at #363, and the Monópolio Turismo Câmbio (for exchanging money) at #325. Turn left on Rua Santo Antônio, a cobblestone street with no cars, down the middle of which are the remains of 19th-century trolley tracks. As the principal shopping avenue of the city (also called Comércio), the street overflows with shops and vendors hawking all kinds of third-world quality goods. As you wander, look up at the second-story houses, once fashionable 19th-century homes and still adorned with exquisite tile work and pastel-colored balconies and shutters.

Restaurante Vegetariano e Mercadinho Natural

Rua Santo Antônio, 264. Lunch Mon.-Fri. 11:30 a.m.-3 p.m.

A vegetarian market where you can stock up on natural shampoos, whole foods and Amazon teas. Upstairs, the restaurant serves only lunch.

Paris N'América

Down the street from the market, peek inside the Paris N'América, today a dry goods store but once a beautiful home constructed in 1906 for Francisco Castro by the Portuguese master Ricardo Salvador Fernandes Mesquita. From the sculptured ceilings to the dramatic grilled stairway, many of the original architectural details are still intact. The steel was imported from Scotland, the ceramic-tiled floor and mechanical clock from Germany, the bronze light fixtures from France, the crystal mirrors from Belgium, and the outside wall tiles from Portugal.

Praça Mercês

A few steps further on, you'll reach Praça Mercês, home to many finely restored buildings. Dominating the plaza is the church known as Mercês, founded in 1640. Despite the graffiti, you can see that the facade is still intact. This may be just the time that you need an ice-cold *água de coco*, which can be bought in front of the church.

Travessa Frutuoso Guimarães

Next, walk in front of the church on Rua Gaspar Viana and turn right on Travessa Frutuoso Guimarães. At #63, you can pick up decent mosquito nets and hammocks for good prices.

Ver-O-Peso Market

Nearby, along Av. Castilhos, facing the pier, you'll enter into one of the great third-world marketplaces of all time. To a first-world eye, the open-air market may look like a den of iniquity, but it's actually the epitome of Amazonian life: hundreds of tiny stalls selling anything and everything that floats up the river – from fruits and vegetables and Brazil nuts to snake skins, turtle soap, and dolphin eyes (the last three items being all contraband materials). Begun as a checkpoint in 1688, the market received its name ("watch the weight") from the Portuguese habit of weighing all merchandise that passed through the port for taxation. Today, the market is also a food bazaar, with scores of native women cooking aromatic dishes for the workers who cram into the tiny pathways. The air in the market is hot and dense and barely conducive to dining, but if you're brave enough, browse around until you find something that looks edible. The dark-maroon, soup-like juice sitting in the large tin pans is *açaí*, a true Amazon delicacy made with sugar and manioc juice (it tastes

Outside the market of Belém – where anything is for sale.

a bit like avocado and goes well with fried fish). Take a moment to watch the workers squeeze the water out of the ground manioc with a long straw tool called a *tipiti,* which works something like an accordion.

As you walk through the market, each section will resound with its own sounds and smells. Not just business, but the very dramas of daily life are carried on here, with lots of flirting and cursing going on between stalls. A perusal of the tropical fruit stands will give you an idea of the enormous variety available here; note the Brazil nuts that come lodged in big brown shells, just as they're found in the forest. The large green spiny-looking fruit is a graviola. The herb section is particularly ripe with superstition and folklore. Good buys are small bottles of concentrated oils, such as *baunilha* (vanilla) and jasmine or more potent love potions such as the Corre Atrás, designed to make a man "Run After" you. *Tamaquaré* powder is a cooked lizard powder sprinkled on husbands to make them calm down sexually – a hot-selling item in the Amazon. (Some women actually buy the live lizards you see in the market and cook them into potions themselves. Another trick is to place the live lizard in the same water where the man regularly washes his clothes.) On the opposite extreme, stall #54 sells perfume that comes complete with a boa constrictor inside, well known as a "fatal attraction" potion.

UP CLOSE TIP: *Due to the tight space and general mayhem, this market can be dangerous. Go with little money on you, do not wear gold chains or jewelry, keep your bag close to you at all times, and be cautious about taking photos. Since a number of vendors trade in contraband items (such an endangered species), they do not care to have their business recorded.*

Meat Market

Don't miss the meat market nearby, a chrome-grilled structure brought from England in 1909; its cast-iron frame and Victorian turrets are souvenirs from the time when the British built most of the port a century ago. Inside, individual stands are manned by brawny workers who constantly yell at each other while slicing carcasses hanging from wires. The wet, smelly fish market in the same complex opens in the early morning and closes by 1 p.m.; here you can view full-sized samples of the region's most common fish. Buyers receive their merchandise wrapped in large leaves from the guarumã bush, then supply their own plastic bag – a traditional Amazonian way of economizing on paper.

In general, the entire area near the pier is endlessly fascinating and ripe with photo ops. Outside the market you may see baby monkeys for sale (illegal) or even baby sloths (also illegal).

Boulevard Castilhos França

Make sure you walk down this boulevard next to the bay, where fishermen and merchants dock their schooners and canoes laden with goods. Unfortunately, a lot of trash litters the portside here, even though (or because) many people use their boats as floating lodges. You may even see rats scurrying about these barges to no one's apparent dismay. Do note the Texaco floating gas station in the bay, an omnipresent reminder of Western influence.

Praça do Relógio (Clock Square)

Across from the pier near the market, this square, with its large, monumental clock tower, is often used by guides as a meeting place.

> **UP CLOSE TIP:** *ENASA boats to Marajó Island leave from the port on the other side of the market.*

Praça Frei Caetano Brandão

Walk from the market past the mango and bamboo tree-filled Dom Pedro II Park to the Praça Frei Caetano Brandão, dominated by the 19th-century Catedral de Nossa Senhora da Graça. Sadly run-down on the outside, the cathedral boasts some of Brazil's finest paintings inside, though the lights are rarely turned on. Hours for mass are Tues.-Thurs. 5:30 p.m., Sat. 6:30 a.m., and 7 p.m., and Sun. 7 a.m., 9 a.m., 5 p.m., and 8 p.m. It's from here that nearly one million faithful begin their journey to the basílica each year during the Círio festival in Oct. Nearby is the Igreja Santo Alexandrian, an 18th-century church, whose small collection of religious art may be open.

Forte do Castelo

Open daily 8 a.m.-noon, 2-6 p.m.; restaurant 11:30 a.m.-3 p.m., 6:30-11:30 p.m.

This is a good place to end the walking tour. This fort marks the city's founding, as it was the first building constructed in Belém, strategically located at the confluence of the Guajará Bay and Guamá River on a hill commanding a view of the bay. Once headquarters for the military operations that expelled the English, French, and Dutch, it also provided a refuge for the Caabanagem revolutionaries. Now the fort houses the Circulo Militar Club and Restaurant, open to the public. Actually, there's nothing to do here but sit and drink (better at night when the weather is cooler, though during the day the view of the port below is fantastic). From the perimeter of the fort you can also see the Feira d'Açai down below, where boats loaded with raw *açaí* start arriving as early as 4:30 a.m. You can also see large cargo boats transporting ceramics from the nearby islands and returning home laden with mineral water and sodas.

Cidade Velha (Old City)

The area around the market and cathedral is full of quaint squares and colonial homes with grilled balconies and colorful shutters. Browse at will, but do try to avoid Rua da Ladeira – not a safe street to walk through due to the prostitutes and homeless who frequent its alleyways. (During the day, it's more or less okay, but avoid it completely at night.)

More Sights

Basílica de Nossa Senhora de Nazaré

Praça Justo Chermont. 6:30-11:30 a.m., 3-9 p.m.

One of the most stunning churches in Brazil, this *basílica* is the end point for the annual procession of Círio de Nazaré on the second Sun. in Oct. The church, which was initiated in 1909, took 40 years to build – a majestic blending of Italian granite and mosaics, French stained glass, and a ceiling of red cedar taken from the forest. The idolized statue of the Madonna, which is carried through the streets, rests above the altar in a circle of cherubs (a photo showing details can be found to the right of the altar). Devotion to the statue is so intense that you might see petitioners dragging themselves on their knees to the altar in payment of a promise. In front of the *basílica* is a modern, open-air complex consisting of high altar, amphitheater, pantheon, and war monument, where mass during the Círio festival is held

Don't forget to visit the sacred-art museum downstairs, called **Museu do Círio**. It's open Tues.-Fri. 8 a.m.-6 p.m., weekends 8 a.m.-noon. A fine gift to take home are the *briquedos de abaetuba*, toys made of balsa wood sold by street vendors during the Círio Festival.

Palácio Antônio Lemos

Between Praça Dom Pedro and Praça Felipe Patroni; ☎ 223-5664. Tues.-Fri. 9 a.m.-noon, 1-6 p.m., weekends 9 a.m.-noon. Admission free.

Originally built during the second half of the 19th century, this former palace had been in such demise that wild animals had taken up residence. Refurbished in 1993, it now artistically reflects the Belle Epoque era, with a grand marble staircase and Louis XVI furniture. The mayor's office is also located here.

Museu Paraense Emilio Goeldi

Parque Zoobotânico, Av. Magalhães Barata, 376; ☎ 249-1233. Closed Mon.

Belém's premier museum was initiated in 1866 to record the richness of Amazônia's flora, fauna, rocks, indigenous culture, and folklore.

The multi-media complex embraces a park, zoo, and indoor museum. The park, modeled after an Amazonian jungle, has fewer trees per square foot than the forest, but offers more species, including rubber trees, guaraná (from which the herbal stimulant is taken), pau-brasil, cedro vermelho, castanha-do-pará (Brazil nut), and the huge sumaumeira (the biggest tree in the South American jungle). At the desk of the permanent exhibition, ask for a guidebook in English, then tour the fine displays of stuffed birds, basketry, Indian artifacts, and jewelry. Running freely outside in the zoo are cutias (a type of small anteater with the frisky personality of a raccoon). Also to be seen is a dazzling array of tropical birds, alligators, cats, tapirs, manatees, and electric eels. The souvenir shop is excellent.

Parque Dos Igarapés

Conjunto Satélite WE 12, # 1000, Ananindeua, Pará. Office: Rua 223 Manoel Barata, 704, Edifício Paes de Carvalho, # 403, Belém, CEP 66020; ☎ *235-1910, 223-8324, 227-2588. Reserve only on Sun. or for groups.*

This tropical park owned by a private family is a welcome respite from the heat of the city and the ruggedness of the jungle. The $10 entrance fee goes toward food and beverages taken in the excellent open-air restaurant or beside the natural swimming pool (whose water was pronounced cleaner than the drinking water in Belém). Ecological walks can be taken through the forested grounds or you can hop in a canoe and navigate the narrow *igarapés* (streams) that seem to go everywhere and nowhere. Children will love the wood-log playground and there are so many animals here – including an *atú* (armadillo), *creatipurí* (squirrel), and *preguiçosa* (sloth) – that a staff vet is required by law. Belemites flock to this complex on weekends, when live bands turn the main arena into a outdoor nightclub.

AN UP CLOSE JUNGLE ADVENTURE
from the author

Jungle adventures start early in Belém – 4 a.m. at the Hilton, when my young handsome guide Tony Rocha picks me up, threading his way through late-night revelers on their way to bed. We drive to the docks, then board a skiff in the moonlight, the humidity dense around us. Illuminating our way with flashlights, we set off down the Guamá River, passing *caboclos* (jungle-dwellers) already on their way to market. A mere 15 minutes later, Tony is pointing out a "new" island, recently sculpted by the six-hour tides that continually change the face of Amazônia.

As the sky turns luminescent pink we settle in front of another island called Ilha dos Papagaios and watch as thousands of green parrots awake, then fly off squawking in pairs. As the sun rises, we catch glimpses of river life – women carrying baskets, children paddling to school. Soon we bank and I take my first plunge into the jungle.

The feeling of being surrounded by literally millions of life forms – trees, shrubs, vines, birds, ants, bugs, and whatever is flying in my face – is absolutely thrilling, though not unscary. Cutting the path with a machete, Tony leads us deeper into the darkened jungle, pointing out the sumaumeira tree, an elephantine monster whose trunks are used by natives to beat out messages. We inspect the leaves of the guaramá tree, which are used to wrap fish at market, and another tree whose bark exudes a drinkable milky substance. My boots sink deep into fungus; my arms get scratched. Despite the incessant cawing of birds, it's difficult not to appreciate the eery green silence of the forest – what writer Peter Mathiesson once described as the "stillness of a cathedral."

Cruising down the river again, we make a pitstop at a riverside grocery – a mere counter crammed with *pinga*, the jungle's alcoholic cure – made from sugarcane. The owners are an elderly couple whose eyes are incredibly similar – wet and suspiciously shiny. "Maybe we are brother and sister," Senhor Tomé laughs. "When we were young, my father was very active!" Their grand-children, visiting from the city, scamper about in their marvelous backyard – the jungle! Dona Palmira

Dona Palmìra welcoming visitors to her home in the Amazon jungle.

talks about the time she saw a white-suited stranger dive into the river ("obviously," according to her, an enchanted *boto*, or dolphin). As a full eclipse of the sun is about to occur, we rush to the pier of an abandoned pepper plantation to catch the magical display of fading color.

At dusk, Branco, our boatman, invites us to sleep at his riverside house. As the sun sets, mosquitoes attack us in droves, but we bat them off long enough to devour an excellent dinner of fried catfish. Before retiring, we pump Branco for tales of the *curupira*, the legendary master of the forest whose feet are turned backwards and who loves to befuddle humans. Branco tells of his troubles with a *matinta pereira*, a forest witch who wouldn't stop seducing him until he finally married. At midnight I wake up terrified. My hammock, which is strung over a boat, is swinging wildly – and for no apparent reason. Soon Tony's hammock, next to mine, also goes out of control, driving us both to hysterics. Then, all of a sudden, both hammocks stop swinging. Paralyzed with fear, neither of us can speak or go back to sleep. In the morning, over breakfast, Branco frowns darkly when he hears the story, mumbling into his coffee that the *matinta pereira* – without a doubt – had paid us a visit. Nobody is laughing now.

After breakfast, we head out to the tiny streams, or *igarapés*, overhung with luscious green vines just as in a Tarzan movie. Branco's nine-year-old nephew Fernando shows me how to climb a palm tree with a rope made from leaves – a true jungle monkey. After a hot, sweaty trek over *terra firma*, we reach a *casa de farinha*, a manioc plantation run by Dona Paula, a powerfully built woman with two grown daughters, and her much smaller husband.

Incredibly, the talk turns to the Gulf War. "I was so happy that President Bush decided to end it," she says in Portuguese to my utter amazement, though I soon learn she has watched the entire war on her battery-operated TV – accompanied, I am sure, by a hefty diet of Brazilian soap operas. Before we head back to our boat, she primes us with a delicious plate of hot manioc and beans, then warns us to look out for cobras – "It's the only thing I worry about with my daughter." The thought does not make me a happy camper. This time, however, the way back, through tangled vines and overgrown moss, with one eye out for fat snakes, seems a lot shorter. By the time we return to the dock only 24 hours after we began, it feels as though we've been gone a few lifetimes.

Something similar to the above tour can be arranged through **Amazon Star Turismo**, Rua Carlos Gomes, 14; ☎ and fax 224-6244, who offers four kinds of tours:

- ☐ A half-day tour around Belém, in front of the Guamá River, including a forest walk (price includes hotel pickup and two guides).
- ☐ A full-day (eight-hour) tour down the Guamá and Acará rivers, including a walk in the forest and lunch.
- ☐ An overnight stay on the Guamá River and Parrot Island.
- ☐ An early morning jaunt to Parrot Island, leaving at 4:15 a.m. and returning 8:30 a.m.

Arrangements with Amazon Star Turismo can also be made in Rio through **Expeditours**, Rua Visconde de Pirajá 414; ☎ (21) 287-9697.

Excursions

River Travel

The most utilized form of transportation in this region is the boat. Wooden multi-deck cruisers (*gaiolas*) regularly make trips down the Amazon River from Belém to Santarém and Manaus – a colorful way to make friends and enter into the heart of Amazonian life. Along with grandmothers, babies, and traveling salesmen, you might share quarters with dogs, chickens, and the family pig. Some boats rent only hammock space (you must provide your own hammock); others offer a few private cabins just big enough for a sink and two bunk beds, with a key to the private toilet. (Note well that the communal toilet is usually beyond description.) You might consider renting a cabin (for the privacy and the bathroom) and also hang your hammock in the main galley.

During sunlight hours, the boats usually cruise near the banks so you can spot wildlife and peek inside the native homes; people hang out on the top deck, where you can buy beer and snacks. Most exciting are the brief stops at port, where you can watch lovers parting, children hawking fruits and homemade foods, and dockworkers loading the ship's goods.

ENASA touring boats with air-conditioned cabins and private bathrooms are popular ways to cruise from Belém to Manuas through Santarém. In Belém, contact **ENASA** at Av. Presidente Vargas, 41; ☎ (91) 222-3995/224-0528.

The *Amazon Clipper* is a riverboat built along traditional lines for cruising the Amazon and its tributaries. Eight double cabins with bunks accommodate 16 passengers, with night-time air conditioning and private toilet facilities. Outboard-powered canoes are used for trips into lagoons, channels, and flooded forest. There's also an open salon, video library, and sundeck. Cruises run three, four, and six days. Four-day trips include meeting native *caboclo* families to see jungle life up close. Contact Expeditours in Rio for more information ☎ *(21) 287-9697, fax 521-4388.*

Safari Ecológico, Rua Monsenhor Coutinho, 119; ☎ *(92) 233-3739;* fax *233-3739,* also offers two double-decked vessels – the *Tunã* and *Fagra II* – regional vessels with air conditioning, fully equipped kitchen, video lounge, and library. These penetrate the tributaries of the Amazon. Cruises from two to 15 days include close contact with local people; crews include a multilingual guide and a trained biologist. Day and half-day excursions can be taken on the *Jacaré-Cu.*

Mosqueiro Island

Fifty-three miles (86 km.) from Belém is Mosqueiro Island, the main bathing beach of the capital that is well-connected by road and bridges. Back in the 19th century, the first tourists to the island were Portuguese, French, and English rubber barons enjoying the boom; today most of the village has retained its mud-hut look. The hour's drive from the city takes you over a decent highway (BR 360) lined with verdant forests full of *açaí* and *dendê* palm trees (the red flag in front of houses signifies they sell *açaí*); after you pass over the nearly mile-long bridge, you'll be besieged by young boys hawking beer and bags of sun-dried shrimps. The bus from Belém stops at **Areão Beach**, where the city's main square and market are located. However, most of the popular beach action takes place at **Farol Beach**, where the sand is the widest and rock concerts last all night. The bay here is where all rivers meet and flow to the ocean, causing an intense wave reaction big enough for surfing. **Murubira Beach** is considered the chic beach, where most of the jetskiers, ultraleve daredevils, and windsurfers hang out. Swimming is considered relatively safe. During Carnaval, this beach is one of the hottest in the Amazon.

Since there are 16 *igarapés* in the middle of the island, the landscape is perfect for short jungle tours, which can be arranged through **Carlos Alberto Ribeiro**, owner of the Maresia Restaurant. For about $20 he'll take you on a 4½-hour tour of the *igarapés* by canoe, visiting a *caboclo's* house and wheat plantation, and fishing for fresh shrimp (you must provide your own transportation to the island). If you would like to spend the night, Senhor Carlos Alberto's colonial-style *pousada* offers an exotic hideaway on the beach for remarkably low prices. The restaurant itself, on Farol Beach, serves a fine *caldeirada* (soup stew with fish, octopus, egg, potatoes, onions, shrimps, and manioc flour) and a delicious *peixe tropical,* fish with Brazil nuts and the cream of Brazil nuts. Buffalo steak, another rare delicacy, must be ordered four to five hours in advance. For reservations for the tour and *pousada* contact the **Restaurante Maresia,** Av. Beira Mar, 29; ☎ *(91) 771-1463.* Crafts can be found on the **Praça da Matriz** from 8 a.m. to 9 p.m., daily.

When To Go

Mosqueiro Island seemed even hotter to me than Belém. After it rains at 1 or 2 p.m. (every day), the temperature cools a bit, making strolling more palatable. (In Belém the same shower is called the "three o'clock rain.") Oct. is the hottest month, when crabs appear in the saltier water. High season lasts from July to Nov., with the best months of sunshine being Aug. and Sept. The months notorious for rain are Jan. and Feb.

❖ **GETTING HERE:** *Buses leave hourly from the bus station in Belém (during vacations, every 15 min.). The trip takes about 1½ hours by bus, or one hour by car. Return buses can be found on the Praça da Matriz;* ☎ *(91) 771-1204.*

Marajó Island

Just across the bay from Belém is Marajó, an island the size of Switzerland, and fast becoming the major tourist destination of the North. The major attractions are the water buffalo ranches, where enormous herds graze the open plains – a species that first came to the island by way of shipwreck. Also in profusion are hundreds of rare bird specimens, as well as numerous alligators, and monkeys, more easily seen here than in the jungle. Those who choose to stay along the coast are awarded with a rolling sea, whose crashing waves result from the confluence of the inland rivers and the ocean seas.

Those who want to truly feel the life of Marajó should go to Bonjardim, the most famous of the buffalo ranches. The owners, Eduardo and Eunice Ribeiro, are a charming couple who speak English, French, and Spanish and love to sit down for lunch and dinner with their guests (invariably a groaning table of fine delicacies). During the day you can ride the range with the staff, birdwatch, and fish for piranha; at night there are organized alligator hunts. Bookings can be made most easily through **Amazon Star Turismo** in Belém ☎ *(91) 224-6244.*

Beyond the ranch, the best pousada in the main town of Soure is **Pousada Marjoara**, Rua de Soure, 33; ☎ *(91) 741-1287; in Belém,* ☎ (91) 223-8369. It's walking distance from the waterfront and the center of town.

❖ **GETTING HERE:** *The fastest way to reach Marajó Island is by plane. Air taxis, which can be reserved for any time, run about $200. Much cheaper are the regularly scheduled flights on TABA (about $30), which leave Mon. and Wed. from Belém at 7 a.m. and return at 7:40 p.m. from Soure. On Fri. the flight leaves Belém at 4 p.m. and returns on Sun at 4 p.m.*

You can also go by bus. Service leaves from Belém's bus terminal at 5 a.m. and includes a bus to Iguraci, a ferry boat to Câmara (across the Marajó Bay, about 3 hrs.), then a bus to Salvaterra and a small ferry to Soure. The return trip leaves from Soure at 2 p.m. Mon.-Sat.

ENASA boats leave Belém Wed. and Fri. at 8 p.m. and return on Thurs. and Sun. at 4 p.m., as well as Sat. at 2 p.m., returning at 5 or 6 p.m. (from Soure). The trip is colorful, usually accompanied by screaming babies, squawking chickens, and quacking ducks. Regional class is about $8, but tourist class (much preferred) runs about $18.

The easiest way to visit Marajó is to arrange a package deal through **Amazon Star Turismo,** ☎ *224-6624, who will provide transfer to the pier in Belém, trip by ferry boat to the island (3 hrs., 2 buses) or boat (5 hrs.), city tour, lodge with breakfast, half-day tour to a fazenda to see buffalos and horses, stops at one or two beaches, and a folklore show on Sat. night.*

Salinas

Situated 124 miles (200 kms) from Belém, Salinas has one of the most beautiful and longest Brazilian beaches (at nine miles/15 km.). The water changes its color and taste according to the season, due to the influence of the Amazon River. The best hotel is **Brasil Palace**, Rua Ver. Corinto Pereira de Castro, 70 (Alvorado); ☎ *891-1064.* An exuberant folklore festival with capoeira (the Brazilian martial art) takes place in Aug.

Where To Stay

Accommodations in Belém run from the ever-efficient, luxurious Hilton to the modest pousada. Air conditioning is a necessity. See page v, at the beginning of this book, for price chart.

Belém Hilton

Av. Pres. Vargas, 882 (Praça da Rep., Centro); ☎ *(91) 242-6500; fax 225-2942.*

The Hilton is Belém's first and only five-star, a luxurious relief from the heat and humidity of the cityscape. Service is geared towards those who wake up at dawn for river tours or stay up till dawn to dance; breakfast opens at 4 a.m. An impressive underground mall includes a deli, famous for salamis, cheeses, and exquisite pastries. The pool is small and unusually shaped; it serves as a magnet on the weekends for chic cruisers. The gym is the best in the city, with free weights, aerobic classes, sauna, and massage. An elegant club serves exotic tropical drinks and offers live music on the weekends. Apartments are plush, with marble-topped bathrooms and comfortable beds. *361 apts. Expensive. All cards.*

Equatorial Palace

Av. Braz de Aguiar, 612 (Nazaré); ☎ *(91) 241-2000, fax (091) 223-5222.*

This traditional four-star is located in a prime area of shady streets and chic stores, four blocks from downtown. Smaller and more intimate than the Hilton, the hotel boasts a fine, old-world restaurant, called 1900, famous for its Portuguese codfish. The circular, blue-tiled swimming pool is surrounded by a *churrascaria* and pool bar. The romantic piano bar is a favorite in the city. The older rooms, mostly used for long-term residences, have an old-world charm the newer apartments lack. Ignore the tacky lobby. *296 apts. Expensive. All cards.*

Novotel Belém

Av. Bernardo Sayão, 4804 (Guamá), 4 km.; ☎ *(91) 229-8011, fax 229-8709.*

Near the University of Belém, the Novotel is a good, medium-priced hotel, particularly suitable for families who make a one-day stop in Belém; most three-hour river tours leave from the harbor located in the hotel's backyard. The pool area, lined with açaí trees, is extensive, with a children's pool, playground, and volleyball court. All rooms are air conditioned, and come with two double beds and an extra couch bed, color TV, and a large desk. Make sure you ask for a room with a view of the river. Laundry service available. *121 apts. Moderate. All cards.*

Zoghbi Park Hotel

Rua Pe. Prudêncio, 220 (Centro); fax and ☎ (91) 241-1800.

This small but adequate three-star offers a good low-priced option for discerning travelers. Rooms, all air conditioned, are clean, with finely finished wood doors, closets, and headboards. A good buy is the *especial*, with a fascinating view of the city's back streets. The bar doubles as a TV lounge. All room keys are electronic and safes are available at reception. *36 apts. Moderate-inexpensive. V.*

Regente Hotel

Av. Gov. José Malcher, 485 (Centro); ☎ (91) 241-1222; fax 224-0343.

Centrally located within walking distance of the Praça da República, the Regente is a reliable low-priced hotel; nearby is the fine restaurant Lá Em Casa. Apartments, with color TV and mini-bar, are cheerful and overlook the city's rooftops. A good budget idea is the standard central. Noise from the city traffic may filter up to the rooms. The restaurant offers standard fare without much style. Safes at reception. *149 apts. Inexpensive. All cards.*

Manacá

Rua Quintino Bocaiúva, 1645; ☎ 223-3335.

An old reformed house with large room, and an interior garden where breakfast is served. This hotel-residence is an oasis in busy downtown. You pay extra for breakfast and TV. *Inexpensive. No cards.*

Vidonho's

Rua O' de Almeida, 476 (Centro); ☎ (91) 225-1444.

A simple, small hotel with rock-bottom rates that can't be beat (without being seedy). Apartments come with mini-bar and color TV, and furniture in good shape. The only drawback is the small windows. Safes at the reception. *48 apts. Inexpensive. DC, MC, V.*

Where To Eat

Belém is one of the best places in the Amazon to sample native cuisine. Fish is excellent. Do try the native fruit juices, such as *cupuaçu* or *taperebá*, from the cashew family. You can't come to the Amazon, however, without tasting its most famous delicacy – ice cream made from tropical fruit flavors. Needless to say, it's the best way to beat the heat (and the parlors are usually air-cooled). See page v, at the beginning of this book, for price chart.

Lá Em Casa/O Outro

Av. Gov. José Malcheer, 247(Centro); ☎ *223-1212. Noon-3 p.m., 7p.m-midnight.*

Some folks say the only native food in Brazil can be found in Belém, where it was taught to the first colonists by the Indians. Owner Ana Maria Martin, who learned to cook from her grandmother (she even went upstream to the family farm to learn from Indian women), has received international raves for her *maniçoba*, a concoction of meat or fish mushed with manioc leaves that must be cooked for four to five days to extract the poison. Warm and voluble, Dona Ana Maria has installed two restaurants in this colonial-style house: the air-conditioned salon, called *O Outro* (The Other), which serves hot and cold buffets; and the back patio, *Lá em Casa* (There at Home), with its gargantuan flamboyant tree in the middle. The Menu Paraense gives you a chance to try all the different regional tastes. A special lunch plate is a steal. *Pato no tucupi* (duck made with a manioc sauce available only in Belém) and *patinhas de carangueijo à Milanesa* (fried crab legs) are excellent. The fish *tucunaré* is best eaten in Santarém. *Moderate-expensive. All cards.*

Restaurante Círculo Militar

Praça Frei Caetano Brandão (Forte de Castelo); ☎ *223-4374.*
Noon-4 p.m. and 6:30 p.m.-midnight.

With its balcony-like salon overlooking the bay, this is the perfect place to lunch away from the hubbub of the marketplace. Located in the Castelo Fort, it's especially romantic at night, but also good for light lunches. *Lagostim* is a small freshwater shrimp breaded with egg and stuffed with cheese. *Moderate. All cards.*

Augustus

Av. Almirante Barroso, 493 (Marco); ☎ *226-8317. Noon-2:30 p.m., 7:30-11:30 p.m.;*
Sat. 7 p.m.-midnight, Sun. noon-3 p.m.

Dark wood-beamed ceilings vie with tropical gardens in this chic restaurant. A specialty is brochette misto à Piamonteza, a mixed grill of steak, pork, and sausage. Don't miss the *coco branco*, an intensely sweet concoction of shredded coconut glazed in sugar and spiked with cloves. *Moderate. All cards.*

Miralha Bar e Restaurante

Av. Doca de Souza Franco, 194; ☎ *241-4832. 8 a.m.-4 a.m.*

Hip Belémites come to this tropical beer garden near the docks in the Umarizal district for a drink after work (and a pickup). Families, however, will also feel at home. Music (usually MPB) is the best in the city, with live bands starting at 9:30 p.m.; a small cover is charged after 9:45 p.m. The special is Japanese food: *camarão na chapa miralha* comes with super-sized shrimp, vegetables, and fries on a simmering grill. *Moderate. No cards.*

Na Brasa

Av. Nazaré, 124; ☎ 225-4541. Closed Mon.

A reasonably priced *rodízio* for barbecued meat (all you can eat), with one salon for the young and noisy, and the other for the discreet. *Moderate. All cards.*

Hilton Delicatessen

Av. Pres. Vargas, 882 (Praça da República). 11 a.m.-9 p.m., Sun. 10 a.m.-2 p.m.

Takeout deli in the Hilton Hotel. Excellent pastries, salamis, and cheese. Stock up if you're planning a river trip. *Moderate. All cards.*

Panela de Barro

Av. Dq. de Caxias, 602; ☎ 246-2733. Dinner only, closed Sun.

A fish house known for its good food, in particular regional cuisine. *Inexpensive. No cards.*

Alternativa Natural

Rua O. de Almeida, 306. Mon.-Fri. 11:30 a.m.-3 p.m.

A nice, quick alternative for vegetarians – a natural foods buffet, including tropical fruit juices, noodles, soy meat, fried macaxeira, soup, salad, and dessert. The post office is nearby. *Inexpensive. No cards.*

Nutribem Ltda.

Rua Santo Antônio, 264; ☎ 224-3429.

Vegetarian restaurant and market for natural products.

Tip Top

Travessa Pariquis at the corner of Padre Eutiquip (Batista Campos).

A tip-top ice cream parlor 4½ blocks from the Hilton, with more than 150 exotic flavors. *Bacuri*, made from the hard-shelled fruit, is particularly delicious.

UP CLOSE TIP: Street Food

You're sure to see folks on the street slurping something from a shell. It's tacacá, made with dried shrimps and tucupí (a sauce made from manioc), served in a cuia, the dried shell of the fruit of the calabaça tree. Tacacá runs hot (both in temperature and in spices), and if you add pepper, you'll have even more sweat running down your brow – an effect strangely adored by locals.

Nightlife

Sabor da Terra

Av. Visconde de Souza Franco, 685 (Umarizal); ☎ *223-8620.*
Mon.-Sat. 8 p.m.-midnight.

Come to dine on traditional Amazonian dishes or just enjoy the city's best folklore show, featuring backland dances such as *xote, forró, lundi, carimbó,* and *lambada.* The eight dancers are young, attractive, and lively. The show lasts about two hours; one fine number is a cowboy dance with lassos straight from Marajó Island.

Boite Lapinha

Trav. Padre Eutíquio, 3901; ☎ *229-3290. Shows: Mon.-Sat. 8:30 p.m.*

The city's most famous nightclub hangs somewhere between funky and old-fashioned. A statue of Iemanjá surrounded by live ducks greets arrivals, while inside, a 50s silver ball dominates the stage. The shows change every half-hour, from comedy to live bands to striptease after 11:30 p.m., all introduced by a transvestite MC.

The specialty is *língua de bumba-meu-boi* (bull's tongue), served with mashed potatoes. Dancing is fun, but beware of mosquitoes and be extra careful when you go to the bathroom: There are three of them (men, women, and "others"), considered a major accomplishment by gays in Belém. Bermudas are not allowed for men.

> **UP CLOSE TIP:** *Check the newspaper for listings of local musicians such as Nilson Choves, a singer/guitarist; Jane du Boc, an ex-volleyball player who sings like Zizi Possi; Rosanna, a wonderful singer of versatile styles; Alibi de Orfeu, who sings Portuguese blues; Debson Tayonara, who sings MPB; and Officina de Samba, an eight-man group that performs popular sambas.*

Other nightclubs, called *boites,* or *boates,* include **Olé-Olá,** Avenida Tavares Bastos, 1234, ☎ *243-0129* and **Escápole,** Rodovia Montenegro, km. 7, no 400, ☎ *248-2217.* Bohemian intellectuals tend to hang at the **Cosanostra Caffé,** Travessa Benjamin Constant 1499; ☎ *241-1068,* which features live instumentals nightly of all types, plus a bar and restaurant. Best on weekends for live music is **Au Bar,** Travessa Benjamin Constant 1843; ☎ *224-0777.*

If you hit Belém around Carnaval time, don't miss experiencing the rehearsals at such samba clubs as **Quem São Eles,** Avenida Almirante Wandenkol, 680 (in the Umarizal district); ☎ *225-1131* and **Rancho Não Posso me Amofiná,** Travessa Honório José dos

Santos 764; ☎ *225-0918.* During other times of the year, go on the weekends.

Local singers and groups worth paying attention to are **Banda Nova, Marcos Monetiro, Nilson Cahaves** and **Grupo Oficina.** The tourist board or the local newspapers can give you schedules.

Shopping

Markets

The main city market is the **Ver-o-Peso** (see under Belém On Foot). There's also an **Artisan Fair** on Praça da República on Fri. and Sat. – not so big, but worth a look. Good buys here are drums, flutes, handmade leather-tooled jewelry, fiber crafts, and semi-precious stones. Aromatic oil essences, made from Amazonian plants, are popular. Many of these oils are related to *candomblé* practices (Afro-Brazilian voodoo worship), and often come packaged with promises of love, money, or good health. Roots and barks are also ground into pleasant-smelling powders and fashioned into dolls or simple sachets.

Pottery is particularly fine in Belém. One style, *tapajônica*, is characterized by fine line carvings and sculptured decorations, originally from Santarém but now made in Belém; they often resemble ceramics made by ancient civilizations. Of wider, heavier design – more colorful and slightly more modern – is the marajoara style. It can be recognized by its low relief sculptures, often brightly patterned in red, black, and white. Both can be seen at the PARATUR tourist office (see under *Hands-On Belém*).

The Palha Market takes place every day near the Novotel Hotel. It is small but exceedingly third-world, with the intense smell of fish and dried spices.

> **UP CLOSE TIP:** *If you're in the market for an Amazonian icon, look for a muiraquitã – a piece of green jade (or ceramic) in the shape of a frog. Legend has it that once upon a time in the middle of the Amazon forest, a tribe of female warriors were desperately in search of men for reproduction. One full moon they waited for Yara, goddess of the water, who unearthed some green stones from the depths of the river. The women dove into the river to retrieve the stones, then shaped the jade (or malachite) into a frog, which they then wore as an amulet. (Since the jungle later became populated, we can assume the fetish worked.) Anyone who wears it today is said to enjoy protection and good luck. (Specimens in the museum were found on Marajó Island by the Aruã tribe who used them).*

Cacique

Av. Presidente Vargas, 892; ☎ *222-1144.*

This is the best artisan shop in Belém.

Herbs

Casa Das Ervas Medicinais

Rua Gaspar Viana, 230.

This "House of Medicinal Herbs" is veritably crammed with wooden bins of dried leaves, herbs, barks, and seeds for every illness imaginable – even cancer. The owner has been in business for years, and even makes mixtures that come refrigerated in tall glass bottles (the tonic I bought did wonders for me). You can also buy a two-volume book (Portuguese only), *A Flora Nacional na Medicina Doméstica,* which tells the story of each herb and the disease it cures.

Perfumaria Chamma

Rua Boaventura da Silva, 606; ☎ *224-7298 and Artesanato Juruá, across the street from the Equatorial Palace Hotel on Avenida Brás de Aguiar.*

Well known for natural soaps, shampoos, cosmetics, and perfumes made from Amazonian plants. Celebrities and actresses, in particular, swear by the products at Juruá.

Pottery

Stúdio Rosemiro Pinheiro

 # 100, Soledade (past Espírito Santo).

On a backroad 11 miles from downtown Belém (a half-hour by car) is the village of Icoracy, an unusual community of craftsmen who maintain the age-old tradition of handmade pottery. One of about 20 master artisans in the area, 50-year-old Rosemiro Pinheiro works in a rundown shack that belies the extraordinary output of his "factory." (He personally makes 200 vases a day, while his 25-man team produces over 2,300 pieces a month.) Young boys take their canoes down the *igarapé* in the backyard to find clay, which is then cleaned, fashioned on wheels, and baked in brick ovens fueled by wood scraps. Children play around Senhor Pinheiro's feet while he creates vases in the marajoara style, a technique he learned from his father, though he is constantly experimenting. In the front room is a showcase, from which you may purchase 45-piece *feijoada* sets, vases of all sizes, commemorative plates, and even erotic beer mugs. Prices are extraordinarily low; shipping to the US doubles the price.

Hands-On Belém

Airlines Serving Belém

Varig/Cruzeiro
Av. Pres. Vargas (opposite Praça da República)
.... ☎ 768-3363
(airport)......................... ☎ 233-3941
TABA
Av. Gov. José Malcher, 883 .... ☎ 223-6300
(airport). .... ☎ 244-2866
 Transbrasil
Av. Presidente Vargas, 780 .... ☎ 224-6977
(airport). .... ☎ 233-3941
VASP
Av. Presidente Vargas, 620, loja B. ... ☎ 224-5588
(airport)......................... ☎ 233-0941
TAP
Rua Senador M. Barata, 704, # 1401 .. ☎ 222-5304

Arrivals

Cooperativos Taxis, ☎ 233-4941. Located at the airport, taxis run about $11-$12 into town and can be hired at the last counter near the Paratur office. Buses run every five min. from the airport for about 25 cents. The name of the bus to downtown is "Perpétuo Socorro" (Perpetual Help).

Car Rental

Avis
Av. Brazil de Aguiar, 621 .... ☎ 233-2066
at Hilton Hotel .... ☎ 223-1276
.... (ext. 7573)

City Transportation

Taxis .... ☎ 224-5444
.... ☎ 229-4799

Points Beyond

The *rodoviária* (bus station) is at the end of Av. Gov. José Malcher, five km. (three miles) from downtown (☎ 228-0500). Buses are available to Brasília, Santarém, Salvador, Recife, Fortaleza, and Belo Horizonte, among other places.

Climate

Temperatures range from 82°F in the Amazonian winter (June-Aug.) to 90-93°F in summer (Dec.-Jan.). Rain occurs nearly every day around 3 p.m.; the months with heaviest rainfall are Jan. and Feb.

Consulates

U.S.A.
Av. Oswaldo Cruz, 165 . . . .   ☎ 223-0800
Great Britain
Rua Gaspar Viana, 490. . . . .   ☎ 223-4353
South Africa
Av. Presidente Vargas, 351 . . . .   ☎ 224-8282

Money Exchange

Monopólio Turismo e Câmbio
Av. Pres. Vargas, 325 . . . .   ☎ 223-3177

Police

POLITUR, ☎ 224-9469, this is a special division of the local police force that provides security for tourists.

Private Guide

Tony Rocha gets my vote for best English-speaking guide in Brazil. A tall order to live up to, but his charm, knowledge, and consideration made my first foray into the jungle a joy to remember. He can be reached through **Amazon Star Turismo,** ☎ *224-6244.*

Time

Belém is one hour later than Santarém.

Tourist Information

A visit to **PARATUR,** Praça Kennedy, ☎ *223-6118* (Mon.-Fri. 8 a.m.-6 p.m.), won't be your typical boring trip to the tourist office.

An ancillary park is full of native animals, particularly little monkeys called saguis, who will come eat from your hand. (They love peanut candy.) The primary handicrafts of the area are sold in an adjacent gallery. Of particular value are the ceramics, whose designs are native to the area. You can also stock up on machetes and bows and arrows authentically crafted by native tribes in Amazonas. Brochures in English can be picked up at the information desk in the artisan store.

Travel Agency/Tours

Most hotels do not have sufficient information regarding river and jungle tours. For the best service in Belém, contact **Amazon Star Turismo Ltda.**, Rua Carlos Gomes, 14; ☎ and fax 224-6244. Owned by French immigrant Patrick Barbier, the agency offers four kinds of river/jungle tours as well as package deals to Marajó and Mosqueiros islands. Special chartered tours can be arranged for specific needs.

Other agencies are: **Carimbó Viagens,** Travessa Piedade, ☎/fax 223-6464; **Neytour Turismo**, Rua Caros Gomes 300; ☎ 241-0777, fax 241-5669.

When To Go

The best time to visit Belém is June-Aug., when there is sun in the morning and a little rain in the afternoon. Dec.-Mar. you'll experience the very wet side of the rainforest and will need rubber boots and ponchos.

Don't miss the **Círio de Nazaré** procession on the second Sun. in Oct., which attracts over a million religious devotees. The last two weeks of Oct. are filled with celebrations. Make hotel reservations far in advance.

MANAUS

Cruising into Manaus along the Rio Negro is an awesome sight after spending even a few days in the jungle. I've often wondered what Indian or *caboclo* children feel when they first glimpse that skyline of 20 skyscrapers, the yellow construction cranes stretching to heaven, the improbable gold dome of the Opera House, all towering over the pastel-colored shacks that cling precariously to the hillside.

How could they possibly grasp the meaning of all that black smoke pouring from the refineries, the multicolored boats bobbing in the floating docks, the desfile of cars and trucks on the steel-girded bridge? One look, I think, and some of them must go reeling straight back to the forest.

Arriving in Manaus: Skyscrapers in the shade of the jungle.

For others, however, Manaus is the technological oasis of the Amazon. Located on the left bank of the Rio Negro, just above its junction with the Amazon River, Manaus is not only the political capital of Amazonas, it's practically the only city with any gusto of civilization. During the rubber boom, it enjoyed a few decades of *nouveau-riche* expansion. After a long decline, it's been gaining a grittier, if just as economically voracious, reputation ever since the the military regime of 1967 declared it a free trade zone to help develop the jungle by exempting the city form Brazil's once-onerous tariff.

Not far from the docks, the center of the city is a beehive of activity – noisy stalls and shops selling everything from knock-off electronic equipment to Persian rugs and Taiwanese toys. Indeed, a few years back, the international airport used to resemble the remains of a wholesale festival as passengers boarded planes loaded with enormous packages.

Today Manaus has itself evolved into the largest manufacturing center in Brazil north of São Paulo and one of South America's high-tech hot spots; while plenty of its inhabitants still live in boats

and stilt houses along the Amazon River, they work at factories churning out five million TV sets a year, not to mention microwaves, components for audio equipment , fax machines and VCRs. Manaus is a huge producer of cars, trucks, motorcycles and even bicycles. Three billion dollars worth of foreign goods now pass through the port, domestic companies add another $7 billion a year.

Typical stilt houses along the Amazon River.

The money shows. While you can still buy hammocks and açai ice cream from street vendors, you can also cool off in a splashy new mall – complete with indoor carnival rides – and a $28 million carnival Sambadrome to complement its opulent rubber-era opera house.

But urban problems have mushroomed exponentially alongside economic progress. Lured by the promise of jobs, migrants from as far as southern Brazil have swarmed into Manaus, swelling its population from 300,000 in 1970 to 1.5 million in 1996. Despite the expansion, the job demand cannot be met and unemployment now tops 30%. As in other major Brazilian cities, shantytowns lacking sewage treatment or garbage pickup, have sprouted up across the city and pushed into the edges of the forest, and traffic jams have become crushing. City officials have started begging for solutions, at the very least trying to encourage the economy to develop in the rest of the state. Otherwise, they fear in 20 years the city's population will swell to an impossible 5 million.

A possible solution to the growth problem has already proven controversial – the proposed paving of a 375-mile gravel gap in the asphalt road linking Manaus with Venezuela and South America's northern coast. The $40 million project would land-link Manaus to its first ocean port so the city's manufactured goods could bypass the lugubrious 1,000-mile trek down the Amazon to Belém. Proponents of the plan enthusiastically claim the road would also open up the rainforest to agricultural prospects, a badly needed source of revenue and employment. Of course, environmentalists charge that the road, like others that have been cut through the Brasilian Amazon, would merely further the incontrovertible damage of the rainforest as farmers burn the jungle for grazing and planting.

(According to a report in the *Chicago Tribune* in late 1996, such fires reached a new peak in the Amazon as smoke clouded up to 2 million square miles of land at a time during the July-November burning season.)

A Bird's-Eye View

The eccentricities of the Rio Negro's ebb and flow sculpt the ever-changing face of Manaus' port. Subject to biannual tides, the river rises and falls as much as 40 feet within a six-month period; hence, the necessity of floating docks, a marvelous feat of British engineering (installed during the rubber boom), that respond to the tiniest variation. Many huts along the shore are actually built on rafts, some merely strung together by chains.

The so-called "meeting of the waters" is the junction of the Rio Negro and the Amazon, where two rivers of different colors flow together without mixing for miles. Blessed with mosquito-free environs, the jungles around Manaus attract most of the Amazon's tourists, who usually head for the jungle lodges located three to six hours away by boat. Many visitors spend their first night in Manaus at the famed Tropical Hotel, a veritable palace replete with its own zoo. My suggestion is to stay there after your jungle expedition to slowly acclimate yourself back to the luxuries of civilization.

Nineteenth-century biologists Wallace, Bates and Spruce all set out from Manaus; today the city is home to several hundred international scientists who actively study the forest in the hope of preserving both its fauna and flora. Though severely underfunded, INPA, the National Institute of Amazonian Research, staunchly perseveres in its multi-environmental projects, including raising manatees, dolphins and rare sea otters that have been confiscated from illegal fishing expeditions. Many are on display to the public, and a swim-with-the-dolphins project is presently being planned, though its future may be bleak: Brazilians are uncommonly suspicious of the breed.

Due to the presence of susbtantial jungle lodges and river excursions on offer, many people book forest expeditions out of Manaus. Unfortunately, the prospects for seeing substantial numbers of animals in their natural habitat near the city are somewhat discouraging. Frightened by loud motors and the sound of crunching boots, the smaller, more timid animals have retreated from the banks of the river, while most of the birds are so high up in the canopy they are difficult to see. (If you are desperate for fauna, head for the Pantanal.) Sadly, many animals in the Amazon have already become extinct; the endangered manatee, common in the time of Henry Bates, is now being illegally slaughtered by *caboclo* fishermen, who often torture the babies to attract the mother. More often seen on excursions (and definitely heard) are screeching howler monkeys and also capybaras, bear-sized rodents who can sometimes be glimpsed poking their snouts into vegetation. Jaguars are rarely encountered by tourists, but I was once lucky enough to be handed a live sloth to cuddle – an experience no one should ever pass up.

History

In the early 19th century, what is today known as Manaus was a garrison village named Barra that grew from a small fort the **Portuguese** had built in 1669 to monitor **Spanish** invaders. When botanist d'Orbigny stopped there in 1830, he noted that its 3,000 ragtag inhabitants were impassioned traders in everything the region had to offer: dried fish, sarsaparilla, Brazil nuts, and turtle oil. As **rubber** became an exportable commodity, Barra evolved into the provincial capital of **Manaus**, shipping nearly 20,000 tons of rubber abroad by the turn of the century. As rubber barons swelled the city to a population of 50,000, well-attired citizens in European fashions transacted business in gold coins. In 1897 electric trolleys clanged down 10 miles of tree-shaded avenues, and there were even 300 telephones used by international stock houses competing for the price of rubber. In 1900 a chicken in Manaus cost about $27, and a bunch of carrots went for $9.

Between 1908 and 1910, when Manaus was at its peak, over 1.2 million square miles of forest, housing 80 million rubber trees, were being developed. With 80,000 tons of rubber now being exported annually, the country heavily depended on the city's export duties, which covered 40% of the national debt. But the rubber bust in 1923 sent Manaus reeling, with many companies declaring bankruptcy. Ironically, that very year, the 200-mile **Madeira-Mamoré Railway** was inaugurated 1,200 miles away to create an easier transport between Bolivia and the Brazilian city of Porto Velho. Called *Mad Maria*, it was an awesome accomplishment since everything –

charcoal from Wales, steel from Pittsburgh, and termite-resistant wood from Australia – had been shipped in by necessity. Sadly, the construction cost the lives of 6,000 laborers and the collapsed market deadened any interest in pursuing the connection.

Sights

Manaus is a jumping-off point for excursions into the jungle (most visitors stay in lodges several hours by boat from the city), but the urban area is worth serious attention. Don't miss a stroll around the port area and the various markets. The Teatro Amazonas is fantastic. Do take care for your belongings.

Teatro Amazonas

Praça Sebastião; ☎ *234-2776. 9 a.m.-6 p.m.*

Imagine the chutzpah, the ingenuity, and the sheer persistence it took to build a grand opera house in the middle of the jungle. Inaugurated after 12 years of construction on Dec. 31, 1896, the Teatro Amazonas (660 seats, including boxes) is still a wonder of artful design, built completely with materials imported from Europe, except for the wood, which came from the Amazon forest. The original curtains, still intact, were painted by the Brazilian artist Crispim do Amaral in 1896 and represent the meeting of the waters of the Rio Negro and the Rio Solimões (the goddess in the middle is Yara, the water princess). The bronze chandeliers, which descend for cleaning, are from France; the pillars are made of English cast iron; and the ceiling was painted in Paris by two Italians, showing the arts of opera, tragedy, dance, and music. Except for the chairs, everything in the house is original (the old wood and cane chairs were replaced when air conditioning was installed under the seats). The ballroom, now only used as a showpiece, consists of 12,000 pieces of Amazon mahogany. The wrought-iron staircases are covered with guaraná plants. The wall painting showing a group of Indians saving some desperate-looking Europeans is a scene from the Brazilian opera *I Guarani*, by Carlos Gomes. In olden times, musicians used to serenade guests from the balcony. In 1947 the Governor declared all public buildings should be colored gray; it wasn't until 40 years later that the front facade was restored to its original light mauve. The first opera given in the house was *La Gioconda*, performed by an Italian troupe imported for the occasion. Tours are given throughout the day at regular intervals (though rarely in English). The air conditioning is only turned on for performances, so bring a fan and prepare to swelter. The view from the balcony is wonderful, but be careful of flying pigeons, who may decide to use your shirt as a toilet.

The Port

The docks in Manaus often look as if somebody threw all the people and goods up in the air and then let them fall back down willy-nilly. But actually there's a consumer's intelligence organizing the activity lining the waterfront. A stroll down the waterfront to the **Municipal Market** may well be one of your best moments in Manaus, as you elbow past brawny dockers, tired fishermen, and even steely-eyed sailors eyeing the crowd for a little companionship. If you're daring, ask around to see which boats may be going out for the day; you could probably hitch a ride or, at the very least, charter one. During the day, walking around here is reasonably safe, but at night do avoid loitering. Despite the enormous fluctuation in river traffic volume, these floating docks, a miracle of British invention, can accommodate anything from canoes to ocean liners all year round. Nearby is the Customs House, prefabricated in Britain, then shipped to Manaus piece by piece.

Feira da Manaus Moderna

Around 10 p.m. nightly a fantastic commotion takes place behind the Municipal Market as the port fills up with fishermen unloading their day's catch from canoes. Often, they throw some of their fish away, and dolphins lurking nearby leap out of the water to catch them. You can even rent canoes here and row around to inspect the activity. Make sure, however, that your boat doesn't have a hole in it, and take precautions with your valuables. A block away is the new market where the fish are sold.

Mercado Municipal

Located at the corner of Rua Rochas dos Santos and Rua dos Barés, the Mercado Municipal is a concrete-and-steel structure built in 1906 and painted the pastel gray of all government buildings. Small cubbyholes manned by swarthy-looking merchants sell fruits, beans, wheat, sweets, and popcorn in big burlap sacks; it's a good place to stock up on supplies if you're headed for the jungle. You can also buy camping gear here, including paddles and hammocks. Good prices for Indian and *caboclo* crafts can be found (bargaining is essential). Check out Store #67, teeming with fresh and dried herbs for medicinal purposes; #30 is an *umbanda* store selling candles, incense, and other paraphernalia for calling up the spirits. Be careful with your own worldly goods here; one merchant cautioned me to carry my backpack in front of me because several people were eyeing it longingly.

Fish Market

The fish market next door to the Mercado Municipal is wet and slimy, full of merchants, women and children all juggling for a good price. Here you'll see *pirarucu* just off the boat, as well as many fresh counterparts to the stuffed fish on view at the Science Museum.

The fish market in Manaus – wet, slimy and smelly.

Praça 24 Horas Desembargador Mário Verçosa

This historical plaza, formerly called Praça Sesquicentenário, has undergone a recent renewal from a garbage-strewn slum to an impressive sports and leisure complex. Located in Conjunto Dom Pedro, it comes complete with 18 snack bars, numerous stores, pharmacy, florist, public baths, police post, a taxi point, and open-air theatre for 3,000. Check the newspaper for a list of cultural and sports events that occur here.

Beaches

Manaus is hot and humid because it labors three degrees south of the equator, 100 feet above sea level and 1,000 miles from the ocean. But you can find a beach, nearby **Ponta Negra**, to which locals flock during the dry season (June-November). Now refurbished by the administration of Mayor Eduardo Braga, this beach, near the Tropical Hotel, has become not only an interesting tourist complex, but an impressive cultural space for the city of Manuas. From March-June the beach practically disappears and the water reaches all the way to the stone barriers. It's a perfect place to head for when the heat rises, especially for the new bars with live music; you'll also find restaurants, snack bars, banks, stalls for coco water, post office, and public telephones. Music shows are often performed in the ampitheatre, which seats 15,000.

Located in the district of Educandos, this traditional beach, **Praia do Amerelinho**, now a totally urbanized beach, was opened to the public in 1996. A walkway runs along Boulevard Rio Negro, offering fantastic views of the Rio Negro. The neighboring avenues have also been spruced up to accommodate shoppers and strollers, including Avenidas Leopoldo Peres, President Kennedy and Adalberto Valle, Ruas São Benedito, Branco E Silva, Amância de Miranda, and Inocéncio de Araújo.

Museums

Flora & Fauna

Museu de Ciências Naturais (Museum of National Science)

Colônia Cachoeira Grande (Aleixo); ☎ *244-2799. Tues.-Sun. 9 a.m.-5 p.m., closed Mon. Small fee.*

Founded in 1988, this exceedingly creative and well-maintained museum was the brainchild of a Japanese businessman who came to Brazil 15 years ago and immediately fell in love with Amazônia's flora and fauna. Located 15 min. from downtown, the museum is situated in a Japanese community where children still speak Japanese and traditional customs are maintained. The museum's air conditioning makes it a most attractive location to plant an overheated nervous system. If you're heading off for some serious fishing, this is a great place to get oriented. All notations are in English, Japanese and Portuguese. Among the 20 stuffed and 15 live species of fish housed in a gorgeous outdoor aquarium you'll see the *pirarucu*, the largest scaled fish in the world (up to 440 lbs.); the vicious *canjirú*, a small leathery fish that is extremely carnivorous (the species of the genus *Vanellia* are feared by people living along the river because they can enter the genitals of unsuspecting swimmers); the *tucunaré*, a very delicious fish whose coloring confuses other fish as to which end is its head. The insect room is straight out of a horror movie, featuring locusts, scarabs, and elephantine beetles. The butterfly mounts are extraordinary, including some species whose coloring resembles leaves and owls. The souvenir shop is one of the finest artisan stores in Manaus; though the goods are pricey, the quality is superlative. Groups may make arrangements to come at night.

INPA

Al. Cosme Ferreira, 1756; ☎ *236-9400. Mon.-Fri. 8 a.m.-noon, 2-6 p.m. Tours 9-11 a.m. only. Free lectures (some in English) are given every Tues. at 3 p.m.*

The Instituto Nacional Pesquisada Amazônia (the National Institute of Amazonian Research) is a forested park utilized by research scientists studying the survival and maintenance of the Amazon region. Many foreign scientists are working here, and guests are welcome from 9-11 a.m., when free tours are given. You may see manatee pups in captivity that have been saved from fishermen who tried to use them as bait to capture their mothers, and there are usually several tanks of dolphins. A good show is always given by the *arainha*, a diva-like otter who has a special ability to amuse himself in front of adoring onlookers. In the past, tours of the sawmill belonging to the Center for the Study of Forest Products have been given upon request, and guests have sometimes been presented with free boxes containing many different types of Amazonian wood. Fine T-shirts with slogans like "Preserve the Manatee" can be purchased on the grounds. Permission to enter the INPA must be obtained from the security police at the front gate. Call about programs open to the public.

Eco Park

Praça Auxiliadora, 4, AP 203; ☎ *234-0939; fax 633-3170.*

You will probably see more animals at this privately owned 4,500-acre preserve operated by the nonprofit Living Rainforest Foundation than in the "real" jungle. Opened in 1991 for purposes of conservation and education, the aquarium and botanical garden are still under construction; the orchid garden is complete. There's also a visitor center, bird sanctuary, a restaurant designed as a gigantic Indian hut, and even bungalows to house overnight guests in the forest. The 150 monkeys in the monkey jungle, who might use your back as a rest stop, were rescued from areas that have been flooded or burned down as a result of development. They receive medical attention and are given time to acclimate in the region before being released into the wild. You can hike six miles of trails leading through the forest, accompanied by trained guides; a full-day "survival course" emphasizes the techniques of indigenous people in obtaining food, water, shelter, and medicine from the forest.

Half-day excursions run about $25, full day $50, boat transportation included. Two-day/one-night stays cost $155 per person, based on double occupancy, and include two-day tours and all meals. A five-day/four-night visit (which requires a minimum of eight persons) is $425 per person and includes two days in the park and a two-day river cruise. The Tropical Hotel also offers packages starting at about $180 a person (double occupancy). Each night includes a one-day tour of the park with lunch. Another package features a night tour with dinner and an Indian dance show.

For more information regarding Eco Park or the package tours listed, contact Max Blankenfeld at Eco Park's office in the US: 9434 Old Katy Road, Suite 230, Houston, TX 77055-6300; ☎ *800-255-4326, fax (713) 468-1213.*

❖ **GETTING HERE:** *To reach the park, you must take a half-hour boat ride from the Hotel Tropical.*

Native Crafts

Museu do Homem do Norte

Av. 7 de Setembro, 1385 (Centro); ☎ *232-5373. Mon. 8 a.m.-noon, 1-6 p.m., Fri. 1-5 p.m. Minimal fee.*

This hot and sweaty, two-room museum was founded in 1985 to show the culture and way of life in the north. If you can brave the heat, you'll find the Indian artifacts fascinating, especially those from the Xingú tribe, which Noel Nutel collected over a 30-year period. Most impressive are the ritual clothes, and masks, among them an exquisitely beaded mask used to celebrate a girl's passage to puberty, and an ant-filled glove called a *Luva de Tocandira*, into which young boys put their hands to prove their manhood. There is also a room full of *bumba-meu-boi* costumes and a typical manioc house. A guaraná display shows the development of the plant as well as its many uses. There is no guide, but we did locate a worker who spoke a little English.

Museu do Indio

Rua Dq. de Caxias/Av. 7 de Setembro; ☎ *234-1422. Mon.-Fri. 8:30-11:30 a.m., 2-4:30 p.m., Sat. 8:30-11:30 p.m. Minimal fee.*

Another non-air-conditioned museum in Manaus – this one is owned by the Salesian nuns, who run an Indian mission along the Rio Negro. Each of the six rooms is dedicated to various facets of Indian life; there are fantastic ceramics, baskets, and weapons, and even a model of a Yanomami house, a circular, straw-roofed dwelling housing between 30 and 250 people. The museum's store sells crafts from tribes up the Rio Negro and from *cablocos*. Rumor has it you can buy here the best guaraná (an herbal stimulant) in Amazonas (called Marou de Maués). One interesting novelty is a *Pega Moça* ("catch the girl"), an Indian wedding ring that looks like a Chinese knot and is placed on the woman's finger to pull her along. Also fascinating is the display of a *paje*'s instruments – the magical tools of the tribal shaman, including various powders, rattles, and medicine pouches. Among the musical instruments are panpipes, maracas, turtle-shell rattles, rain sticks and instruments made out of the brain of a buck. The last room is full of neon-colored butterflies and humongous-sized creepy crawlers. To film or take pictures, you must pay an extra 30 cents.

> **UP CLOSE TIP:** *Ponta Negra, the river beach next door to the Hotel Tropical, is the city's hot spot on weekends. Between Oct. and Mar., when the river is low, you'll even find sand for fresh-water swimming.*

Jungle Excursions

What's the best way to "do" the jungle near Manaus? You have basically two choices: lodges or package cruises. Jungle lodges are pousada-type accommodations deep in the jungle (usually near the shore of a tributary), where trekkers stay for two to three days. Quality ranges from the semi-luxurious to the primitive; meals are generally served in an open-air communal dining room. If you like to cruise, you may be happier (and cooler) if you take a package boat tour, where you sleep in tight (usually cramped) quarters and take meals on board prepared by a crew member. (The schedule may include a night of sleeping in the forest.) Excursions from the lodge and boat tours are usually similar: canoe treks through tiny streams, piranha fishing in the afternoon, alligator hunts at night, and the proverbial walk through the forest. During rainy season, consider that the lounging space on a boat becomes even more cramped. Private boat cruises usually sleep up to eight, not including crew.

A third category of tourists fantasize about renting their own canoes, meeting up with crazy explorers and riding the rapids to the mouth of the Amazon. Before you do this, make sure you read Joe Kane's compelling account of his own hazardous trip in *Running the Amazon*. The Polish daredevils he traveled with now have their own agency, **CanoAndes**, 310 Madison Avenue, NY, NY 10017; ☎ *212-286-9415*. They arrange trekking, rafting and wildlife and cultural expeditions for all levels of fitness and expertise. Just be forewarned that their guides run on the wild side.

Cruise Packages

There are over 150 travel agencies in Manaus offering river excursions. Some of the best are listed below.

For those in a hurry, there are excellent one-day cruises out of Manaus, which go to the **January Ecological Park**, leaving from the docks at 9 a.m. and returning at 3 or 4 p.m. (lunch included, about $20). You see the Meeting of the Waters, tour around water lilies and take a canoe ride to the *igapós*. For more information, call **Selvatur**, Av. Gétulio Vargas, 725 A; ☎ *(92) 233-8044, fax 622-2177*. Also try **Amazon Explorers**, Rua Nhamunda, 21 (Centro); ☎ *(92) 233-4418, fax (92) 233-4418*.

Several different cruises are offered by **Fontur**, located at the Hotel Tropical, Estrada da Ponta Negra; ☎ *(92) 656-2167, fax (92) 656-2167*.

Some of the best tours outside Manaus these days are run by **Amazon Nut Safari**, Av. Beira Mar, 43 (São Raimundo); ☎ *(92) 671-3525, fax 671-1415*. It's best to write or fax for their itineraries, but schedules vary from three days and two nights to five days and four nights. They also have private rentals. (The five-day jaunt tours the **Anavilhanas Arquipelago**, the biggest archipelago in fresh water, formed by 400 islands.) Among their boats is the *Cassiquiari*, a double-decker river schooner that sleeps 24, with private, air-conditioned cabins. Trips leave from the Tropical Hotel, and include a visit to **Novo Ayrão**, a tiny town where the company's owner maintains a farm inhabited by an Indian family. The *Iguana* is a 10-person boat, with remote engine controls, hydraulic steering, and a satellite navigation center. You can also hire *Catuque*, a small motor boat, for about $100 a day.

For information about Amazon Nut Safari's jungle lodge, see "Apurissara Floating Lodge" under Jungle Lodges in the Manaus section.

Other tour operators are:

Rio Amazonas Turismo (Francisco Ritta Bernadino, director), Rua Silva Ramos, 41; ☎ *(92) 234-7308 or 232-4160, fax (92) 233-5615 or 622-1415;* e-mail:treetop@internext.com.br; web site: www Internext.com.br/ariaú. The owner of the Ariaú Jungle Tower Lodge (see under *Lodges*) also operates this travel agency, which can make arrangements for jungle cruises.

Fontur (Fontes Turismo) Estrada da Ponta Negra, s/n; ☎ *656-2807, 656-2167.* Located at the Tropical Hotel, this travel agency provides day excursions and can make arrangements at any lodge.

Fishing Packages

The Amazon boasts 1,500 different species of fish to catch on the end of your line. A favorite catch of sports fishermen is the *tucunaré*, (peacock bass), which is also delicious to eat. The best season to fish is August-December. Among special operators for fishing expeditions are **Amazon Explorers** (see address above), Solição Assessoria e Planejamento, ☎ *(92) 234-5995/5400, fax 233-7470;* and **Negrotours** (Mr. Phillip Marsteller) Rua Marquês de Erval, 01 (Parque das Laranjeiras), ☎/fax *(92) 236-1411.*

(Also see tips on fly fishing, page 126.)

Riverboat & Jungle Touring

Swallows & Amazons Tours

Operating out of Manaus, this company specializes in private and small group river and jungle tours. They use classic Amazon houseboats and do treks and overnight camping, providing meals and all the necessities. Visits to river families can be arranged and guides are multilingual. They offer tours of the Rio Negro on a daily basis, extended tours, birdwatching tours and make packages to meet the needs of individuals. Their ultimate destination is the beautiful **Anavilhanas Archipelago**, where you spend three nights sleeping on board the boat in hammocks and beds, with two nights at their special jungle lodge (Over Look Lodge) at Arara. Located on the Rio Negro, the lodge has 10 single beds, showers and bathrooms, meals on the balcony with river and island view. Tania and Mark Aitchinson are the owners and can be reached in the US at ☎ *(508) 255-1886, (800) 356 1121;* fax *(508) 240-0345.* The contact in Manaus, Brazil is ☎ *(92) 622-1246.*

Jungle Survival Training Course

Those of you who are would-be guerillas (or is that gorillas?) will love the **Jungle Warfare Instruction Center** (CIGS) in Manaus, considered the most advanced center for the transforming of soldiers into jungle fighters. Today, several tour operators arrange 1- , 2- and 3-day programs for civilians, taught by scientists and military men who indoctrinate the visitor into the hard-core facts of jungle survival. Among the skills imparted are how to discern what paths to follow, how to find drinking water, what to eat, how to make a fire, how to build shelters, and how to fight stress. Do ask ahead of time what level of fitness you should have to endure this training. For more information contact: **Natureza Camp**, c/o Solução Assessoria e Planejamento, Rua Coronel Salgado, 63 (Aparecida); ☎ *(92) 234-5995/234-5400/981-0961, fax 233-7470.* Full-day program featuring scientific lectures and jungle survival techniques. Tailored groups can be arranged for scientific or alumni groups.

Excursions

Ornamental Fish

Ever wonder where the neon fish in your aquarium come from? Thousands of collectors and vendors swarm the area near Barcelos, Amazonas (pop. 7,000), 300 miles northwest of Manaus, along the Rio Negro, for its enormous stock of ornamental fish. In 1993 about 16 million cardinals were exported. The first annual ornamental fish festival was held in Jan. 1994. Studying these fish at the Dr. Herbert R. Axelrod Foundation in Barcelos is Dr. Ning Labbish Chao, who can be reached through his organization Bio-Amazonia Conservation International, Caixa Postal 2310, 69, 061, Manaus, Amazonas; ☎ and fax *(92) 644-1138*, or 3204 Beaumont Drive, Tallahassee, FL 32308-2806, USA; ☎ and fax *904-668-8225.* Arrangements can be made for groups (such as aquarium societies or classes) to visit Barcelos and work at Dr. Chao's lab. Charter boats to Barcelos are also available.

During Jan., the city of Barcelos hosts the annual **Festa de Peixes Ornamentais** (Festival of Ornamental Fish). Participants can buy aquarium fish collected by *piabeiros,* or collect their own (a license is required). Visit the fish and plant show, trade crafts, workshops, contests for children, sportfishing, and boat excursions, music, dancing, and a tour of the aquarium business in Manaus. Beautiful water and bog plants, and especially wild orchids and bromeliads, are everywhere. Turtles may be available for sale, but do note that their trade or transportation is illegal. For more information contact: Il Festa de Peixes Ornamentais, Prefeitura do Municipio de Barcelos, Av. Tenreiro Aranha, 204; Barcelos, Amazonas Brazil (CEP 69, 700); ☎ (only Portuguese) *011-55-92-7221/1200, fax 721-1191.*

Travel arrangements and boating accommodations can be made through Miguel Rocha da Silva, **Amazon Nut Safari**, Av. Beira Mar, 43 (São Raimundo) Manaus, Brazil; ☎ *(92) 671-3525/233-7282; fax 671-1415.*

Where To Stay

Manaus is one of the hottest places in the world (and I grew up in Houston!). So, there are several points to remember in selecting a hotel.

- ☐ The air conditioning must work.
- ☐ A good pool will be appreciated.
- ☐ Cleanliness is sacred (this close to the jungle, you should think twice about the type of bug in your bed).
- ☐ Laundry (no one has ever returned from the jungle without the devastating need to wash clothes).

Considering all that, good deals can be found in Manaus, but at least one night at the Tropical is a must. If you can't afford it, just drop by for a drink beside the fantastic wave-pool. See page v, at the beginning of this book, for price chart.

Tropical Manaus

Estrada da Ponta Negra (Ponta Negra), 18 km., ☎ (92) 658-5000; fax 658-5026.

The palatial oasis of the Amazon jungle. If you have the money, spend it here. The hacienda-like hotel is a sprawling maze of 608 rooms; a newer building added six years ago doubled the capacity. Dominating the lobby is a three-story atrium housing a great white heron and tropical ducks that perform tricks between 6 and 7 a.m. A magnificent pool complex famous throughout Brazil sports waterfalls gushing over rock cliffs. A mini-zoo features jaguars and pumas.

Minimal differences exist between standard and deluxe rooms, both lavishly appointed, with a chic-rustic allure. (Rooms in the older section are slightly more expensive, but sometimes retain a musty smell.) The three restaurants are spectacular: a barbecue buffet poolside for about $16, a candlelit gourmet restaurant, and a charming coffee shop. Tennis courts are open from 9 a.m.-9 p.m. daily. A travel agency arranges river and jungle tours, and a Varig office is open during business hours. *605 apts. Very expensive. All cards.*

Taj Mahal Continental

Av. Getúlio Vargas, 741 (Centro); ☎ *(92) 633-1010; fax 233-0068.*

Opened in 1991, the Taj Mahal is the premier property of a famous Indian family who also owns the Plaza and the Imperial. All apartments have a view of the city; standards and deluxes barely differ. Furniture is streamlined and functional. Special rooms are available for the handicapped. The roof pool is about three strokes long. A nightclub is being built here. The restaurant delivers a fantastic lookout over the opera house, and an upper level slowly rotates for a panoramic view. *190 apts. Expensive. All cards.*

Imperial Hotel

Av. Getúlio Vargas, 227 (Centro), ☎ *(92) 622-3112; fax 622-4857.*

Brass sculptures of Buddha adorn the lobby of this Indian-owned hotel in downtown Manaus. Standard rooms sport brightly flowered spreads, but the rugs are not uniformly clean. The medium-sized pool looks up to the hanging laundry of the neighboring apartment. The best *tacacá* in Manaus – a native dish of tapioca, manioc juice, garlic shrimps, and pepper – can be purchased right outside the front door, between the Plaza and the Imperial. 10% tax charged. *100 apts. Expensive. All cards.*

Plaza Hotel

Av. Getúlio Vargas, 215 (Centro), ☎ *(92) 232-7766; fax 622-1761.*

Owned by the same family as the Taj Mahal, the Plaza carries over the Indian decor in its colorful tapestries and bedspreads. Service is friendly. Superior rooms are substantially larger than deluxes, with an extended area for an extra couch bed. Although the rooms are well cooled, the corridors are as hot as a sauna. A rectangular pool is covered by a glass ceiling, which keeps the pollution out. Laundry service, a travel agency, and an imported-foods store are also on premises. Deluxe doubles run about $71, superiors about $86. *80 apts. Expensive. All cards.*

Hotel Amazonas

Praça Adalberto Vale (Centro), ☎ *(92) 622-2233; fax 622-2064.*

This four-star seems to be particularly accommodating to children, who were running their electric cars all over the lobby when I visited. Deluxes feature verandas offering a fantastic view of the port; standards are a bit depressing. Special discounts are available for those who eat lunch and dinner. A hair salon, barbershop, pool, luncheonette, and drugstore accommodate guests. Children up to age five stay free; those aged between five and 12 are charged half-price. *182 apts. Moderate-expensive. All cards.*

Slaass Flat Hotel

Av. Boulevard Alvaro Maia, 1442; ☎ *(92) 633-3520; fax 633-1088.*

This gorgeous three-star is such a steal that one is left wondering what's wrong with this picture. Built initially as an apart-hotel (with kitchenettes), the Slaass, about six minutes by car from downtown, suggests an elegance almost unknown in Manaus. Doubles are incredibly spacious, with attractive wooden floors and a breezy veranda overlooking the city's rooftops. Apartments for four include three bedrooms, two bathrooms, kitchen, and living room. Special long-term rates are available. The rooftop bar makes a great perch. A pool and shopping center are being planned. Restaurants within walking distance include Florentina (Italian), Canto do Peixada (fish), and Miako (Japanese). *Moderate. All cards.*

Hotel Monaco

Rua Silva Ramos, 20 (Centro); ☎ *(92) 622-3446; fax 622-1415.*

The classic Hotel Monaco is something out of a Jim Jarmusch movie, where the receptionist resembles a hooker and the quirkiest people emerge from the rooms. Still, the rooftop restaurant is one of the great spots to witness the city's fabulous sunsets, and you're sure to meet some real characters. *112 apts. Moderate. No cards.*

Pousada Montemurro

Rua Emilio Moreira, 1442 (Praça 14 de Janeiro); ☎ *(92) 233-4564.*

This *pousada*, in a middle-to-low-class residential neighborhood, is a viable budget option. A white stucco building holds six kitchenettes and three suites, all air conditioned, with sculptured stained-glass windows. Suites are the best bet, with an outer room that includes a couch, dining table, and crazy photos of the Swiss Alps. All apartments have color TV and tiled bathrooms; only the suite has a phone. Breakfast (included in the rate) is the only meal served, but a tiny luncheonette is across the street. A sunning patio with potted plants relieves any sense of claustrophobia. *Inexpensive. No cards.*

Hotel Dona Joana

Rua dos Andrades, 553; ☎ (92) 233-7553.

If you're looking for a cheap night, this simple three-story pension might do, but check your room before you sign in; grunginess is in the mind of the beholder. There's no elevator, and the stairs are steep, but the deluxe room on the third floor has a good breeze and great view of the river. You pay extra for hot water, but the spacious rooms should all have air conditioning. Across the street is a famous fish restaurant. The lobby is more funky than tasteless, but do note: This is no place to leave valuables. *60 apts. Inexpensive. No cards.*

Hotel Rio Branco

Rua dos Andradas, 484; ☎ (92) 233-4019.

Located across the street from the Dona Joana Hotel, this pension is the hangout for hard-core adventurers, with 90% of the clientele European. All rooms have private bathrooms, and if you're seriously backpacking, who cares if the rooms are a little musty, the showers cold, and the breakfast room small? PR man Christopher Charles Gomes organizes jungle tours with expert guides; among his best is Jerry Hardy (part Brit, Indian, and Brazilian) who has his own boat. Three-day/two-night tours run about $150. Reports from the bush have been raves. Doubles with air conditioning run $10, with fan $8; singles $5-$6. Bedrooms with three or four beds, called *coletivas*, are the cheapest; all rates include breakfast (coffee, bread and milk only). A pay telephone, which you can use for three minutes a shot, is in the lobby, as are safes. *Inexpensive. No cards.*

Hospedaria de Turismo Dez de Julho

Rua 10 de Julho, 679; ☎ (92) 232-6280.

Located within walking distance from downtown, this youth hostel for all ages is perfect for trekkers. All rooms are air conditioned and come with tile floor, two beds, and clean baths. Breakfast is included, and laundry service is available. Pay phone in the lobby. Janete Tôrres, the director, is a lovely, gray-haired lady who speaks some English. *13 apts. Inexpensive. No cards.*

Jungle Lodges Outside Manaus

Ariaú Jungle Tower

2 km. from the archipelago of Anavilhanas; 60 km. (37 miles) from Manaus; 3 hrs. by boat.

The Amazon jungle's premier accommodation, Ariaú is the brainchild of a Brazilian businessman who longed to be not only in the jungle but above it. The entire complex of 45 wood apartments are interlinked by wooden catwalks between the trees, affording a unique communication with the flora and fauna. Towering 130 feet above ground is an observation deck (the only one in Amazonas), which allows you to see the magnificent canopy of the forest from above – a thrilling experience. A special Tarzan House on top of a 120-foot chestnut tree was especially erected for guests who want to live out tree house fantasies. All rooms, with air-ventilators only, have private bathrooms and verandas. The duplex Presidential Suite, where the owner stays when he visits, boasts a downstairs dining room, TV, VCR, and lush leather furniture. Upon arrival from the river, you'll no doubt be greeted by the resident monkeys, macaws, and coatis (charming anteaters with raccoon tails); just watch out for the monkeys, who love to rip off eyeglasses and throw them in the water. Two-day/one-night packages include all meals (except drinks), a visit to a *caboclo* village, an alligator hunt at night, forest walks, and fishing. (Longer packages are available.)

For reservations in the US, contact **F&H Consulting**, 2441 Janin Way, Solvang, CA 93464; ☎ *(800) 544-5503, fax (805) 688-1021.* The main office in Manaus: **Rio Amazonas Turismo**, Rua Silva Ramos, 41 (Centro) ☎ *(92) 234-7308; fax (92) 233-5615.*

Don't be fooled by these cute creatures; their other trick is to throw your eyeglasses in the water!

Amazon Lodge

Lago do Juma, 100 km. (62 miles) from Manaus (4½ hrs. by boat).

This is a two-story rustic pousada that actually floats on the water. The 17 apartments share two bathrooms (cold water only) and use candles for illumination. Various treks into the jungle are part of a package.

In Manaus, contact: **Transamazonas Turismo**, Rua Leonardo Malcher, 734 (Centro); ☎ *(92) 622-4144; fax 622-1420.* In the US contact **Brazil Nuts**, ☎ *(800) 533-9959* or **Expeditours in Rio**, ☎ *(21) 287-9697, fax 521-4388* or direct *(92) 622-4144; fax 622-1420.*

Amazon Village

Lago do Puraquequara, 60 km. (37 miles) from Manaus (2 hrs. by boat).

These 64 wooden apartments in neat cabanas are favorites of Germans and Swiss. who appreciate the excellent service and reputedly good food. Perched on a small hill at the bend of an *igarapé*, it's two to four hours from Manaus, depending on the river's condition. There are no electric lights, no air conditioning, no doors, and no windows. The "main building" is a large, open-thatched shed with a dining area, living room, bar and mini-museum, all open to the wind. Guests sleep in cottages scattered around the main building, easy to find with flashlights. The house jaguar eats in the dining area and loves to be stroked like a kitten. A five-star banquet can be held in the middle of the jungle if you ask.

In Manaus, contact: **Transamazonas Turismo**, Rua Leonardo Malcher, 734 (Centro); ☎ *(92) 622-4144; fax 622-1420.* In the States contact **Brazil Nuts**, ☎ *(800) 533-9959*, or **Expeditours in Rio**, ☎ *(21) 287-9697, fax 521-4388* or direct, ☎ *(92) 622-4144; fax 622-1420.*

Acajatuba Jungle Lodge

Lago Acajatuba, Rio Negro, 70 km. (44 miles) from Manaus (4 hrs. by boat).

More primitive than the Ariaú, these 16 apartments with bathrooms were built recently and are contained in three grass-roofed huts, all illuminated by gas lanterns. Two-day/one-night packages for $140 include all food and mineral water, as well as piranha fishing, alligator hunts, a river tour, and a jungle walk. No cards accepted, but travelers cheques, dollars and *cruzeiros* are welcome.

In Manaus, contact: **ECOTEIS**, Rua Dr. Alminio, 30 (Centro); ☎ (92) 233-7642, fax 233-7642. Contact **Expeditours** in Rio, ☎ *(21) 287-9697, fax 521-4388,* or **Amazon Explorers** in Manaus, ☎ *(92) 232-3052.*

Pousada dos Guanavenas

Ilha de Silves, 320 km. (200 miles) from Manaus (4½ hrs. by car).

The Hilton Hotel of jungle lodges, these 20 apartments overlooking the Urubu River sometimes embarrass tourists who come to the forest to escape air conditioning, mini-bars, and excellent food. On the other hand, the two-story roundhouse with screened porches and hewn-log verandas made entirely from regional materials, has received architectural raves.

❖ **GETTING HERE:** *From Manaus, it's a 3½-hour trip by jitney to Itaquatiara, where you must board a flat-bottomed boat for another 1½-hr. ride. You may also arrive by sea plane or take a bus to Itaqoatiara and continue by boat.*

Packages include all meals and guided jungle excursions, such as alligator hunts and piranha fishing.

In Manaus, contact the main office: Rua Ferreira Pena, 755, ☎ *233-5558;* or **Expeditours in Rio,** ☎ *(21) 287-9697, fax 521-4388.*

Terra Verde Lodge

This is an attractive lodge with two towers and five exotic grass-topped cabins on stilts in The Forest of Life, a large ecological reserve of virgin jungle situated among the richly contrasting ecosystems of the Negro and Solimões rivers. Electric lights, complete bathroom facilities, floating pool for swimming, and facilities for fishing and horseback riding are available. The owner is the famous film director and ecologist Zygmunt Subitrowsky. Contact **Agencia de Viagens e Turismo Terra Verde**, Rua Dr. Moreira 270/207; ☎ *(92) 234-0148; fax (92) 238-1742.*

Apurissara Floating Lodge

Rio Cueiras.

Owner Miguel Rocha was a world traveler who used to invite his friends to cruise the Amazon with him. Today he still leads tours, along with his sons and daughters, using a squad of four kinds of boats. Their flagship property is a floating lodge (about five hours by slow boat, one hour by fast boat) on the Rio Cueiras, a tributary of the Rio Negro. The style is primitive chic, with 14 beds, some private bathrooms, and a thatched-roof dining area with a 360° view of the river. A four-day program includes transfer from Manaus, a canoe trip through the woodlands, night-time alligator hunts, a visit to a native house, an orchid search, and an overnight stay in the jungle. The lunch I ate here, cooked by a local, was verging on haute cuisine. Swimming in the river is encouraged, and kayaks are available. On rainy afternoons you can curl up with one of the many ecological books on board. For more information on their cruising boats, see above, under Cruising. For reservations, contact in Manaus: Miguel Rocha da Silva, c/o **Amazon Nut Safari,** Av. Beira Mar, 43 (São Raimundo); ☎ *(92) 671-3525/233-7282; fax 671-1415.*

Lago Salvador

On the right bank of the Rio Negro.

This floating restaurant on the banks of the river, with 12 cabanas, is more luxurious than the average. An excellent resting place with a superb view; locals go just to feel at home in the jungle. For reservations, contact: **Fontur** (Hotel Tropical), ☎ *(92) 658-5000, fax 658-5026.*

Where To Eat

I once wrote in a previous edition that no one goes to Manaus for a memorable meal. With more and more attention given to tourism in the Amazon, however, options for dining in Manaus are now growing in quantity and sophistication, providing something a little more tasty than that ham sandwich in your backpack. Tropical fish have an exotic flavor, especially when seasoned with local spices; among the best are *pirarucu* (called the "codfish of the Amazon"), *tambaqui, tucunaré* (especially delicious), and the more common *jaraqui* and *pacu. Molho de tucupi,* a sauce extracted from the manioc plant, is also ubiquitous. Many entreés come with *farinha,* a flour made from cassava.

Regional fruits, like cupuaçu, taperebá, pupunha, graviola and jaca, are prepared as excellent ice creams, juices and cream desserts (see under *Ice Cream,* below).

The streets of Manaus are filled with tasty, if exotic, treats. (Just be careful to eat only well-cooked food.) *Quebra-queixo* (literally "jawbreaker") is a mixture of sugar and Brazil nuts, cut into slices with a spatula; it's a great treat to munch while strolling the city streets. Less sweet is a type of biscuit, called *broas,* rumored to melt in your mouth. In the open markets, try a *pamonhas,* a sweet corncake wrapped in corn leaves. When the heat starts to get to you, head for an ice-grinding machine which dishes out a treat of shaved ice and flavored syrup called *rala-rala;* they are usually located in front of movie houses, discos and schools. And if you haven't eaten breakfast at your hotel, there are always push-cart vendors selling *mingau,* a type of porridge with banana, tapioca or corn.

Also, don't leave the region without tasting *tacacá* – a street dish famous in the region, made with tapioca, *cupí* (manioc juice and pepper), garlic and shrimps. The most famous vendor is located on the corner between the Plaza and the Imperial Hotels.

UP CLOSE TIP: *Sometimes a type of ginger candy called* mangarataia, *normally wrapped in wax paper, is given instead of small change. It's especially good for alleviating voice and throat discomfort.*

See page v, at the beginning of this book, for price chart.

La Barca

Rua Recife, 684 (Parque 10); ☎ *236-8544. Daily 11:30 a.m. -3:30 p.m., 7 p.m. midnight, Sun. 11:30 a.m. 4 p.m.*

This popular fishery is set in an open-air, white stucco building, with a glimpse of the encroaching forest seen through open arches. *Costela de tambaqui grelhado* (grilled fish) is native to the Amazon, big enough for three, and one of the best fish I had in Brazil. People with colds (everyone seems to get one in Manaus because of the heat and the air conditioning) will love the steaming bowl of *canja da galinha* (chicken soup). Beef or chicken strogonof and omelettes are also available. Those who can't take the heat or the traffic noise can escape into an air-conditioned salon. *Moderate. All cards.*

Churrasco/Tropical Hotel

Estrada da Ponta Negra (Ponta Negra); ☎ *238-5757. Daily 7 p.m.-midnight.*

This barbecue buffet held under a tent-like roof is a little steep, but the quality of the meats, fish, chicken and salad bar is superb. One meal could last you two days. *Expensive. All cards.*

Churrascaria Búfalo

Rua Joaquim Nabuco, 628A (Centro); ☎ *232-3773. Daily 11 a.m.-3 a.m., 6 p.m.-11:30 p.m., Sun. 11 a.m.-3:45 p.m.*

An air-conditioned *rodízio* – all-you-can-eat meat for reasonable prices. *Moderate. All cards.*

Tarumã

Tropical Hotel, Estrada da Ponta Negra; ☎ *238-5757. Daily 7 p.m.-midnight.*

Old-world romance with Spanish-style lanterns and high-beamed ceilings makes a welcome (i.e., air-conditioned) oasis. The cuisine rates as one of the best in the city: roasted duck with a cashew-spiked sauce was memorable. Desserts are first class. Music from a grand piano and strings wafts down from the upper staircase. *Moderate. All cards.*

Fiorentina

Praça da Polícia, 44 (centro); ☎ *232-1295. Daily 11:30 a.m.-11 p.m., closed Monday and first Sunday of the month.*

In the heart of the duty-free zone, this is the closest you'll get to an Italian cantina in the Amazon, with cheerful tablecloths, bustling waiters, wood-slat chairs and the inevitable fan. Air-conditioned room upstairs. Menu in English and Portuguese. *Moderate. All cards.*

Hakata

Rua Jonathas Pedrosa, 1800; ☎ *233-3608. 11:30 a.m.-2 p.m., 6:30 p.m.-10:30 p.m., closed Monday.*

Na chapa (or table-grilled) is the specialty at this air-conditioned Japanese restaurant. *Camarão na chapa* comes with six shrimps, fried cabbage, and fried rice. It's a bit greasy, but filling. *Moderate. No cards.*

Restaurant Palhoça

Estrada da Ponta Negra; ☎ *238-3831.*

An open-air restaurant with excellent views overlooking the river and obsequious waiters who present your fish to you before cooking it. Specialties include the *caldeiradas* (fish stews) and *pato no tucupi* (spicy duck). *Moderate. All cards.*

Panorama

Rio Negro Boulevard, 199; ☎ *624-4626.*

Half the price of La Barca (see above) and Amazonian fare almost as impressive. Plus a wonderful view of the city. *Moderate.*

Canto da Peixada

Rua Emilio Moreira, 1677 E; ☎ *234-3021.*

Situated in an old house with a veranda, this very good fish house specializes in such Amazonian delicacies as *caldeirada*, a kind of fish stew. *Moderate.*

Restaurante Suzuran

Rua Senador Alvaro Maia, 1683 (Adrianópolis); ☎ *234-1693. 11:30 a.m.-2 p.m., 6:30-11 p.m. Closed Tuesday.*

Best Japanese restaurant in the city. Personally, I wouldn't eat raw fish here, but then I'm not sure I'd eat it anywhere. *Expensive.*

Bar Galo Carijó

Rua dos Andradas, 536. Daily 10:30 a.m.-3 p.m., 5:30-9 p.m., closed Sun.

Also known as O Rei Jaraqui Frito, this open-air dive across from the Hotel Dona Joana is just a roof and tables, but it's famous citywide for fish. The ones I saw were bigger than the plates, with the head and tail hanging over. Tastiest is the pirarucú, one of the largest fresh-water species; one of the cheapest is the small jaraqui. Fish is normally served lightly fried, with tomatoes, onions and a mixture of rice and beans. *Inexpensive. No cards.*

O Picanha da Pedra

Av. Efigênio Sales, 3050 (Aleixo); Tues.-Sat. open at 6 p.m., Sun, open at noon.

The reputable kitchen here specializes in well-selected *picanha* (a delicious cut of beef), served on stone grills. Chicken, pork, shrimp, mussels and sausage are also served on their own grills. Live music Fri. and Sat. *Moderate.*

Restaurant Mouraria

Rua Pará,440 (Vieiraives); ☎ 233-1419. Tues.-Sat. 11 a.m.- 3 p.m. and 7 p.m.-midnight. Lunch on Sat., Sun. and holidays.

Menu specializes in Portuguese fare. *Moderate.*

Agua na Boca

Rua Pará,415 (Vieiraives). ☎ 232-6383. Tues.-Sun. 11:30 a.m.-3 p.m., 6:30 p.m.-midnight.

Regional dishes incorporating local fish as well traditional *feijoada* on Sat. *Moderate.*

Ice Cream

Beijo Frio Ice Cream Parlor

Av. Getúlio Vargas, 1289 (Centro). Daily 8 a.m. midnight.

People go to Manaus just to indulge in the numerous tropical fruit-flavored ice creams. This air-cooled parlor features 36 exotic tastes, including cupuaçu, goiaba, tucumã, tapioca, graviola, castanha de cajú, açai, and maracujá, as well as five diet flavors. Sundaes and banana splits are delicious. Take your time tasting flavors.

Alema

Rua José Paranaguá at the corner of Doutor Moreira.

Located near the Free Zone, this is a good pit stop for cold tropical juices, desserts and ice cream.

Nightlife

Nightlife in Manaus is also getting hotter, but don't expect the va-va-va-voom of Rio. Clubs appear and disappear in less than a year, so check out the latest hot spots when you arrive. Besides the clubs listed below, also head for **Ponta Negra Beach** on the weekends, which has a club with a Caribbean flair.

El Mosquiton

Ponta Negra Beach. Thurs.-Sun.

Set beachside, this is one of the latest fun spots to kick up your heels to a Caribbean beat.

Da Vinci Hotel

Rua Belo Horizonte,240 (Adnanópolis); ☎ *663-1213.*

The disco and piano bar here are considered a good place to meet locals.

Clube Nativagos

Rua Wilkens de Mattos, 431 (Aparecida). Fri.-Sun., fee $10.

A gay club where straights are made very welcome, with live performers, techno music and dark rooms to smooch in.

Coração Blue

Estrada da Ponta Negra, s/n. Wed.-Sun.

Outdoor café with sidewalk tables. Mostly attracts the young crowd.

Flet's

Estrada da Ponta Negra, s/n.

Great place to catch live Northeastern music.

Gay Manaus

Turbo 7, a well-known gay bar, has served at least three generations of gay clientele, near the docks.

Shopping

Downtown

The main street downtown is **Rua Eduardo Ribeiro**, full of large department stores like Mesbla (the Macy's of Brazil), and the even cheaper Lojas Americanas. The majority of **banks** are located along **Rua Djalma Batista**. Duty-free shopping (not of particular value to the foreign tourist) is concentrated in the **Calçadão area** around the streets of Doutor Moreira, Marcilio Dias, and Guilherme Moreira, crossed by Quintino Bocaiuva.

Native Crafts

Centro de Artesanato Banco e Silva

Rua Recife (no number); ☎ *236-1241. Mon.-Fri. 8 a.m.-7 p.m.; Sat. 8 a.m.-1 p.m.*

Located in Parque 10 de Novembro, these 20 stores carry various indigenous Indian and *caboclo* artisanry.

Museu do Indio

Av. 7 de Setembro at the corner of Duque de Caxias.

Fine Indian artisanry, such as headdresses, bows and arrows, and jewelry have been collected by the Salesians nuns who run the museum. Reasonable prices; considerably cheaper than the Science Museum store.

Eco Shop

Amazonas Shopping Mall.

Unbelievably expensive, but you'll find lots of good quality handicrafts from Amazônia and Alta Floresta, including fine pieces of Indian art.

Artindia

Praça Aldaberto Vale, 2; ☎ *232-4890. Mon. 8 a.m.-noon and 2-6 p.m.*

In front of the Amazon Hotel, this old white building houses the Funai store, with excellent prices and good variety. Amazon Indians from all over provide earrings, necklaces, pottery, straw baskets, bows and arrow, and tangas made from seed. The ambiance has the boisterous spirit of an outdoor market.

Herbs, Cosmetics & Whole Foods

Chapaty

Rua Saldanha Marinho, 702-A (Centro), ☎ *233-7610.*

This natural health food store specializes in herbal medicines, teas, whole breads, wholewheat pastas, and natural sweets, as well as extraordinary shampoos made from Amazon products.

Pronatus do Amazonas

Rua Costa Azevedo, 11 (Centro), factory at Rua 223, Esconde de Porto Alegre, 440 (Centro); ☎ *234-8754.*

Inspired by the richness of Amazônia, this company has an exclusive line of herbal pills and cosmetics culled from the jungle plants. All products are hypo-allergenic, and their processing is all timed to the natural cycles of the forest. Soaps made from tropical herbs make great gifts, as do herbal formulas for anything from impotence and diabetes to weight control.

Shopping Malls

Amazonas Shopping Mall

Rua Djalma Batista, on the corner of Rua Darcy Vargas (Chapada). Mon.-Sat. 10 a.m.-10 p.m. On Sun. movies open at noon, shops 3-9 p.m.

Ten minutes from downtown by car (20 minutes from the Tropical Hotel), this new shopping mall is shockingly chic for Manaus. Six movie theaters, food fairs, fine clothes stores, a one-hour photo shop, pharmacies, and a store that sells American cosmetics. Go just to get out of the heat.

> **UP CLOSE TIP:** *Best place to buy hammocks is along Rua dos Bares. For international magazines and newspapers, try the* **Livraria Nacional** *on Rua de Maio and the kiosk near the Teatro Amazonas.*

Hands-On Manaus

Arrivals

Aeroporto Internacional Eduardo Gomes (Av. Santos Dumont; ☎ 212-1431) receives flights from Rio, Belém, Brasília, Campo Grande, Cuiabá, Fortaleza, Natal, Recife, Porto Velho, and a few other towns. From the United States, Varig flies direct from Miami, and a new flight was recently installed from San Francisco and Los Angeles. Hotel Tropical provides shuttle bus service to and from the airport for guests.

Airlines Serving Manaus

Varig
Rua Guilherme Moreira, 278/86. . . . .   ☎ 621-1136
VASP
Rua Guilherme Moreira, 179 . . . .   ☎ 621-1355
Transbrasil
Rua Guilherme Moreira, 150 . . . .   ☎ 621-1356
TABA
Av. Ed. Ribeiro, 664. . . . .   ☎ 621-1480
Air France
Rua dos Andradas, 371, first floor . . . .   ☎ 234-2798

LAB
Av. Gétulio Vargas, 759 . . . .   ☎ 633-4200
VIASA
Rua Dona Libânia, 215 . . . .   ☎ 622-2427
American Airlines
Av. Eduardo Ribeiro, 620, loja F . . . .   ☎ 633-3363

Business Hours

Banks are open Mon.-Fri. 9 a.m.-3 p.m. Stores are also open Mon.-Fri., 8 a.m.-noon and 2-6 p.m., and Sat. from 8 a.m.-1 p.m.

City Transportation

Car Rentals

Hertz . . . .   ☎ 621-1376
Nobre . . . .   ☎ 233-6056

Taxis

Amazonas . . . .   ☎ 232-3005
Coopertaxi . . . .   ☎ 621-1544
Manaus Radio Taxi . . . .   ☎ 235-4220

Buses

City buses run from 5 a.m.-midnight.

Climate

Manaus is a sauna – hot and humid all year long with temperatures that start at 80°F and rise without mercy, sometimes up to 115°F. Nov.-Mar. is the rainy season, with precipitation a daily occurrence.

Temperatures are a bit cooler in May and June, with the water level reaching its peak in June. Dry season occurs July-Nov. During dry season, you may have to change routes. Canoe trips may be cancelled in downpours. In an open river with a real storm, strong winds can make canoeing dangerous.

Luxury Cruise Liners

A number of luxury cruise liners dock in Manaus or travel up the Amazon River, among them: Odessa America Service Co., Sun Line Cruises, Regency, Royal Viking, Ocean Princess, Society Explorers, Sagafjord, Stella Solaris, Berlim, and Fairwind.

Money Exchange

Casa Cortez
Av. 7 de Setembro, 199 . . . .   ☎ 232-2695
Banco do Brasil
Rua Marechal Deodoro and at the airport (24 hrs.)
Exchanges dollars at the tourist rate.

Mosquitoes

The Amazon River has an acidity content that prevents the breeding of mosquitoes, but the white waters of the Solimões are seriously infested. There, mosquitoes attack mostly at dusk and after dark, when repellent is absolutely necessary. Most legitimate tours avoid this area at those times. (Also see the Amazon Survival Kit, under Amazônia.)

Yellow fever, transmitted by mosquitoes, is considered endemic in Brazil, except around the coastal shores. Health authorities advise that the most infected areas are Acre, Amazonas, Goiás, Maranhão, Mato Grosso, Mato Grosso do Sul, Pará, Rondônia, and the territories of Amapá and Roraima. Vaccinations are good for 10 years and are essential if you are traveling either to the Amazon or the Pantanal. You may be required to show proof of vaccination when entering the country from Venezuela, Colombia, Ecuador, and Bolivia; it's best to always travel with the document. (For more information on malaria, see the *Amazon Survival Kit*, page 132.)

Photo Development

Foto Nascimento

Av. 7 de Setembro, 1194; ☎ *234-4660, 234-4995.*

Film development in one hour. Major makes of cameras are for sale.

Private Guides

EMAMTUR, the official tourist board, requires officially sanctioned guides to take three months of training, including courses in history, jungle survival, ecology, and Red Cross. If you hire a non-official guide, make sure he is reliable and knowledgeable or you will regret it dearly. Some recommended private guides are: **John Harwood** (☎ *236-5133*), a British scientist formerly at INPA, who now works with cruise lines as well as individuals; Brazilian-born **Claudia Roedel** (☎ 244-2455), formerly an ecology student, who now guides treks into the jungle with her husband; **Christopher Charles Gomes**, who conducts tours and individual expeditions that may be reserved through the Hotel Rio Branco, Rua dos Andradas, 484; ☎ 233-4019. (See more information under *Where To Stay*.)

Special interest groups may contact **Sherre P. Nelson** at Solução, Rua Monsenhor Coutinho, 1141; ☎ 234-5955/5400.

Telephones

To make international calls, head for the telephone company, **Telamazonas**, Rua Guilherme Moreira, 326 (downtown), open daily 6 a.m.-11:30 p.m. Another branch is on the corner of Av. Getúlio Vargas and Leonardo Malche. Both are downtown.

Time

Manaus is one hour behind Brazilian standard time (two hours behind between Oct.-Mar., when the rest of Brazil is on summer time).

Tourist Information

EMAMTUR (State Tourist Board) is located at Av. 7 de Setembro, 1546 (Vila Ninita/Centro) 69005/141; ☎ *(92) 633-2850* and *633-1367*, *fax (92) 233-9973*. An information post is located at the airport Eduardo Gomes. Tourist information can also be obtained at the head office (address above). For information regarding native tribes and permission to visit reservations, contact **FUNAI**, Rua dos Andradas, 473; ☎ *234-7632*.

Travel Agencies

Amazon Explorers, Rua Quintino Bocaiúva, 189, ☎ *232-3511*, arranges boat excursions, overnight jungle treks, fishing trips, city tours and excursions specially tailored to the needs of clients. English-speaking staff available.

The **Hotel Tropical**, ☎ *238-5757*, maintains a fine agency for guests and non-guests alike.

Another full-service agency is **Selvatur**, Praça Adalberto Vale (Hotel Amazonas), ☎ *234-8984*.

When To Go

The best months with least rainfall are August and December. In July the river starts to recede and beaches sprout up.

JUNE 12-30: **Folklore Festival of Paratins.** Often as spectacular as Carnaval in Rio, these festivities divide the cities into rivaling groups with parades, typical foods, and music. The best time to go is the last three days.

JULY 15-30: **Folklore Festival of Amazonas.**
SEPTEMBER 21-28: **Agricultural Fair.**
SEPTEMBER 27-29: **Itacoatiara Festival of Song.**
JANUARY (last weekend): **Ornamental (Aquarium) Fish Festival**, in Barcelos.

ALTA FLORESTA

In the southernmost part of the state of Mato Grosso, the grit-and-grizzle town of Alta Floresta is something right out of the Old West. The business at hand is gold. For the last 20 years, thousands have converged on the area to try their luck; some make it after two years; others are still following pipe dreams. Luck, not persistence, seems to be the deciding factor and, as one local explained, a kind of inbred culture prevails where rules are not made to be broken. "There are no thieves here," he told me matter-of-factly, "because if someone takes something, he dies." A pale orange dust storm seems to have perpetually enveloped the city; even the children playing outside are covered with it. The major activity during the day takes place at the **Aurim Gold Exchange**, where *garimpeiros*, from the slick to the mud-slung, come to exchange their gold nuggets for cash. Around 10:30 in the morning, you'll see *garimpeiro* wives, dressed in cut-offs, high heels, and lots of gold jewelry, forking over the husbands' hard-earned nuggets to be weighed and processed.

Alta Floresta is also fascinating because you can actually see rainforest burning. Perhaps that's not everyone's dream vacation, but there's nothing like ramming home the reality of the earth's plight than by seeing it up close and in your face. Just traveling the roads out of town will bring you past scorched earth and burnt trunks, and you'll no doubt see not only smoldering grass but groves of trees and shrubs in actual flames. I actually saw one farmer setting fire to a plot of land so he could plant cotton, but the most shocking scene I witnessed was that of a three-year-old playfully setting a tiny pile of twigs on fire with a match – obviously imitating the gestures of his dad.

There is, however, access to a wonderful jungle near Alta Floresta and the best way to see it is by staying at the Floresta Amazônica Hotel. This resort, unusually stylish for the area, is located at the junction of the TeleSpires and Cristalina rivers and is owned by a large landholder who is passionate about preserving the forest (she even hires young professional botanists as guides who do extensive research over their six-month internships). The complex is unique for the multidimensional perspectives of Amazonian life it offers its guests, who can look forward to widely different adventures, depending on the season (routes navigated during the dry season by jeep are cruised by canoe during the rainy season). A day trip may be taken to a nearby *fazenda* (farm) that features an unusual zoo as well as an exciting display of *garças* roosting in the leafy trees at dusk. Other excursions include a coffee plantation and the muddy dregs of a gold mine, where you'll probably get a chance to speak with miners. Overnight excursions into the jungle are the most exciting: Guests are escorted down the Cristalina River in a canoe to a location in the jungle, where they bed down dormitory-style (beds or hammocks). Just waking up to the symphony of cawing birds is thrilling, not to mention the nightly orchestra of bullfrogs. Fishing expeditions and fresh-water swimming are also available. This resort is particularly fine for families.

Culture

The Forest People

The following interview was made with Luiz Pereira Andrade, a 57-year-old guide who lives with his wife, daughter, son-in-law, and grandchild in the forest connected to the Floresta Amazônica Hotel. He is a burly man with gray, bushy eyebrows and a paunch that pushes out of his shirt. He has lived in the forest for over 25 years.

Spirits of the Forest

"Here, in Alta Floresta, we call the *matinta pereira* (forest witch) the *pai do mato* (father of the forest). The first clue to being in contact with him is when you suddenly feel lost in the forest. You go home and get something to give him – food, anything – and put it where you felt strange. If you don't do this, you'll be lost forever and won't find your way home. He's invisible but you can feel him. When I fish at night, sometimes I hear strange sounds, like tools falling, or somebody coughing. I never feel afraid – I just don't know what it means. Many times I've seen strange lights. When I'm fishing at night, a spot of light, yellowish with a blue tail, comes up behind me, goes to the river and disappears in the water. This light is strong and illuminates the whole river. Some people say it's the Gold Mother. I don't know.

"Do trees and animals have spirits? *Com certeza* (certainly)! If they are alive, they have spirits. Trees have a natural capacity to take energy, others to receive. When I embrace a tree, I feel it. I learned this by myself because one time I went to the shade of a tree when I was very nervous and suddenly calmed down. You saw that, when you went to hug the embauba tree, it released your negative energy and when you hugged the castanha it gave you positive energy. How could trees do this if they don't have souls?

"When you go to the forest and watch birds, they are happy, so you feel happy. You start to join with their happiness. When you are unhappy and you

Luiz shows how to bleed "milk" from a tree.

go to the forest and look around, you know a human is not that big. You are just a small piece in this world. I will live in this forest till I am 90 because here the old people become young. We don't miss anything from the city. I just feel unhappy I didn't come sooner."

A Gold Miner

The following is an interview with the owner of a gold mine in Alta Floresta, a well-dressed man in his late 50s waiting to exchange gold. His slicked-back gray hair, good linen clothes, diamond ring and gold watch made a sharp contrast to the rough, desperate-looking young men with muddy feet who were also waiting in line.

Garimpo

"I came here nine years ago from Paraná just for gold – eight in the mine, one year making money. In the beginning you don't know much. You usually lose money. You get friends to work for you, but usually they steal from you. But I was lucky. I have a good life now – a good house, a car. I was rich also in Paraná – I had a shop of tools for cars. But I think life was better there. The city here doesn't have much society, but my wife likes it better here because it's hotter. I had malaria five times. Only last year did I have it badly – at Christmas, I was very ill. Is it worth the pain? For me it's been good. *Garimpo* is like a vice. When you start you can't stop. And sometimes you lose all your money just because you have to reinvest it to try again."

Where To Stay

Floresta Amazônica Hotel

Av. Perimetral Oeste, 2001; ☎ *(65) 521-3601; fax 521-3801.*

A clean, cheerful resort – the most comfortable you'll find for thousands of miles. An outdoor dining area looks onto a pleasant pool complex; meals can also be eaten inside a stylishly rustic restaurant. Excursions include jungle hikes, coffee farm, and gold mine. The landscape is an ebullient profusion of pink and blue flowers and the lobby sports a few caged spiders and snakes. Trained biologists serve as guides. Fishing and swimming in fresh water are included.

An oasis in the middle of nowhere.

Reservations can be made through **Expeditours** in Rio, ☎ *(21) 287-9697, fax 521-4388.* The following rates include a 50% discount: single deluxes run $24, doubles $30, VIP apartment $43. *Moderate. V.*

Hands-On Alta Floresta

Arrival

By Air

Alta Floresta is serviced by the airline **TABA**, Av. Ariosto de Riva; ☎ *(65) 521-3360/521-3222* (airport), with flights from Altamira, Belém, Cuiabá, Itaituba, Jacareacanga, Juará, and Santarém.

By Bus

The bus station is on Av. Ariosto da Riva; ☎ *521-3177/2710*. Connections can be made from Campo Grande, Cuiabá, Paranaiba, and other towns. Some parts of the road from Cuiabá are not paved. "Luxury" buses, *leitos*, are available from São Paulo to Cuiabá, where you must change buses. At Colida, you change to an even more primitive bus for another three hours (total trip from São Paulo runs 12-14 hrs., about $76).

Air Taxis

Jato . . . . ☎ 521-3903

Penna . . . . ☎ 521-2584

When To Go

The rainy season runs Oct.-Mar.; mosquitoes are rampant after heavy rains. Best time to visit is May-Oct. The coolest months are Aug.-Oct.

> **UP CLOSE TIP:** *Mato Grosso is one of the most malaria-infected states in Brazil, and Alta Floresta has its fair share (mostly around the gold mines). Do come protected and wear plenty of mosquito repellent, reapplying it before dusk. Keep windows shut at night. Personally, I never had a problem, but I did take precautions. (See Health Kit in the back of the book.)*

THE PANTANAL

Although nearly obscured by the eco-media's blitz on the Amazon rainforest, the Pantanal – an immense kidney-shaped swampland in western Brazil – is perhaps the country's greatest natural resource. Officially known as *O Grande Pantanal*, the region, which cuts across the states of Mato Grosso and Matto Grosso do Sul (as well as western Bolivia and northeastern Paraguay) is a multi-faceted ecosystem that changes its alluvial face every six months – not unlike the Everglades in Florida. During the rainy season (Oct. through Mar.) torrential rains inundate up to 85% of this region, causing rivers, lakes and ponds to merge into an inland sea. Five months later, the effect of the burning tropical sun and the north-south flow gives way to verdant grassy plains dotted by water holes teeming with fish, tall wading birds and alligators. As such, the Pantanal during the dry season becomes an acutely visible arena for the playing out of Mother Nature's food chain. Simply, what the Amazon is to flora, the Pantanal is to fauna. If you want to see Brazilian wildlife at its most exotic, come to the Pantanal.

A BIRD'S-EYE VIEW

There are many ways to visit the Pantanal – all of them rugged, muddy affairs, but well worth the effort for a die-hard eco-tourist. The city of **Cuiabá** is only one of three gateways to the Pantanal; the other jumping-off points are **Campo Grande** and **Corumbá**. From any one of these cities you can journey into the interior and choose among several types of accommodations, from four-day cruises on fishing boats to lodges that allow you to comb the countryside on horseback, foot, and boat. Each of these accommodations has its own benefits and disadvantages, and each can be tailor-made to your level of physical fitness.

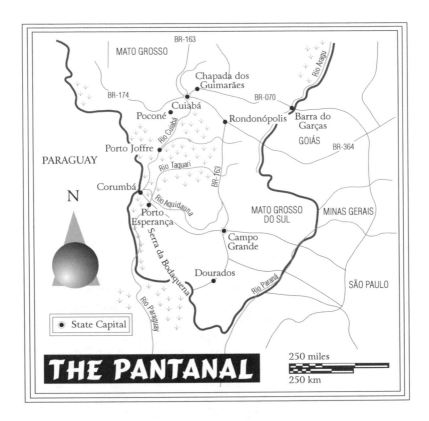

THE PANTANAL

250 miles
250 km

UP CLOSE TIP: *Avoid Jan., when there are the most mosquitoes. Aug. and Sept. are the coolest months.*

The Transpantaneira Highway

At least once in your stay, arrange to traverse the grand Transpantaneira Highway, a feat of civil engineering completed during the dictatorship (1964-85) that unwittingly led to the creation of a stunning reserve. Accessed from the city of Cuiabá, the 150-km./93-mile road, elevated 8½ feet above the flooded plains, starts right after the quaint village of **Poconé**, where the asphalt road suddenly turns into what Pantanal vets sardonically call an "all-weather" highway.

In the rainy season, the road becomes a linear refuge for wildlife; when the waters recede, millions of fish are trapped in the roadside trenches, offering a smorgasbord for predator and scavenger alike. During the dry season, riding over the bumpy highway with its bomb-sized craters is like journeying through a zoo on the moon – every few feet brings another "oh-oh-oh" experience. Large mounds become islands of refuge for snakes, capybaras, antbears, and jaguars, while caimans and great wading birds retreat to the artificial pools below to wait out the dry season. Seeds borne on the wind and in the guts of birds create the landscape of squat trees and scrub – a dried-out *cerrado* that nearly resembles parts of East Africa. The highway ends abruptly 150 km./93 miles south of Poconé at **Porto Jofre** on the banks of the Cuiabá River.

Transportation can be as primitive as ox carts in the Pantanal.

There are few people and no other towns in the Pantanal, so a look around Poconé is well warranted. Dating back to the 18th century, Poconé is a picturesque, well-kept colonial town, where most of the houses have traditional roofs and horse-drawn carts still meander down the cobblestone streets. A blue church dominates the main square, around which are general stores and the mayor's office. Just as it was 150 years ago, gold was "rediscovered" in Poconé about five years ago, turning the town upside down. Convinced there was gold hidden in the walls of the church, miners actually tore it down, finding only enough to rebuild a new church. Today, signs of *garimpeiros* (gold miners) are everywhere, from the picks and axes in the country stores to the smell of mercury in the air.

UP CLOSE TIP: *Hitchhiking the Transpantaneira Highway (as opposed to going with a pre-arranged tour) seems to be the beloved pastime of male travel writers and gonzo photo-journalists who are mad for adventure and great photo-ops. Maybe I'm a sissy, but frankly I wouldn't suggest hitchhiking, at least not on your first trip to the region. Sure, you'll find a friendly ride eventually, and you're bound to meet lots of colorful cowboys, native fishermen, and even a few federal agents, but in the meantime you could be overcome by sunstroke, exhaustion, bee attacks, hungry capybaras, dazed crocodiles, and even swarms of malaria-ridden mosquitoes, not to mention sudden floodings. You might even stumble on illegal poachers who would like to scramble you for breakfast. You'd be better off with a reputable guide in a well-maintained vehicle (truck, boat, or plane) and a responsible driver who knows the terrain. The driving is rough; even Brazilian tourists have been known to topple over in their jeeps. Since there are no towns, restaurants, or phones on the highway, getting stuck will mean a very long wait.*

HISTORY

Although the word *"pantanal"* is usually translated as swampland, in actuality the Pantanal is a sedimentary basin into which numerous rivers drain, including the Rio Paraguay and its tributaries, as they make their way south to the Rio de la Plata and the Atlantic Ocean. More than 65 million years ago, the region was completely ocean; 7,500-year-old animal bones have been found here, as well as the remains of a 10,000-year-old human fetus. As recently as 500 years ago, Kayapó, Iguato, and other tribes were known to migrate along the border with Amazonas. In the early 18th century, rumors of fist-sized emeralds and diamonds galvanized the first *bandeirantes* (pioneers) from São Paulo, though it was gold that was finally discovered along the Cuiabá River. After a 30-year rush, most miners moved on, but the few who stayed started sugarcane plantations and huge cattle ranches, piquing the interest of the King of Portugal, who established a captaincy in 1719 to collect taxes.

A Wild West Fantasy

It would take another century before anyone intentionally returned to the Pantanal. As 17th- and 18th-century expeditions found the way nearly impassable, the region gained a certain wildcat reputation. In 1925, **Lt. Colonel Percy Fawcett**, one of the most indefatigable explorers, mysteriously disappeared while searching for the legendary city of El Dorado, but that didn't deter big-city slickers during the 1930s and 40s from zooming down in their German-made seaplanes to fish and bag game. With the construction of the highways between Cuiabá-Santarém and Cuiabá-Porto Velho, the Pantanal's fortunes, and especially those of Cuiabá (Mato Grosso's capital) improved dramatically. The booming frontier town, situated on the banks of the Cuiabá River, became a symbol of Manifest Destiny, a Wild West fantasy for those trapped in the drought-ravaged Northeast. Roads were planned for 150,000 new residents, but many thousands more were spellbound by the lure of gold, lumber, cattle, and diamonds. Nearly all had to pass through Cuiabá on their way to the yellow-brick plains.

Today, as the Pantanal loses its reputation as an intractable swamp, it is fast becoming the focus of enormous political and economic intrigue. Although two Brazilian areas are officially protected – a remote national park near Bolivia and a small ecological reserve in Mato Grosso – the rest remains the property of private cattle ranches, where frontier law prevails. Illegal hunters, miners, and commercial fishermen continue to blatantly exploit the region in the face of lax federal enforcement. The health of residents is threatened by mercury poisoning from gold mining, agrochemical pollution from crops, and malaria epidemics. Violent outbreaks take place daily between gold miners and native tribes, the latter being forced further and further into the interior. Sadly, with the exception of **Pantanal Alert**, an activist group made up of artists and musicians in São Paulo, there are very few private organizations dedicated to conserving the Pantanal with the same fervor as that of the Amazon rainforest.

Whether the land in the Pantanal is even economically viable is being hotly debated today behind closed doors. Although most of the land had been traditionally owned by a few families, it is now being divvied up into smaller plots, at great loss to the new owners. Rumor has it that, since such a large percentage of the land is flooded for most of the year, substantial agriculture is nearly impossible, and the exorbitant cost of constantly relocating grazing cattle makes for unprofitable business. Some factory owners are now using their newly claimed property merely as tax dodges. Beyond the great ranches, the only other residents of the region are poor fishermen, who eke out a subsistence level of existence. **Eco-tourism** is the Pantanal's brightest hope for the future.

CULTURE

Cowboy Culture Of The Pantanal

The rugged, die-hard faces of the Pantanal's cowboys, farmers and fishermen tell it all. Due to the great distance between ranches the typical inhabitants of the region have accustomed themselves to lives of solitude and isolation. Facing daily facing the unforgiving climate and obstinate terrain has created a breed of resourceful, independent people. By inter-marrying with the Guarani, Paiaguá and Guiaiató Indians, the Pantanal local has inherited physical agility and a deep respect for nature, though a certain streak of hunter's machismo still reigns supreme. Among the skills of the typical resident are the ability to deftly maneuver a flat-bottomed boat or canoe, horsebackriding, and oxen-herding over both dry and swampy terrain. Most locals drive jeeps with wavering courage and seem to preternaturally know when and where fauna will appear.

A Pantanal cowboy rides the swampy range.

The typical Pantanal farmhand primarily chows down on meat. A local breakfast might include jerked beef with rice, coffee and milk, and a typical biscuit of the region called *maria-chica*. Before he sets off for a day of work in the fields, a farmer will pack an *empamonado* (made of minced jerked beef and manioc flour). Barbecues are thrown at even the hint of potential celebration. To offset the overconsumption of beef and aid in digestion, residents in the northern section of the Pantanal drink a mixture of guaraná powder, water and sugar. In the South, the *tereré-mate* is preferred, a Paraguayan tea brewed in cold water and served in a bull's horn.

Because roads are often impassable, the majority of farms communicate by radio and even have their own airstrip to avoid complete isolation. Due to the lonely life-style, women traveling alone through the region should be careful how they conduct themselves. From experience, I suggest to women that they travel in the company of a known and trustworthy male companion or take a package trip outlined in the *Options for Travel* and the *Where to Go* sections (even then, be careful around guides).

A Pantanal Indian Speaks Out

On May 10, 1994, Marta Silva Vito Guarani, President of the Kaguateca Association for Displaced Indians-Marçal de Souza, delivered the following prepared statement before the Subcommittee on Western Hemisphere Affairs, Committee on Foreign Affairs, U.S. House of Representatives, Washington, D.C. It is reprinted here with permission from the Amanaka'a Amazon Network in order to give voice to a shameful side of Pantanal politics that has been readily ignored. When I first heard Marta speak at an Amanaka'a Conference on the Amazon, I was deeply moved by her presence and her plea for help for her tribe, which was threatening to commit mass suicide unless their lands were returned to them.

~

"I have come before this tribunal to speak about the life of the Indians who live in the state of Mato Grosso do Sul, in a region known as the Pantanal. There are nearly 60,000 Indians, of the Guarani, Nhandeva, Kaiowá, Ofaié-xavante, Guató, Kadiwéu, Quinikinawa, Quaxi and other nations.

They are courageous and brave Indians, who were able to survive the violent attacks of our enemies – white men who in their ambition of land have evicted us. They kill and degrade. If today the world knows about the beautiful Pantanal (Wetlands) of Mato Grosso – one of the last ecological reserves of the planet – it is because we Indians defend and preserve it.

Much Indian blood has run, and still runs, on the ground of that land. Millions of Indians were killed, and the majority of the different nations were decimated. But there are still many survivors.

The Ofaié-Xavante, the people with lips of honey, are a gentle people who have spent the last 100 years being kicked out of one place to another. Today, they live on the Paraná River. The government has now taken them from their lands, because it will be flooded in order to build a factory. The Guató also live there, one of the last Canoeiro tribes left in the world. They were the first inhabitants of the Pantanal. Today, they live on the borders of the Paraguai River, in the city of Corumbá, and some on Insua Island, where they wish to return and live their culture. Their lands are in the process of demarcation on this island. The Kadiwéu live in Mato Grosso. They are known for the warrior spirit and for the beauty of their pottery decorated with natural paints. The Terene, who were able to survive from their gardens and planting, live in Mato Grosso. They also have problems with the invasion of their lands.

Now I want to speak of my people: the Guarani Nhandeva and Kaiowá. There are statistics which show that we are the poorest and most abandoned peoples in Brazil. We are a people with an ancient culture, descendants of the people of the Sun. There are Guarani in all of Brazil, especially in the southern part of the country. The Guarani are a great indigenous nation, which has been able to survive the conquest, perhaps by their nomadic life.

For the Guarani, the core of resistance is religion. But today there are many Protestant churches that come to our communities with the same discourse as the Jesuits who came during the "discovery" of Brazil. They are killing our religion, killing our culture. Without a cultural identity, our people wander the highways and streets of the cities, drinking, begging and being ridiculed by the white society.

I am the niece of Marcal de Souza, who was murdered in 1983 by gunmen hired by rich and owners. They wanted him to shut up, because he was denouncing to Brazil and to the world the disrespect with which we are treated in our own country. In Brazil, the murder of Indians doesn't shock anymore. Not the politicians or the goverment or the civil population. There is a minority concerned with indigenous people and for this, we need to sensitize the whole world. And that is what we are doing now.

At the government level, FUNAI (the National Indian Foundation) is in charge of Indian issues. We also have a chapter in the Brazilian Constitution. But if we continue dying, suffering and living is misery, if we are marginalized, we must ask:

- *Why the Chapter in the Constitution?*
- *Why FUNAI?*

The lands of my people were occupied by large land owners, who have lands that go as far as the eye can see, full of well-treated and well-fed cattle. On my land, cattle is worth more than Indians. Many Indians in Mato Grosso do Sul are leaving their communities and moving to urban centers. They go to live in the slums, and little by little they start losing their cultural identity and become "nobodies." In the villages they live surrounded by gunmen and by the rancher's cattle. The cattle stomp on their gardens and tractors knock down their houses. The rivers are dirty with the waste from the large farms in the region: pesticides, mercury, etc. They finished with our forest, they are finishing with what is left of our savannahs. They killed our birds and our animals. And they say that we are no longer Indians because we wear clothes...

Over seven thousand Indians are working in the charcoal factories and in the sugar cane processing plants. They live in a state of slavery. This is the integration that white society offers us. But we Indians, the first owners of this land, cannot accept this humiliating and inhuman integration!

For this reason, young Guarani are killing themselves, they are searching for the end, hanging themselves. The women from the community of Jaguapiré told me that they will kill their children and kill themselves afterwards if they try to take their lands away again. I cannot cross my arms before the massacre of my people. It is for them that I am here to tell the world that the Indians of Brazil do not see lands as private property. Land is important for peoples to survive culturally and in their humanity. To populate an area is to give human value to a place, to complete a stage in our evolution – therefore, taking away the means to kill the people. For this, it is necessary to demarcate the indigenous lands in Brazil. It is necessary to secure the land for our survival.

Land is culture and culture is life for us. Brazil needs to stop being the nation which least respects its native peoples on the face of this earth. The true history of the Brazilian Indian remains to be told. We have resisted for 400 years. We are not enemies, we want to live in peace in this country, with enough ground for all:white, black and yellow. Along with me, all the Indians are dreaming of this moment. Marçal de Souza, Angelo Krata, Simão Bororoo and so many other anonymous heroes have shared this dream with us. "

~

WHAT'S WHAT: A GUIDE TO FAUNA & FLORA

Fauna

The changeability of the Pantanal's weather patterns and ecology means that you will see wildlife here in a dramatic life-and-death struggle. While the following guide to the region's abundant animal life emphasizes individual characteristics, do stay attuned as you travel through the countryside; just how each animal plays its role in the overall plan of ecological balance is awe-inspiring – what in the words of one poet has been called the "terrifying beauty of God's irrevocable Plan." In that way, you may come to see and feel and hear the Pantanal as intimately as its own inhabitants do.

Mammals

Capybara

The world's largest rodent is not shy and may well be the animal you most sight on your Pantanal voyage. The name means "master of the grasses" in the native dialect of the Guarani Indians and perfectly describes how the mammal mows down tall grasses with its four large incisors and grinds them with a set of specialized molars. Looking lovable, but dumb and extremely slow-moving, this bear-like creature always lives near water and is often seen from canoes, but it flees when threatened, letting loose a series of grunts, snorts and snuffles. Capybaras are expert swimmers and divers and tend to rove in small bands of up to 20 individuals.

Pantanal Deer

One of the region's most beautiful (and largest) animals, this deer roams the entensive plains where the buriti palm tree is found. Long on the endangered species list, the deer population is fast disappearing, since they succumb to cattle diseases, such as foot-and-mouth.

Felines

Among the felines in the Pantanal are the **ocelot**, the **cougar** and the **jaguar**, the latter now on the endangered species list as a result of hunting. Even today, some farmers will not hesitate to kill a jaguar, claiming it is destroying their herds of cattle. A characteristic figure of the region is the *zagaieiro*, a "jaguar hunter" who kills the feline with a kind of primitive iron spear attached to a long hardwood handle. Locals usually hold the *zagareiro* in awe for his almost inhuman courage. When wounded or cornered, the jaguar hurls itself against the hunter, who is waiting for it with his *zagaia* firmly planted in the ground.

Tapirs

The largest of land mammals, the tapir has a snout that extends into a flexible trunk; its ears are as movable as a horse's. It eats all kinds of vegetable matter, as well as wild fruits. The tapir has been known to invade planted fields.

Reptiles

Jacaré

The Tupi Indians gave the name *jacaré* to the reptiles of the *alligatoridae* family, which includes the African crocodile and the North American alligator. You will see hundreds of jacarés on a boat trip through the Pantanal; the first one will scare the living daylights out of you, particularly if they are following your canoe; by the time you sight the fifth one you'll feel chummy; the 20th, nonchalant, and the 50th, completely bored. Awkward and easily threatened on land, the jacaré gains its true strength in the water. Its best protection is its sharp teeth and thick, leathery skin that is nearly impenetrable. It feeds on whatever it can catch, from fish and birds to mammals and reptiles, as well as decaying meat. Its extreme taste for piranha helps keep the population of the voracious fish relatively balanced. Females can lay up to 30-50 eggs at one time. Since alligators have been known to crawl across roads, where they are sometimes run over by vehicles, be careful if you camp outdoors. At night, if a light is shone on them, their eyes shimmer like a sea of red specks of light, One of the pastimes of some boat tours is to go "alligator hunting" at night in canoes. Don't try this yourself, but your guide will probably stick his hand in the water, pull out a baby and show you the genitals. It's supposed to be very bad luck for men if they pull up a male jacaré.

Sunbathing jacarés *in the Pantanal don't tan.*

Anaconda

Smaller than the Amazonian species, this still enormous snake in the Pantanal reaches 10-13 feet long. It is not poisonous, but uses its tremendous strength to squeeze the life out of hapless victims.

Sinimbu

A member of the iguana family, this prehistoric-looking lizard grows to 3½ feet long, more than half of which is its tail. An expert swimmer and diver, it can leap gracefully over tree branches as well. Its diet consists mainly of fruit, leaves, insects and small animals.

Pantanal Cattle

Bred freely on native pastures and allowed to roam at will, this type of cattle has adapted well to the region's adverse conditions; the first head of cattle, imported in the early part of the 18th century, were from Europe. In the early part of the 20th century, the Pantanal cattle started to crossbreed with zebu, mainly that of the Nelore species. One of the most exciting things to view in the Pantanal is an oncoming herd of cattle being escorted by cowboys on horesback.

Pantanal Horse

This special breed of horse was introduced over four centuries ago. Rustic and rugged, it has an acquired ability to graze below the surface of the water in partially flooded fields.

Fish

There are over 400 species of fish in the Pantanal, making it one of the world's richest resources. There are rigid restrictions on fishing; inquire with local authorities or follow the advice of your hopefully trustworhy guide, who does not want to be fined for illegal actions.

Piranha

This vicious-looking and acting fighter is a committed carnivore, aided by razor-sharp teeth. Amazonian river, marshlands and bays are full of piranhas. They are delicious to eat, but do avoid swimming near them, especially if you have open wounds – they attack ferociously at the smell of blood. The most common species include: **black** or **red piranha**, which measure up to 13 inches in length; the **yellow piranha**, which changes color; and the **white piranha**.

Dourado

Considered by anglers as the "king of the rivers," the dourado in the Pantanal can weigh up to 30 kilos (66 pounds), putting up a huge and valiant struggle when being caught.

Pacu

Pacupeva
This is a round-shaped fish that enjoys digesting the wild fruits of soft fig trees and inga-trees growing on the riverbanks. Pantanal residents adore its savory meat.

Scale Fish

Among the varieties of scale fish are **piraputanga, curimbatá, piau, piava, piavaçu** and **lambari.**

Skin Fish

Also known as siluridians, these skin fish have no scales (hence their name), but rather barbels or "feelers" near the mouth. Nocturnally active, their instincts are driven more by taste and smell. The best representatives of this species are the **jaú** and the **pintado**, the latter of which offers tasty meat. Other skin fish include the **abrado, jurupensen, chara, palmito** and the beautiful **yellow mandi** or **golden mandi.**

Birds

Birding is one of the great joys of Pantanal travel. Aquatic birds that can move easily from place to place are especially adaptable to the demands of the region, with its alternating cycles of flooding and drought. The climate and hydrological changes in the Pantanal strongly affect the feeding and mating habits of birds. As such, the best time for birdwatching is during the mating and egg-laying season. During the dry season, from July to September, thousands of tall-legged birds, from egrets to herons to spoonbills and American wood-storks, come to breed in colonies known as nesting grounds, or bird sanctuaries. At this low-water period, the juvenile fish attempt to return to the rivers, but many fail, crowding into the remaining shallow bodies of water and becoming easy prey for scavenging birds.

The dry season is also a marvelous time to glimpse nests, wonders of construction and resourcefulness. Mud, wood chips, grass and twigs are made into a variety of shapes and sizes, from the spacious two-room "house" made of earth and cow dung by the rufoud hornero to the hollow made in the grass by the southern lapwing. Saliva is often used by hummingbirds and swallows for gluing material together. Some interesting nests to look for are the sack-like structures of all the *icteridae* species (orange-backed

A lone parrot in the Pantanal.

orioles, crested oropendola and yellow-rumped cacique) that dangle from the tips of long palm branches by bunching together the individual strands of leaf. During the dry season, nests of different species sometimes occupy the same branch. A highly dramatic scene, the nesting ground, full of thousands of birds, is also stalked by a vicious round of natural selection, as crested caracas and black vultures snatch eggs and chicks directly from the nests. Down below on the ground, alligators wait patiently for any helpless chick that has fallen out of its safety zone. Excellent places to sight birds are along the shores of the **Miranda River**, downstream from **Passo do Lontra** along the Vermelho and Cuiabá rivers, and down the **Transpantaneira Highway**.

Egrets & Herons

Dynamic symbols of the Pantanal, these graceful, svelte, lanky-legged birds with multicolored plumage are omnipresent, but often difficult to photograph. They usually live near water, especially shallow swamp waters or marshes, where they search for prey, in particular small fish and insects. To keep their luscious plumage looking good, nature has provided them with a kind of comb alongside their toes. To watch a heron walk slowly and pointedly is a lesson in meditation. At dusk, a memorable sight is a flock's return en masse to its collective roost high up in a tree.

Great Egret

One of the symbols of the Pantanal, this entirely white bird has a yellow/orange bill, legs and feet. They are the most commonly found species in the Pantanal, and can be seen especially well during the dry season – July to October – when hundreds travel side by side next to alligators, around a *coriso* or bays swarming with fish. During the breeding season, they develop decorative dorsal feathers, called "egret," whose plumes flow down their backs like a wedding veil.

Cattle Egret

This idiosyncratic egret also has white plumage, but is less slender than the snowy egret, has a thicker neck, and a yellow bill and legs. It was first sighted in Brazil in September, 1964, on the island of Marajó, in association with buffaloes. The species walks in the fields following cattle and eating insects (for example, grasshoppers), which they rout.

Whistling Heron

Also known as the "singing heron" because it sings as it flies, this species has a distinctly melodious whistling voice and a spectacular multicolored plumage. Often seen in couples, it hunts for insects in dry fields, where it sometimes is associated with buff-necked ibises.

White-Necked Heron

The largest of the herons, it boasts a six-foot wingspread. It has no song, and makes only noise, a shrill cry, when frightened and sometimes while flying.

Black-Crowned Night Heron

This heron of the night boasts large red eyes, gray wings, black crown and back, and a white underbelly. A voracious eater, it has been known to gobble up an enormous number of frogs, as well as fish longer than its own body.

Ruffescent Tiger-Heron

Young specimens can often look like leopard-skin due to their brown and beige-patterned plumage. The name "socó-bumba-meu-boi" (ox heron) was derived from its cry, a deep monosyllablic mooing, resembling that of an ox. When attacked, it tends to stand motionless, as if in hope that its cryptic plumage will succeed in camouflaging it from an observant predator. Its neck can often resemble a perfect "S."

Storks

Storks, from the ciconidae family, are master gliders, all the more impressive since they have robust, big bodies, long bills and elongated necks.

Tuiuiú

Pronounced "too-yoo-yoo," this stork is the largest of the species and is considered the symbol of the Pantanal. Also called jabiru, it is forced to build its nest on very tall, leafless trees because of its huge size. A jabiru builds one nest in a lifetime and refurbishes it every year at mating season, which usually starts in June. Their nests can often be found near a jatobá or a piuva tree destroyed by the floods. Though they mostly feed on fish, they sometimes catch baby alligators and steal small specimens of anacondas. When frightened, they clasp their bill, emitting a sound like that of a castanet. Rumors abound in the Pantanal about a jabiru that actually attacked a horse and rider.

Ibises

Ibises belong to the same family as the sacred ibis (*Threskiornis aethiopicus*), the ibis found in Egyptian hieroglyphics, a startling-looking bird with a snow-white plumage that was revered as a god of wisdom. Ibises are characterized by their long legs, elongated, curved bill, slender, graceful bodies and varied colored plumage. They build their nests in redbuds, bushes or trees, in large colonies, in small groups or alone.

Roseate Spoonbill

This ibis sports a remarkable bill that resembles a long cooking spoon and a magnificent pink plumage, which darkens during the breeding season. Searching for food in shallow waters, they revolve the mud with their spatula-like bills, looking for small fish, crustaceans and mollusks, plankton, insects and larvae. The number of roseate spoonbills in the Pantanal has been sadly reduced as their nests are constantly plundered by crested cascaras and black vultures.

Buff-Necked Ibis

The "alarm clock" of the Pantanal is often seen carousing with the plumous ibis. When the flock comes together to spend the night, they screech in unison and throw their heads back at the peak of passion. This buff-necked bird will scour dry fields, looking for spiders, snakes, mice, sand-lizards, and toads. Upon sensing human presence, it emits a shrill cry.

Green Ibis

A dark shiny green, this ibis also sports a jade-colored bill and legs. A forest species, it prefers to remain close to river shores and lakes deep inside the forest. Its diet consists of worms, plants and insects.

Bare-faced Ibis

Black-greenish plumage with a light red forehead and a curved whitish bill are the identifying features of this ibis. It lives in the marshland, feeding upon seeds and leaves which it finds by walking slowly along the shallows with its bill in the water. At certain times of the year it is one of the most frequently seen birds.

Passerines

The living jewels of the Pantanal, the passerines are arguably the most attractive and ornamental of all birds. They also are essential to ecological balance, forming a protective shield against the invasion of the planet by insects. There are nearly 400 species in the Pantanal (5,100 worldwide). Among them:

Black-Capped Mockingthrush

Part of the *Mimidae* family, this is a singular bird that lives in marshes and along riverbanks where the piri plant grows. Both sexes rise early and sing magnificently in unison while flitting through tall grasses. Sometimes they even dance together, fanning and swinging their tails.

River Warbler

A species of the *Parulidae* family, this bird measures only a third of an inch in length. It can be found along the forest creeks, groves of buriti palm trees, and flooded riparian forests. It skips and hops onto roots and alights on branches overhanging the water, rapidly flicking its tail and flapping its wings.

Yellow-Throated Spinetail

About 5½-inches long, this passarine of the *Furnariidae* family sports a rusty red color. Its nest, built above or very near the water, consists of a mound of twigs accessed through a vertical tube or chimney. The male and female sing in unison.

White-Headed Marsh-Tyrant

This species inhabits swamps and marshes, usually perching on branches as opposed to scavenging the ground. The male is easily recognized by its white head and black coat; the female is ash-gray in color.

Chestnut-Capped Blackbird

This passerine is glossy black with crown, throat and breast a tawny-rufous to chestnut. It often sings while gliding with wings and tail tautly stretched. They are often seen in flocks numbering hundreds.

Gulls & Terns

Terns consist of several species of long-winged birds of the *Laridae* family (the same as gulls).

Of 10 species living today in Brazil, two can be found in internal waters, on the shores of major rivers and their tributaries, and in the Amazon and the Pantanal. In general, their color is white mixed with pale gray; the bill and legs are yellow. Feeding on fish and crustaceans, they fly low and quite slowly over the water searching for prey. Without warning, you might see them suddenly flapping their wings while hovering over water and swaying their bodies vertically, with the head at a right angle to the body, as if their gaze is penetrating the river floor. Then, like a missile, they will dive straight down, up to 3½ feet below the surface, to snag their dinner. They build their nests – little more than holes dug into the sand – on the ground close to the water's edge. Varieties include:

Black Skimmer

This species spends most of the day lying in the sand, waiting till twilight to search for food. Its extremely narrow bill sports a mandible (lower part) much longer than the mazilla (upper part). Flying just above the surface of the water, it keeps the mandible partially below the water's surface, as if it were plowing.

Large-Billed Tern

This tern is unmistakable due to the considerable size of its lemon-yellow tail. It may be glimpsed in the company of common stilts or the caraúna.

Jaçaná & Lapwings

Closely related to collard plovers, brown snipes, gulls and terns, these *Charadriiformes* comprise a large number of cosmopolitan birds of heterogeneous characteristics, usually aquatic, both in salt and fresh water. Many have the capacity to fly great distnces.

Southern Lapwing

A graceful and perky resident of marshes and pastures, this species is characterized by long feathers on the back of its head and a red spur on the bend of its wings. The bill and legs are remarkably red. Its song is nearly metallic, and closely resembles its name in Portuguese: téu-téu. The bird is often seen squatting, ever watchfull for enemies; when it does sense a threat, it silently runs off along the fields and takes flight a good distance away, then screaming loudly. If a predator ties to snatch its eggs, it swoops down and strikes him with its wing spurs. Humans have been known to be attacked in such a manner.

Wattled Jaçaná

One of the most common birds in the Pantanal, this small waterfowl has a strikingly elegant shape with a very light body, tall thin legs, and a yellow beak topped by a red shield. This bird spends its whole life within a very small area (about one square kilometer). Protective of its environs, it emits a shrill call and simultaneously raises its wings as soon as a threat is sensed. Most wattled jacanas live in pairs along marshes or small bogs, like those formed by excavation alongside roads.

Hawks

Hawks are omnipresent in the Pantanal and it is impossible to travel any distance without seeing one. Species range from the pearl kite, the smallest falcon, to the stately and impressive harpy eagle. Astute hunters, they boast strong hooked bills and powerfully sharp claws that are most suitable for ravaging flesh. Extremely sharp vision and a majestic flight help in their quest for nourishment. Among varieties are:

Crested Caracará

Plentiful in the Pantanal, this bird takes its name from the sound of its call. A voracious eater, it often preys onthe catch of black vultures and has been known to wander into houses to snatch food off the table. Large numbers often gather on riverbanks when fishermen clean their catch, patiently waiting to feast on the discards.

Sail Kite

This is one of two species of hawks in the Pantanal that can also be considered aquatic birds, since they feed on mollusks. The plumage of the adult male is slate-gray. The female and the fledgling have whitish eyebrows and throat, underparts streaked buff, resembling an immature savannah hawk. A mound of crab and mollusk shells around a fence post is often the sign that a snail kite had been feeding. During the breeding season, they often perform elegant exhibition flights, full of loops and dashes.

Harpy Eagle

The world's most powerful hawk, the harpy eagle has a majestic strength. Its wingspan can reach as much as seven feet. Like most hawks, its retinas are four to eight times more sensitive than a human's, making it the creature endowed with the greatest visual acuity.

Black-Collared Hawk

Often seen in the Pantanal, this species haunts the bays and swamps, using long claws to catch mollusks. The adult has a buffy white head and a black patch on its throat. Fine, thorn-like warts cover the underside of their toes, enabling them to easily hold onto fish they catch.

Turkey Vulture

Known in the Pantanal as "sole-leather head," this vulture can often be sighted standing over the carcass of alligators.

Cormorants & Anhingas

Relatives of the pelican, cormorants are expert fishermen; indeed they eat only fish. Unlike the majority of other waterfowl, they will descend underwater and swim while chasing a fish. Since their feathers are not waterproof, you can often see them perched on a rock or tree, drying out their spread wings. Among the species are:

Anhinga

Also called a snake-neck bird, this species has a very thin, long neck with 20 vertebrae, which makes it extremely mobile, enabling forceful and rapid strikes similar to those of a snake. Its bill is so straight, sharp and long that the anhinga can directly spear fish. When sensing danger, the anhinga dives under water, then only part of its head emerges some distance away. Because of the shape of its neck, it often resembles a water snake in this position.

Neotropic Cormorant

Basically fish-eaters, groups of neotropics cormorants ban together for collective fishing expeditions, swimming side-by-side in the same direction in order to block a channel or river inlet, thus preventing the fishes' escape. You can often see them flying in V-shaped formation, or lined up one after the other. While underwater, they propel themselves only with their feet and use their long, stiff tail as a rudder.

Owls

Great Horned Owl

This is the largest owl on the continent and lives on the edge of wooded areas, in groves and fields, usually near water.

Burrowing Owl

This owl has daytime habits and builds its nest in holes in the ground.

Ducks

Ducks in the Pantanal are, by necessity, migratory for several reasons: the availability of food changes widely with the water level, as do safe havens for sleeping and the moulting period (when they are unable to fly).

Muscovy Duck

The South American domestic duck is descended from this species, which is found in small groups or sometimes in pairs, in rivers and lakes, surrounded by forests or close to them. They often spend the night perched on defoliated branches, like those of the embaúba; sometimes they use the location as a daytime lookout. Nests are built in trees, which can accommodate up to 14 eggs. Since they are avidly hunted by humans, they have developed skittish and distrustful personalities.

White-Faced Whistling Duck

One of several nocturnal ducks, this species is quite gregarious, forming groups of 10-20. They search for food at night, eating grass seeds, as well as mollusks and small crustaceans. When disturbed, they stand more erect than most ducks, stretch their necks out, and let loose a repeated three-note whistle. Other variaties include the **fulvous whistling duck** and the **black-bellied whistling duck**.

Brazilian Duck

A small duck of about 16 inches in length, this species roams the swamps and weirs of the Pantanal, which are chock full of low, dense vegetation. Depending on how the sunlight hits them, their wing cover can appear black, green or shiny blue. The female sports a blue-tinted bill and two white spots on her face, while the male's bill is red.

Flora

The vegetation of the Pantanal is not a typical homogeneous mix; rather, the unusual combination of plants and flowering trees is known as the **Pantanal Complex**. Patches of forest, thick brush and open prairie vie for space through a vast plain. Elements characteristic of the shrub lands in the Amazon forest as well as in Central Brazil mix freely with plant species that have adapted to the swampy lowland environment. In addition, a xerophytous flora has developed on shallow calcareous overgrowth and higher terrain, producing a landscape similar to that of the "caatinga," the characteristic dried-out terrain of Northeasern Brazil, a stunning, yet delicate ecological balance.

The **alluvial plain** of the Pantanal lies between 330 and 650 feet above sea level. On the Brazilian side (east, north and west) it is surrounded by a **plateau**, approximately 2,000 feet in altitude, covered with *cerrado* (bush savannah vegetation). To the south, lies the **Paraguayan depression**, a rolling plain with an extensive hydrographic network, formed by countless tributaries of the Paraguay River. Drilling in this area has reached 270 feet without hitting the bedrock.

The Pantanal's vast **prairies**, or *campinas*, are filled with slender meadow grasses, forming a natural pastureland boasting only an occasional ligneous plant. In general, these prairies are found in the more humid areas subjected to flooding. In contrast, the shrub lands, restricted by nature to higher and drier areas, remain out of the water, giving rise to tiny islands of vegetation.

Clusters of thorny bushes, dense forests and palm tree groves complete the terrain of these prairies The most common palm tree is the **carandezaias,** formed by specimens of the **caraná,** a stately palm tree with fan-shaped leaves, that grows to about 35 feet. The **buriti** is another popular palm tree, which also sports fan-shaped leaves. In densely forested areas, called *capóes,* we also find the **aroeira fig** trees marked by twisted, almost sculpture-like trunks; the **piúva,** which blooms flamboyantly in shades of pink, lilac and purple in the months of July and August; and the **cambará,** which is remarkable for its golden yellow flowers.

Another type of grove, called *paratudais,* sports trees with more slender trunks, thick and wrinkled bark and twisted branches. The most common variety is the **yellow ipê,** known in the Pantanal as the *paratudo.*

Flanking the region's many waterways, are the **riparian forests.** Among the trees here are the **genipapo fig trees, inga trees,** the **silver-leafed embaúbas,** which flourish beside anthills, and the **tucum,** a small palm tree of the *Bactris* genus. The **acuri palm tree** provides a delicious fruit for the blue macaws, and the **pau-de-noavto** contributes color to the riverbanks with its clusters of pink or red flowers. The name "novato" (or newcomer) refers to the danger awaiting those who do not know that if you cut the tree down with an axe or hang your hammock there, hundreds of tiny ants will fall upon you without mercy. Their sting is intense and fiery.

On the higher plains, calcareous rock formations pierce the surface, creating a mosaic of xerophytic and deciduous succulent **cacti** and spiny, rigid-leafed **bromeliads.** Here you can find smaller groves of *Bromeliacae* and *Cactacae.*

Among stunning examples of flowers, the **pond-lilies** are floating, aquatic plants typical of the region, forming clusters that collect in ponds and watercourses. Their various blues and purples are a colorful addition to the green vegetation. As in the Amazon, there are numerous *Vitória-régias,* enormous lily pads that look like Alice-in-Wonderland-type pie plants.

OPTIONS FOR TRAVEL

Lodges

Besides trekking the Transpantaneira Highway there are several other travel options you can add to your Pantanal itinerary. First choice, in my opinion, is to book a stay at a rustic lodge. From here, you can initiate treks by foot, horseback, or canoe, always led by a guide – usually preferred by those who sleep more comfortably on dry land. A variety of lodges in all price ranges are available, from the most primitive ranches, where meals are cooked over an open fire, to the luxurious Pousada Caiman, the most famous lodge in the Pantanal. Package deals are usually the cheapest and the most sensible way to go; just make sure the lodge provides transfer from the airport.

The Fazenda Experience

I step off a 10-seater plane in Corumbá and find a rugged, four-word cowboy waiting for me in the lobby. He piles my gear in the back of his truck, and soon we're off on a rollicking ride to reach the Fazenda Xaraes. During rainy season, more than half of this trek would be navigated by canoe, when the annual rains floods the plains leading to the arm. On this Aug. day, the ride gives new meaning to "wear your seatbelt."

After a dead-to-the-world sleep in my air-conditioned cabana, we fortify ourselves with a mule-teamer's breakfast, then hop in his truck to interface with the countryside. Julio, the driver of our jeep, seems to have preternatural sense where the wild animals are lurking, even before he sees them; along the highway we discover just-shed cobra skins, contemplate the jaws of alligators from bridges, and nearly get crushed by herds of cattle running Pamplona-style. Capybaras, bear-like rodents, sometimes plant themselves in our way; birds fly right in front of the windshield, barely surviving. If we were traveling at night, our guide informs us, we'd be running smack into alligators looking for dinner. Twice we catch toucans streaking past. In mid-sentence Julio jumps out of the running jeep to race after an armadillo, catching it by the tail so we can inspect its armored body. If you go to Bolivia by train, he says, they'll serve you armadillo *na casca* (in the shell). Soon we discover it's not just humans who scavenge the Pantanal. We drive past about 20 black *urubus* (vultures), feasting on the remains of a *jacaré* (crocodile).

In the afternoon, a canoe trip glides us through the leafy waterway of an *igarapé* – a miraculous vista at dusk where a crop of trees lining the banks become home to roosting *garças* that fly in for the night. The sight is something out of a tropical Christmas, the white birds hanging like snowy ornaments on the branches.

The next day we comb the enormous grounds of the Xaraes farm on both horseback and foot, exploring forests that seem nearly primeval – home to hundreds of monkeys, capybaras, and rodents that scurry under the brush as we approach. From our guide, we learn that the only way to hear the voice of the Pantanal is to descend into silence – a kind of Zen in the wild. Crouching down behind bushes, we suddenly hear the terrifying screech of howler monkeys, a sound that even terrified the naturalist Henry Bates.

Fazenda Xaraes

Rio Abobral, 130 km. from Corumbá. Reserve in Campo Grande. ☎ (67) 242-1102 or São Paulo, ☎ (11) 246-9934, or through Expeditours, ☎ (21) 287-9697.

This well-maintained, three-star lodge is rustic enough to be authentic and clean enough to be comfortable. Owned by the same group as the Nacional Hotel in Corumbá, it features wood-and-tiled rooms with shutters open to the river. The air conditioning is solid, and whatever dirt you trail in seems to mysteriously disappear in a matter of hours. The dining room is surrounded by screens so you can see and hear the chirping birds. Most impressive is the salt-of-the-earth staff, some of the nicest people I met in Brazil. Packages include all meals and a variety of daily excursions. Rates per person per night range from $58 (doubles $51); transfers from Corumbá $61 per person or $40 for doubles; three-hour horse treks run $8; a boat trip, $40. Two-day / one-night package, including one boat tour, runs $89; three-days/two-nights per person is $200 (doubles $162). (Rates may change.)

If you arrive in Corumbá, the staff will pick you up and transfer you by truck (or canoe during rainy season) to Fazenda Xaraes. You can also take the bus to Morro do Azeite, which leaves you out in the middle of the road, 31 km. (45 min.) from Xaraes, where the staff will pick you up. Flights to Corumbá are offered by VASP from Belo Horizonte, Brasília, Campo Grande, Cuiabá, Goiânia, and São Paulo.

Pousada Caiman

236 km. from Campo Grande, Mato Grosso do Sul.

The five-star accommodation of the southern Pantanal, situated on a serious working ranch, is the eco-dream of Roberto Klabin, the energetic scion of a rich Brazilian family who wanted to create for his friends and tourists the height of luxury-in-the-wild. Of the ranch's 53,000 hectares, 7,000 (17,300 acres) has been set aside as an ecological reserve, but much of the land remains range for the 65 staff cowboys who live in a village adjacent to the lodge. The u-shaped hacienda (formerly the Klabin's family residence) houses 22 guests and offers every deluxe amenity, from swimming pool and Italian-tiled floors to comfy leather furniture, satellite-dish TV, and stylish apartments with excellent air conditioning. The cuisine is superb. The grounds have been called "an oasis for birds," since a large variety of species can easily be seen. Guests are led on morning and afternoon excursions on horseback, in canoe, and on foot. The lodge is about four hours by car from Campo Grande; transfers by air-conditioned micro-buses are offered every Sat. and Wed. from Campo Grande between 1:30-2 p.m., and after breakfast from the lodge. (Campo Grande may be reached by commercial flights from Belém, Brasília, Corumbá, Cuiabá, Rio Branco, Santarém, São Paulo, and others.) Three-day packages run from Wed.-Sat.; four nights from Sat. to Wed. In New York, contact Brazil Nuts (see Specialty Tours, at the end of this book, for address). In São Paulo, contact Roberto Klabin **Hotels e Turismo**, Rua Pedrosa Alvarenga, 1208, first floor, CEP 045531; ☎ *(11) 883-6566.* In Rio contact **Expeditours,** ☎ *(21) 287-9697, fax 521-4388.*

Fazenda Boa Sorte Regilo de Abobral

☎ *231-1120 (in Corumbá); reservations can be made through*
Expeditours, ☎ *(21) 287-9697 (Rio) or (65) 381-4959 (Cuiabá).*

A rustic (read "primitive") farm without frills near the Fazenda Xaraes gives you a home-on-the-range ambiance. Sleep outdoors in hammocks, inside tents, or under grass-roofed huts with wood-slat floors. If you don't want to bathe in the river, there's a communal bath. Three daily meals are cooked over a wood fire; don't pass up a glass of freshly milked cow juice. The farm's parrots will sit happily on your shoulder and even the wild ducks and toucans are friendly. During the day you can make excursions on horseback, sleep in other *fazendas*, and take canoe trips. A three-day package for $70 includes all meals and treks.

Fazenda Beira Rio

Rod Transpantaneira, 150 km. from Poconé, 205 km. from Cuiabá. Reserve: ☎ (65) 322-0948; in São Paulo, ☎ (11) 35-4157, or (67) 725-5267 (in Campo Grande); or through Expeditours in Rio, ☎ (21) 287-9697, fax (21) 521-4389.

Located on 3,700 hectares of land right off the Transpantaneira Highway, this is considered the best pousada in the region for cleanliness and trek options. The hotel is seven years old, owned by the grizzly but *simpatico* Senhor Valdo de Luis. Running next to his property is the Pixaim River, which you can cross by motor boat, or canoe (monkeys upstream, herons downstream). You can also rent horses or explore the grounds by foot. Guides accompany guests without charge. Housed in a one-story white stucco building with traditional tile roofs, the simple rooms are all air conditioned and come with mini-bar, TV, and attractive tile floors. Suites sleep five. If you come through a travel agent, the package deal includes horse treks and boat excursions; otherwise, you pay extra. There are no phones, but there is radio communication with Cuiabá. Rates include all three meals; packages available. *13 apts. Moderate.*

Araras Farm

Reserve through Expeditours in Rio, Rua 223 Visconde de Pirajá, 414 (Ipanema), ☎ (212) 287-9697, fax 521-4388; in Cuiabá, Av. Governador Ponce de Arruda, 670, ☎ (65) 381-4959/381-5674.

After nearly 20 years of working in the Pantanal, André von Thuranyi of Expeditours travel agency has now started his own lodge program in collaboration with native farmers in the Pantanal wetlands. A four-day, three-night package at this private reserve off the Transpantaneira Highway offers treks by foot, canoe, horseback, and jeep. An extra night in Cuiabá and/or a tour of Chapada dos Guimarães (highly recommended) may be added. Transports to the Araras Farm leave from the Expeditours office in Cuiabá each day at 3:30 p.m.

Hotel Santa Rosa do Pantanal

Transpantaneira Highway, 150 km. from Poconé. Reserve in Cuiabá,
☎ *(65) 322-0513/0077; in São Paulo,* ☎ *(11) 231-4511.*

Once a luxurious (for the region) hotel, this is still the best in Porto Jofre, located at the end of the Transpantaneira Highway on the banks of the Cuiabá River. One travel option is to trek or hitch your way here; then rent boats, horses, or guides at the hotel. The owner of the nearby campgrounds also rents boats. *54 apts. Moderate. No cards.*

Botels & Boat Cruises

An alternative to bunking down at lodges is to take a package cruise. Expeditours offers the **Pantanal Ecological Triangle Tour**, a fine five-night/four-day package on the *Pantanal Explorer*, a modest, low-draft boat that sleeps 12, including crew (four air-conditioned bunks for passengers, with two shared bathrooms, sun deck, and kitchen/bar). During the day, you can watch birds and other wildlife from the top deck of the boat; at night, special alligator expeditions are conducted in canoes. Tight quarters make sociable personalities a must, but humor is provided by outgoing guides who are able to identify most of the animals and birds sighted. Food is surprisingly good: a mixture of beef, fish, chicken, and pasta. The most exciting part of the trip is the roller-coaster ride over the Transpantaneira Highway – a must for Pantanal-goers. Among animals to be sighted are savanna hawks, Amazon kingfishers, snowy egrets, toucans, black-headed vultures, wood storks, herons, parrots, woodpeckers, cormorants, marsh deer, capybaras, caimans, iguanas, and lizards. The highway's 114 bridges are sometimes portraits of imminent disaster – weatherbeaten washboard planks crossed by moldy timbers, but the anything-can-happen ambiance is part of the fun. An hour and a half beyond Poconé you'll pass the Sao João ranch, owned by Sebastião Camargo Correia, one of the five richest men in the world. Ask if you can visit. A stop at the gold mines near Cangas, 10 minutes from Cuiabá, is also an eye-opener. (For more information, see *Hands-On Cuiabá*, below.)

> **UP CLOSE TIP:** *If you're traversing the Transpantaneira Highway in a group tour, make sure the driver and guide know you want to savor every last scene. This will slow down the trip considerably, so if you have to catch a flight later in the day, leave a few hours earlier. You may never see anything like it again.*

Independent Travel

The independent's way to see the Pantanal is to combine different options. First, hire a good guide who is ready to go anywhere, then improvise. You can go by car from Poconé to Barão de Melgão, then rent kayaks and paddle to Porto Cercado or, if you're crazy enough, all the way down to Porto Jofre (about four to five days). This way you can stop and take time to talk to the locals, who are usually friendly. Have a car waiting at Porto Jofre and go over the Transpantaneira Highway to Pixaim, camping or staying at a lodge. To do it right, you'll need eight to 10 days. Such a trip, with guide and transportation, will probably cost as much as the Expeditours boat tour, but you must come with your own food. To find a guide, call a travel agency and ask for the names of reliable guides without explaining exactly what you want; then make private arrangements with the guide.

PANTANAL
SURVIVAL KIT

Climate

During the dry season (Apr.-Oct.), temperatures range from 68-75°F, but can rise over 50° in a matter of hours. The hottest months in the Pantanal are Dec.-Feb., when 110-112°F is common. During dry season, it's important to drink lots of liquids to avoid dehydration. Starting in Nov., weather alternates between torrential rains and scalding sun. The most animals can be seen in Dec. and Jan.

Medical Emergencies

It's best not to have them in the Pantanal. Decent hospitals will probably be boats, planes, and torturous jeep rides away. Take your own medicine kit (including gauze, antiseptic, allergy pills, and antihistamines, calamine lotions, aloe vera lotion for cuts and bruises, a snake bite kit, TANG for dehydration, and Pepto-Bismol for diarrhea, etc. Make sure you've had all the necessary inoculations (tetanus, yellow fever, typhoid, polio). And pray. (Hospitals are listed under *Hands-On Cuiabá*.)

Bees

Anyone going to the Pantanal should read Vick Banks' riveting description of the "bees from hell" in his book *The Pantanal* (Sierra Club), 1991. According to Banks, 300-400 people a year die from bee stings in Brazil, more than from any other animal attack. In the Pantanal, Europa honeybees have interbred with African killer bees, making them capable of attacking aggressively en masse, even if just one drone is disturbed. Truly, Banks' encounter was most unfortunate, but frankly, I never met one bee in the Pantanal.

What To Pack

Follow guidelines for Amazon treks (see *Amazônia*), but also dress in layers (for cool nights, a jean jacket and sweater is sufficient). Binoculars, telephoto lenses, and high-speed film are essential in the Pantanal. (Those magnificent close-up shots of birds seen in books and brochures are surely taken by professionals who spend days waiting silently under a bush for just the right moment.)

WHERE TO GO IN THE PANTANAL

CUIABÁ

The capital of **Mato Grosso**, Cuiabá (pronounced Kwee-ah-bah) is the major gateway to the Pantanal, located about 102 km. (63 miles) from the northern entrance of the Transpantaneira Highway. Even so, it's not exactly a destination in itself, though a day or two stuck here won't feel like the end of the world. Most visitors use Cuiabá as a trampoline to visit other parts of the region, such as the magnificent rock sculptures in the national park and the caves and waterfalls of Chapada dos Guimarães, one of the most beautiful sites in all Brazil.

Once a frontier town, Cuiabá has boomed to over 330,000 people (some reports claim up to one million in the surrounding area); you will discover fine regional restaurants here, as well as some of the best crafts stores for Indian artifacts in the region.

The first *bandeirantes* in the early 18th century came in search of Indian slaves, but soon forgot their objective when they discovered **gold**. A Paulista, Pascoal Moreira Cabral, established the first settlement in 1719, having braved disease, mosquitoes, floods, and intense heat through his arduous five-month journey from São Paulo. Soon, thousands more were traveling the 3,000-km./1,865-mile route, boosting the population of Cuiabá far beyond that of São Paulo between 1719 and 1730. Because of the navigation systems, however, ties with Bolivians, Paraguayans, and Argentineans soon became tighter than with fellow Brazilians, resulting in a kind of trans-Latino culture. The flotillas of canoes and medium-sized ships that arrived laden with supplies and slaves invariably departed from Cuiabá groaning with gold.

In 1979, Mato Grosso was divided into two states, **Mato Grosso** in the north and **Mato Grosso do Sul** in the south. Since then, Cuiabá has enjoyed enormous development in education, tourism, and construction. In 1989-1990, three shows on TV claiming that gold had been found on the streets (!) of Cuiabá magnetized a stream of Northeasterners and *Mineiros*, who arrived with little more than dreams in their pockets. As a result, a rash of frontier towns rose up, most of them approximating slums. One such town is **Cangas**, 10 minutes from Cuiabá on the Cuiabá-Santarém Highway, the site of six or seven gold mines. Founded about seven years ago, Cangas today is a scene straight out of a Wild West movie, with two big bars, three small snack bars, one school, three churches, three gas stations, and a single public phone (for all 5,000 people). As one local told

me, "There's only one phone because most people here have no one
to call."

UP CLOSE TIP: *During the dry season, airplane descents into
Cuiabá can be turbulent due to the smoky warm air from fires set
by cattle ranchers every dry season to burn off undesirable
vegetation and promote fresh grass for fodder. Aug. is the peak
month for these fires, and sometimes flights are cancelled for
several weeks, forcing travelers to take five-hour bus trips from
the nearest open airport. During the rainy season, flights may be
delayed due to inclement weather.*

A Bird's-Eye View

Cuiabá is nicknamed the **Garden City** because of its many trees,
including 200-year-old palms. The main plaza, **Praça da República,**
is dominated by an old church, the Hotel Excelsior, and a 12-story
television tower on a nearby hill. Next to the tower is the alabaster
minaret of a Muslim temple. The **Igreja de Bom Jesus dos Passos,**
an 18th-century church with an exquisite Gothic facade, offers a
great vista of the city. The tourist office, **TURIMAT,** is off the main
plaza near the Igreja Matriz.

Sights

Praça Moreira Cabral (Geodesic Center)

Although the mirante in Chapada is considered a more scenic
representation of the geodesic center of South America, the exact
point is here, in Cuiabá. The site is marked by a monument and
pyramid in a small concrete park facing the Legislative Assembly.
It is considered to cover a 50-km./31-mile radius (of which Chapada
forms one end). The *praça* can be entered from Rua Barão de
Melgaço.

Fish Market

Buying and selling the day's fresh catch takes place along the **Rio
Cuiabá** daily from 4 a.m.-6 p.m.

Horto Florestal Bairro Coxipó (City Park)

At the confluence of the Rio Coxipó and Rio Cuiabá; access through Avenida Fernando Correa da Costa. Daily 7 a.m.-5:30 p.m. Guides available 2-5 p.m.

The future park of the city is being planned on this tropical landscape where children can scamper around playgrounds made from logs. On the docket for the future is an orchid greenhouse, an exposition of seeds and plants natural to the forest, and a special display of medicinal plants.

Comunidade São Gonçalo (Crafts Commune)

Located near the Fazenda de Mato Grosso, this primitive community sits on the banks of the Rio Cuiabá and supports itself totally through artisanry (especially pottery) and folkloric presentations. Visitors are always welcome; just seeing the rural lifestyle should prove fascinating. The community's major festival is held on Jan. 10, the **Feast of São Gonçalo**, when colorful boats proceed upriver to herald the arrival of the saint.

Museums & The Zoo

Museu de Artesanato

Rua 13 de Junho, Praça Maj. João Bueno. Tues.-Sun. 10 a.m.-3 p.m., 6-11 p.m.

Next door to the Casa do Artesão (a fine crafts store) is a museum of folkloric art situated in a frontier-styled, brick-and-wood house, complete with an antique kitchen. Featured are ornaments and weapons from the Xavantes and other Mato Grosso tribes, as well as leather goods from the home-on-the-range culture. Especially intriguing is the leather *bornal*, a contraption that was strapped around a horse's mouth so it could walk and eat millet at the same time.

Museu do Índio Marechal Candido Rondón

Located at the University Federal of Mato Grosso.

This museum displays artisanry, weapons, and ornaments crafted by the state's indigenous peoples.

Universidade Federal do Mato Grosso (Mini Zoo)

Av. Fernando Correa da Costa. Best times to visit: 6-8 a.m. and 3:30-7 p.m. to avoid sunstroke (1 p.m. is deadly). Interior is open daily 7-11 a.m. and 1:30-7 p.m. Closed Mon.

UFMT displays the fauna and flora of the region in an outdoor natural environment that features snakes, jaguars, monkeys, birds, and ostriches. On the far side of well-secured fences, animals such as capybaras, egrets, garças, alligators, and land turtles all seem to live in harmony, although some appear to be collapsed from the heat. A university restaurant near the parking lot goes on strike a lot, but is a nice place to meet young people. To reach the zoo, take the city bus labeled "Copamel Universidade" or "Santa Cruz."

Where To Stay

If you don't want to find a veritable zoo in your hotel room (i.e., frogs in your toilet and cockroaches the size of capybaras in the closet), you'll have to pay for a bug-free environment in Cuiabá.

In the hot clime, air conditioning is essential, and if you are returning from an excursion, you'll appreciate a good laundry service. See page v, at the beginning of this book, for price chart.

Veneza Palace Hotel

Av. Coronel Escolástico, 738 (Bandeirantes); ☎ *(65) 321-4847; fax 322-5212.*

This perfectly respectable, impeccably clean three-star has an oriental lobby and a pleasant staff. The carpeted apartments are small, but the air conditioning is ice-cold, and the wood furniture attractive. All rooms come with color TV, mini-bar, and carpet. Safes are at the reception. Laundry is available.

The restaurant, which favors international cuisine, serves an excellent *canja de galinha* (chicken soup). There's also a pool, TV/playroom, and an American bar. Superior singles run $46, doubles $61. *78 apts. Moderate. All cards.*

Hotel Fazenda de Mato Grosso

Rua Antônio Dorileo, 1200 (Coxipó); ☎ *361-2980.*

Only six km. from the city, this farm-like complex is surrounded by 19 hectares of forested land – a kind of "civilized wilderness." The rustic apartments are housed in one- and two-story buildings with traditional tiled roofs; all have air conditioning, color TV, mini-bar, and phone. Clean and attractive, the bathrooms are appointed in tile and marble.

On the grounds is a mini-zoo with snakes, garças and capybaras; there's also a large pool and playground surrounded by tropical vegetation. Horses, paddleboats and other sports are included in the daily rate, as is breakfast. Transportation to the city is provided for convention groups. *50 apts. Moderate. All cards.*

Il Palace Hotel

Rua Alziro Zarur, 312; (Boa Esperança); ☎ *(65) 361-1858.*

For budget travelers only. A single in this three-story hotel is absolutely basic – little closet space, a slight mustiness, somewhat dirty walls, but a well-equipped mini-bar. Location is near a pharmacy and several restaurants. Singles have fans, but the doubles are worth splashing out on for the air conditioning. *Inexpensive. No cards.*

Where To Eat

Recanto do Bosque

Rua Cândido Mariano, 1040; ☎ *323-1468. 11:30 a.m.-3 p.m., 7 p.m.-midnight.*

Trees grow right through the middle of this open-air restaurant, the best rodízio in town, situated under a grass roof. Eighteen cold salads and all-you-can-eat meat; Sat. features *feijoada.*

After 5 p.m., beer is half-price and barbecued fish is included. Discounts for groups of 15 or more. *Inexpensive. All cards.*

Taberna Portuguesa

Av. XV de Novembro, 40; ☎ *321-3661. 11 a.m.-2:30 p.m., 6-11:30 p.m. Mon. lunch only.*

About one km. from the center of town, this cozy, air-conditioned Portuguese tavern is piquant with the smells of home cooking.

Codfish runs about $9, *caldeirada* (a thick fish soup made with white wine, potatoes, onions, pimentos, and tomato sauce) runs about $13, an award-winning paella about $20. Dishes usually serve two. *Moderate. No cards.*

O Regionalíssimo

Rua 13 de Junho (Praça João Bueno); ☎ *322-3908. 11:30 a.m.-2:30 p.m., 7:30-11 p.m. Live music Thurs.-Sun., closed Mon.*

Next to the Casa do Artesão, this charming adega features some of the best regional cuisine in Cuiabá. Local folkloric musicians serenade the buffet, which changes daily; you might find fried fish, *peixe ensopado, farofa de banana, carne de sol,* and other delicacies. Alas, no air conditioning, but a steady breeze whips through the open brick arches. *Moderate. No cards.*

Mamma Aurora

Rua Miranda Reis, 386; ☎ *322-4339. 6 p.m.-midnight.*

Best pizzeria in town. Live music. *Inexpensive. No cards.*

Nightlife

Nightlife in Cuiabá is as hot as you will find in the Pantanal, or even in Mato Grosso – north or south.

Discoteca Logan
Best disco for the 18-40 set.

Get Up Dance
Avenida Fernando Corrêa da Costa, 1953; ☎ *323-3335.*
Another dance spot.

Mirante Bar
Avenida Miguel Smith, in front of the Plaza Motel.
For local bands and solo singers performing MPB.

Shopping

Casa do Guaraná
Avenida Mário Corrêa, 310; ☎ *321-7729.*
Situated in the barrio of Porto, the oldest district in Cuiabá, this "House of Guaraná" makes a fascinating showcase for Brazilian ingenuity, featuring products made from the plant most known for its stimulating kick to the nervous system. Here you can buy "sticks" of guaraná that you can grate into a powder in the traditional way, or you may buy the powder loose. *Xarope de guaraná* is a syrup that is drunk as juice (just add water). The store also features *licor de pequi* (a liqueur made from a typical fruit of the cerrado), and *serrinhas de unha* (nail files made from fish scales). You can stock up on natural herb shampoos and cosmetics, as well as stunning Pantanal T-shirts.

Casa do Artesão
Rua 13 de Junho, 315; ☎ *322-3908, 321-0603.*
Founded on May 15, 1975, this store, situated in an 18th-century blue-and-white colonial house, features some of the best crafts in the region. Good buys include *ganzas* (scraper-like percussion instruments made of wood) and handmade pottery. Absolutely exquisite are the embroidered hammocks that go for about $200 – steep, but so lovely you could hang them on the wall as decoration. Also for sale are indigenous Indian crafts such as bows, arrows, and basketry. A special room features homemade sweets and liqueurs;

don't miss the antique sugarcane machine in the garden. Next door is the Regionalíssimo restaurant.

Artíndia

Rua Comandante Costa, 942; ☎ 321-1348, near the Praça Rachid Jaudy.

The artisan store of FUNAI features crafts from the indigenous tribes of the Pantanal.

Mercearia Banzal

Av. Generoso Ponce (no number), Mercado Municipal Box 1/2/3 (downtown); ☎ 321-7518.

Macrobiotic and natural products, including brown rice, miso, and tofu are sold here.

Healers

Cuiabá and Chapada dos Guimarães have attracted a steady stream of holistic health practitioners during the last 10 years. Among the best are those listed below.

Centro de Vivências Para Integração do Ser

Rua Balneário São João, 323 (Coxipó da Ponte); ☎ 361-2215.

The city's most active alternative health center, offering a fine acupuncturist, Décio Cesar da Silva, as well as other practitioners in the fields of rebirthing, oki-yoga, massage, and more.

Ma Prem Dwari

Rua Doze, 297 (Boa Esperança); ☎ 361-5274.

Excellent masseuse and practitioner of Bach Flower Remedies.

Hands-On Cuiabá

Airlines

Flights to Cuiabá can be arranged from Alta Floresta (TABA), Belém, Belo Horizonte, Brasília, Campo Grande (Varig), Natal, Porto Alegre, Rio Branco, Rio de Janeiro, Salvador, Santarém, and São Paulo, among others.

Airlines Serving Cuiabá

Varig/Cruzeiro
Rua Antônio João, 258 . . . . ☎ 321-7333

VASP
Rua Pedro Celestino, 32 (Downtown)...... ☎ 624-1313
Transbrasil
Rua Barão de Melgaço 3508 .... ☎ 381-3347
TABA
Airport .... ☎ 381-2233

Arrivals

Aeroporto Marechal Rondôn is on Avenida Governador Ponce de Arruda (Várzea Grande); ☎ 381-2211. The *rodoviária* (**bus station**) is on Avenida Mal. Rondôn (on the road to Chapada dos Guima rães); ☎ 624-2085. For more information see *Points Beyond*, below.

Car Rentals

Nobre, ☎ 381-1651, can be found at the airport. There is also an office at Avenida Governador Ponce de Arruda, 980; ☎ 381-2821.
Localiza Nacional, Avenida Dom Bosco, 965; ☎ 381-3773; at the airport, open 24 hours.

Climate

Weather can change very quickly in Cuiabá. Basically, summers (Dec.-Feb.) are hot and humid (over 100°F), while winters (June-Aug.) are cool and dry (dropping to 60°F).

Money Exchange

If you're flying into the state of Mato Grosso from a major Brazilian city, it's best to exchange money before you leave; rates will undoubtedly be better. Traveler's checks can be exchanged at **Banco do Brazil,** Rua Barão de Melgaço, 915. In addition, good exchange rates for dollars are offered at the **Abudi Palace Hotel.**

Medical Emergencies

Hospitals are generally to be avoided in this region. For emergencies:

Hospital Geral e Maternidade
Rua 13 de Junho, 2101 .... ☎ 323-3322
Pronto-Socorro Municipal
Rua Gen. Valle.................... ☎ 321-7404

Pharmacy

Drogaria Avenida
Avenida Getúlio Vargas, 280 . . . .   ☎ 624-1305

Points Beyond Cuiabá

By Bus

Buses run regularly between Cuiabá and Chapada dos Guimarães. (For times, see under *Hands-On Chapada*). Buses are also available to São Felix do Araguaia, São José dos Quatro Marcos, Guiratinga, Rio do Casca, Paranatingam, Paxaréo, and D. Aquino, among other places. You can also reach the Véu de Noiva (a waterfall and mountain) by local bus, which will leave you off after Buriti if you tell the driver in advance.

By Air

Flights are available to Alta Floresta, Belém, Brasília, Belo Horizonte, Corumbá, Fortaleza, Manaus, Porto Alegre, Recife, Porto Velho, Rio Branco, Rio de Janeiro, Salvador, Santarém, São Paulo, and other towns.

Private Guides

Amilton Martins da Silva, ☎ *322-3702*, can provide names of city guides who speak English. He is the president of the local Guide Association, and is a very good guide himself. **Carlos Wolff,** ☎ *661-1469*, is another English-speaking guide.

Telephone

Local and international phone calls can be made from the telephone company **Telemat,** Rua Barão de Melgaço, 3195, during commercial hours. There is also an office at the bus station and the airport.

Travel Agencies

Cidade Turismo

Rua Duque de Caxias, 59 (Alvorada); ☎ *(65) 322-3702.*

Director Amilton Martins da Silva specializes in cinematography, film crews, ecological tours, and VIP service. Arrangements for treks by boat, jeep, or plane can also be made. Four-hour city tours can be arranged, including lunch at a regional restaurant.

Expeditours (Pantanal Explorers)

Av. Ponce de Arruda, 670 (near the airport); ☎ *(65) 381-4959, 381-5674.*

Perhaps the leading eco-tour agency in Brazil, Expeditours mans an office in Cuiabá near the airport, where clients headed for Pantanal river cruises and Chapada dos Guimarães are received. (Their base office is in Rio.) One of the most serious eco-tour operators in Brazil, owner André von Thuranyi is not only deeply committed to preservation, but is also well tuned to the mystical aspects of the countryside. His efficient English-speaking staff can arrange accommodations at any of the *pousadas* listed below, as well as transportation and accommodations throughout the country, including the Amazon.

Tourist Information

The state tourist board, **Turimat**, is at Praça da República, 131 (downtown); ☎ *(65) 322-5363.* Information booths can also be found at the airport and the bus station, offering maps and some general assistance on car rentals and hotels. For major excursions, it's best to contact the travel agencies above.

When To Go

Chapada presents a **Winter Festival** in July.

CHAPADA DOS GUIMARÃES

Chapada dos Guimarães is simply an extraordinary place. More than a half-mile above sea level, it boasts a variety of microclimates that allow for the coexistence of an enormous variety of plants and animals. Geological studies have shown that life existed here over 45,000 years ago, and mystics predict that future civilizations will be born here. Exactly what that means for the average visitor is obscure, but it can't be denied that most tourists immediately feel a strong sense of clarity and well-being here, and many are inclined to stay longer than they had initially planned. Frankly, it's my favorite place in Brazil, if not the world.

Spirits are said to live in the totem-like rock near Chapada dos Guimarães.

Chapada is at the 15th degree parallel, on line with such cities as Porto Seguro, Bahia (the birthplace of Brazil), Brasília (the futuristic capital), and Ilhéus. Such a location has great symbolism among Brazilians; many prophecies have suggested that Chapada dos Guimarães will be the birthplace of the Third Millenium. If you're a fan of Sedona, Arizona, you might recognize the same kinds of vibes here – a mixture of gorgeous landscape and mystical energy generated by numerous psychics, healers, and "Green People," who have moved to Chapada over the last 20 years. Not surprisingly, spiritual beliefs run rampant here. Some locals even believe there is a magnetic hole over Chapada that allows for communications with extraterrestrials. Indeed, something magnetically fishy is going on down here since car batteries and cameras are notorious for malfunctioning on cloudy days (mine did). Without much effort, you're sure to find residents who claim to have personally tape-recorded conversations with ETs; the topics generally seem to concern saving the environment.

History

Chapada's recorded history began when the Jesuits built a little chapel in 1751. By 1779, Chapada had become a primitive baroque city, its newly built cathedral marked by two imposing towers that were later felled by heavy rains. *Bandeirantes* from São Paulo swarmed over the area, looking for gold to mine and Indians to subjugate; the first sugarcane plantation was established, later becoming famous for its *cachaça*. Supplies were so limited in this isolated region that locals were often forced to trade large hunks of gold for the simplest foods imported from São Paulo.

In the 1930s, a group of Americans left Bahia to found an evangelical mission at Buriti, Chapada's first farm. Today, the pastoral estate is an agricultural school, but the American-made church and colonial houses still look like something out of New England. In more recent times, Chapada has become famous for its waterfalls, rock formations, and UFO sightings. Every year a **Winter Festival** brings artists and craftspersons to the region in July.

A Bird's-Eye View

The town of Chapada is 73 km./45 miles north of Cuiabá, (with access on MT 251). No one knows how many people live there; some say about 6,000, but it's rumored another 15,000 live in the surrounding area. The main square is full of flowers and trees and makes a peaceful core to the town; the majority of restaurants are located here, as well as the oldest church in Mato Grosso, the **Igreja de Senhora Sant'Ana**, built in 1779 with the help of the local Indians. Today chickens scratch around in its courtyard, but inside is a magnificent dusty old chapel. Of particular note is the statue of Joseph wearing boots, a symbol of the gold miners who lived in the area. During my visit, an old couple was valiantly trying to clean the church from the soot that continually blows in from the burning fields – a sad reminder of the forest's destruction.

Sights

The drive from Cuiabá to the national park of Chapada dos Guimarães offers some of the most thrilling vistas in Brazil. Taking MT-2551 (Cuiabá-Chapada Road), you'll first pass verdant rolling hills and glimmering lakes, behind which looms a massive mountain range washed in purples and blues. Suddenly, the rocky skyline is accentuated by vertical cliffs standing like sentinels – a dramatic contrast to the shrunken brown-and-green shrubbery lining the highway. This is the beginning of the Planalto Central (Central Plains) of Brazil, a magnificent inland sea 10,000 years ago that gradually dried to its present state.

Salgadeira

The first stop you must make is at this weekend spot, originally built by the government for tourists, but now a private enterprise. Nicknamed the "Beach of Mato Grosso," the area boasts a stupendous man-made waterfall where bathers can take a dip, as well as a restaurant complex with four bars, ice cream stands, bathrooms, and playground. Walking along a path into the forest you'll come upon a turbulent double waterfall, and at every angle another mystical nature scene, including steamy falls, natural grottoes, and *macumba* offerings tucked inside coves. Campgrounds are available, but please don't litter; policemen keep close watch. A few years back, the "green" community made a fuss here when trees were cut down to build the complex, but the environs are still so beautiful that it's hard to complain.

Portão do Inferno (Hells' Gate)

Nearby is this truly awesome canyon sculpted into dramatic shape more than a thousand years ago by natural erosion. The lookout point, a few feet beyond, is the subject of much gossip. Legend has it that the federal police threw "undesirables" off this cliff during the dictatorship, and at the beginning of Sarney's administration, a lot of Brazilians were rumored to have thrown themselves off when they lost all their money. Even today, a yellow car can be seen at the foot of the pit, reputed to have accidentally veered off the cliff, killing four or five people. These days, police maintain strong surveillance to avoid further incidents, but locals claim they can still hear the spirits of the departed crying at night. Three to four centuries ago, Indians roamed these areas, and the rock formations, which rise like phallic symbols along the highway, have helped create a number of legends. Local mystics like to think they are beacons for landing extraterrestrials. The big holes in the ground, however, are definitely made by local rodents. If you're intent on climbing these hills, be careful because the rock is soft.

Cachoeira Véu de Noiva

Six km. after Salgadeira, take a right turn onto a red dirt road and go a few hundred feet from the rock formations. The road takes you down to an open canyon graced with a slender 200-foot waterfall that looks like the veil of a bride (hence its name). During rainy season, the fall is more voluminous, but can become yellow and dirty-looking; in Aug., when I saw it, it was simply stunning, rivaling Iguaçu Falls, perhaps not in volume, but at least in grace. Sturdy trekkers will love the half-hour climb down to the foot of the waterfall (one hour back), but be forewarned: the inclines are abrupt. Also, the route is deceiving and doesn't look the same on the way down – just stick to the wall on the right. The fall is actually a big lake, which you can only see from the base, and the water and surrounding air are always cold, no matter the season. The canyon itself is a natural wonder, embraced by a forest and accentuated by vertical backdrops of red rocks. A snack bar serves beer, light fare, and *galinha com arroz* (chicken with rice).

Cachoerinha (Little Waterfall)

Eight km./five miles before you reach the city of Chapada (and an easy one-hour trek from Véu de Noiva) is this smaller waterfall. The *mata* (forest) here is being reforested by locals, since destruction of this environment could endanger the entire microsystem of the Pantanal. Walking down an idyllic woody path, you'll come upon a small waterfall jutting out of a rocky embankment; facing it is the perfect beachlet. A thatched-roof restaurant surrounded by a mixture of rainforest and cerrado is a perfect place to let the sound of crashing rivulets wash over you. It's also a great place to sun, but weekends are packed. The path to the left above the waterfall goes to Véu de Noiva.

Mirante

Considered the "picturesque" geodesic center of South America, this magnificent rocky cliff and mountain range is felt by many to be a point of high magnetic energy and one of the best places to sight UFOs, particularly at night. At the very least on a clear day you can see Cuiabá, 50 km./31 miles to the southwest. Do take the exhilarating walk down the rocky path to the right, until you reach the half-mile drop-off plateau; the trip back up is tiring but worth it. Hopefully, the litter marring the landscape has been picked up; be careful with cigarettes since fires start fast. Near the rock formations is a large amount of burned land, probably caused by human carelessness.

Parque Nacional

Founded about three years ago, the park covers 33,000 hectares; it is a national park in name only as the government does little to no maintenance. **Eco Turismo** is the only agency that conducts tours to the park's wonderful **Cidades das Pedras**, seven "cities" of rock formations situated among the gnarled trees of the cerrado. During the rainy season, this route, which must be navigated by truck or four-wheel-drive, is considerably less dusty than in dry season, and more animals, such as pigs, foxes, jaguars, tapirs, wolves, and coatis can be seen scurrying over the landscape. But even dry season is exciting. In Aug., the stunted carrado lends an other-worldy air to the forbidding rock formations, which can look variously like sacrificial altars, alligators, or Indian faces. Animals do approach at

An exquisite waterfall near town.

times; we clocked an emu running chase in front of our truck at 50 mph. Many of the rocks are over three million years old; on their side you can often see stratification lines where the ocean left its indelible marks. It's even possible to find chips of hematite and crystals embedded in the ground, as well as fossils engravened with fish shapes.

At the **Nascente do Rio Claro**, you can walk to the edge of a 1,100-foot cliff and witness an awesome vista of rivers and plateaus that could keep you mesmerized for days. The most unforgettable thing I saw here was the **Casa de Pedra**, a natural house of stone situated over a running stream that was surely the home of native peoples thousands of years ago. I dream of making an overnight camp-out here; the nearby waterfalls boast such clean water you could probably safely drink it. Our final trek in Chapada took us down a precipitous descent to what must be the most perfect cove in Brazil – a gorgeous waterfall embraced by a thumb-sized strand of beach, behind which is a craggy outcropping of rock.

Where To Stay

Chapada is a rustic town; so are the hotels. Fortunately, with such cool temperatures, air conditioning is not necessary. No *pousada* or hotel in Chapada has telephones inside the room. See page v, at the beginning of this book, for price chart.

Pousada da Chapada

Rodovia MT-251, km. 63, Estrada Chapada dos Guimarães/ Cuiabá, 2 km.,
☎ *791-1171. Reservations: São Paulo, ☎ (11) 231-4511; fax 791-1299.*

The nicest hotel in Chapada is, unfortunately, half a mile from the city, but the hotel provides free transportation. The red-tile, white stucco complex of four buildings retains a frontier colonial charm. Apartments, with raw wood furniture, are spacious, and tiled floors cut down on dirt. The deluxe suite, which sleeps four, is unusually elegant. On premises is a playground and outdoor pool, along with a restaurant that serves all three meals. The owner also runs the Fazenda Porto Jofre in the Pantanal, as well as the Selva Turismo travel agency. Singles with fan run $27, doubles $32, double the price for air conditioning. *38 apts. Inexpensive. No cards.*

Rios

Rua Tiradentes, 333; ☎ 791-1126.

Among the lesser-priced hotels, Rios rates as the best. A block from the bus station and near the telephone company, it looks like a private residence. Families stay here, as do the kind of hippie clientele that sport feather earrings. Bathrooms are reasonably clean. Rooms with TV are priced higher. Singles and doubles come with air conditioning. *18 apts. Inexpensive. V.*

Hotel Turismo

Rua Fernando Corrêa, 1065; ☎ *791-1176.*

From the street, this small hotel looks like a residential house, complete with crowing roosters. The rooms are simple and clean, if overpriced. The dining room serves lunch, dinner, and a small breakfast of fruit, bread, and coffee). Sun. features all-you-can-eat *comida caseira* (home-cooking). Air-conditioned rooms with mini-bar and TV; some have fans. *14 apts. Inexpensive. No cards.*

Pensão do Povo

Rua Fernando Corrêa, 825.

Located behind the church, Chapada's cheapest rooms are for those who don't care what bites them after they drop dead asleep. One communal bathroom for most rooms; two apartments have private baths. Some rooms have four beds, but there are no phones. *Cheap. No cards.*

Where To Eat

See page v, at the beginning of this book, for price chart.

Taberna Suiça

Rua Fernando Corrêa.

Open only on the weekends, but insiders consider this to be the best restaurant in town for international cuisine. Fri. serves only dinner. *Inexpensive. No cards.*

Nivio's Tour Restaurante

Praça Bispo Dom Wunibaldo, 631; ☎ *791-1206.*

Don't let the word "tour" discourage you. This Portuguese-styled house with blue-tiled walls and white stucco arches offers a veritable feast. No one ever knows what will be served, but it's invariably good in this one-room house. If temperatures rise too high inside, you can sit outside on the veranda on a residential side street overlooking the public swimming pool. (The natural water is piped in from the Prainha River several hundred feet away.) Chicken and rice dishes are excellent, as is the *prato feito* (meal of the day). *Inexpensive. No cards.*

Costelão

Road to Cuiabá, 2 km. (Aldeia Velha); ☎ *791-1102. 11 a.m.-3 p.m., 7-9 p.m.*

Good barbecue styled in a typical *gaúcho* house. *Inexpensive. No cards.*

Chapadense

Rua Ver. José de Souza, 535; ☎ *791-1410.*

Open for lunch, dinner on Sun. only. Small salon with home-style regional cooking. *Inexpensive. No cards.*

Gaia Bar

Off the main plaza.

This green-and-orange house is the hangout for the local "Green People," who are still reading Herman Hesse. Outsiders are sometimes scowled at, but yell *"Preserva natureza!"* and you'll be fine.

Borboleta Casa de Chá

Rua Fernando Corrêa, 446-B; ☎ *321-5307.*

A civilized teahouse in this dirty-boots wilderness is definitely refreshing. Indulge in *bolos* (cakes), *docinhos* (sweets), and *salgadinhos* (salty pastries), washed down with tea or cold beer.

Shopping

Achei Novidades

Praça D. Wunibaldo. 8 a.m.-8 p.m.

Next to the Gaia bar off the main praça, this is the city's premier crafts store, featuring jewelry made by the Xavantes Indians (who live about 750 miles from Chapada) and pottery from the Carajas tribe in the state of Pará. Other great buys are homemade liqueurs with *pequi cristalizado* (a tree typical of the cerrado). You can also buy modern art from regional artists. *No cards.*

Healers

Chapada, like Cuiabá, has a strong Green movement, as well as a New Age/alternative health community. If you ask around, you can easily meet students of various gurus (such as Rajneesh, called Osho here), Zen meditators, yoga enthusiasts, massage therapists, acupuncturists, and even psychic healers. There may also be a few lingering souls who speak Esperanto. The small brochure-like magazine *Tempo de Crescer!* lists various professional holistic practitioners and organizations in the Cuiabá-Chapada region.

Hands-On Chapada dos Guimarães

Arrival

The *rodoviária* (**bus station**) is at Rua Cipriano Curvo; ☎ *791-1280*. Buses run between Cuiabá and Chapada dos Guimaráes, at 7:30, 8 and 10 a.m., at noon, and at 2, 4 and 7 p.m., and returning at 6 and 9 a.m., noon, and at 1, 1:30, 2, 4, and 6 p.m. Buses also run to Brasilândia, Paranatinga, and other places.

Climate

From Apr. to Oct., – the dry season – temperatures range between 68 and 75°F, but temperatures can rise over 50° in just a matter of hours. The hottest months in the Pantanal are Dec.-Feb., when temperatures average 110-112°F. During dry season, it's important to drink lots of liquids to avoid dehydration. Starting in Nov., weather alternates between torrential rains and scalding sun. The most animals can be seen in Dec. and Jan.

Credit Cards

Chapada seems to have trouble processing American Express cards. A few businesses take VISA. (See below.)

Money Exchange

Come with a full stash of cruzeiros; few people accept dollars or credit cards. Even the Banco Brazil will not exchange dollars, though it is rumored the **Hotel Turismo**, Rua Fernando C. da Costa, 1065, ☎ *791-1176*, will.

Taxis

There's only one taxi in Chapada: contact **Eco Turismo**, ☎ *791-1393*, to find out who owns it that week.

Telephone

Posto Telefônico, Rua 223 Tiradentes, 390.

Travel Agency

Eco Turismo Cultural

Praça Dom Wunibaldo, 464; ☎ *(85) 791-1393, 791-1305.*

One of Chapada's premier trek agencies is owned by Jorge Belfort Mattos Jr., a university professor who, despite his Santa Claus girth, scampers up and down steep hills like a master. All his trips last between four and six hours, including transportation, light lunch, and water. Three main tours include the **Parque Nacional** (with the Véu de Noiva), the **Caverna Aroe Jari** with the Lagoa Azul, and the **Cidades das Pedras** (City of Rocks). Exciting two- to five-day packages, from $100-$282, including breakfast and one meal a day, can also be arranged (accommodations at Hotel Pousada or Turismo). Five-day tours include city tour and geodesic site, caverns, National Park, Cidades das Pedras, and horseback riding. *V.*

When To Go

JULY: **Winter Festival** mid-month.

CONTACTS & MORE

SPECIALTY TOURS

Specialty tours, especially those in the Amazon, are often the easiest and safest way to travel. The following agencies, most of them based in the US, are all reputable, but do take precautions. Cancellations and price changes are a way of life in Brazil, so you might consider taking out insurance against cancellation. And do read the fine print of any contract; usually you are required to take responsibility for your own health and property.

Brazil Nuts

79 Stanford St., Fairfield, CT 06450; ☎ (203) 259-7900, (800) 553-9959.

Owner Adam Carter is passionate Brazilophile who offers packaged tours of Rio, the Pantanal, the Amazon, Carnaval in Rio, Salvador, and others. Independent travelers can also take advantage of the "Rio Like a Native" program on a day-by-day basis, which includes various excursions to tourist sites and evening performances. The agency has also sponsored exciting culinary tours of Brazil and now has new adventures through the Amazon that include Gabriel da Cachoeira. Clients rave about their services. To contact the office in Rio upon arrival, ☎ (21) 255-6692.

The Adventurous Appetite

56 West 70th Street, New York, NY 10012; ☎ (212) 873-9067; fax (212) 496-1846.

Owned by Bonnie Kassel, this company specializes in distinctive cooking pleasure trips throughout the world, including an extensive tour of Bahia. Groups of 10 explore local markets and cook in private homes and with chefs of outstanding restaurants. In Brazil, a 15-day tour, costing $3,395 per person, includes Salvador, Praia do Forte, a weekend at Morro de São Paulo, sailing around Parati, and Rio. Next trip: Mar. 15-30, 1997.

Christine Chauvin, Ltd.
Adventures on Horseback-Personalized Travel

430 E. 56 Street, New York, NY 10022; ☎ *(212) 421-0671, fax (212) 935-0559.*

Christine Chauvin both organizes and leads exciting horseback treks over the most exotic landscapes in the world, including South Africa, Uruguay, the Kalahari Desert, and Brazil. In Brazil she has designed two tours: Rio Grande do Sul and the Pantanal, which she leads yearly. She also creates and prepares itineraries for independent travelers on any budget, drawing from her vast international experience in out-of-the-way places. Get on the mailing list for her well-written newsletter, *Travel Log*.

International Expeditions

One Environs Park, Helena, Alabama 35080; ☎ *(205) 428-1700.*

This company usually offers trekking journeys through the Amazon basin in Peru, but may have now extended trips into Brazil.

ICS Scuba and Travel

5254 Merrick Rd, # 5, Massapequa, NY 11758; ☎ *(516) 797-2133, (800) 722-0205.*

This company specializes in scuba expeditions throughout the world, including an extensive program in Fernando de Noronha. (For more information, see the section on Fernando de Noronha.)

Special Expeditions

720 Fifth Avenue, New York, NY 10019; ☎ *(212) 765-7740; (800) 762-0003.*

This company, aimed at the adventurous tourist, offers remarkable 16-day voyages aboard the 80-passenger *M.S. Polaris* from Manaus to Ciudad, Venezuela, traversing a thousand miles on the Amazon. Cost begins at $5,030 per person, double occupancy, including everything but airfare.

Ecotour Expeditions

P.O. Box 1066, Cambridge, MA 02238; ☎ *(617) 876-5817.*

A three-year-old company, Ecotour offers a nine-day Amazon journey with three meals a day, including a tour of Manaus. The cost is about $1,895 (plus airfare to Brazil).

Cosmos

☎ *(800) 851-0728.*

A pioneer of high-quality budget travel, Cosmos has developed seven escorted packages to Latin America. Tour prices, including airfare from Miami or Atlanta, range from $1,038 a person (double occupancy) for the seven-day "Mayan Mysteries of the Yucatan" tour, to $3,521 for the 22-day "South American Odyssey" package (Brazil, Argentina, Chile, and Peru). Airport transfers, accommodations, breakfast, and sights are included.

Rainforest Alliance

65 Bleeker Street, New York City, NY 10012-2420; ☎ (212) 677-1900; fax (212) 677-2187; E-mail: canopy@ra.org.

An international non-profit organization dedicated to the conservation of tropical forests for the benefit of the global community. Among the various programs they sponsor is a Conservation Media Center, the Amazon Rivers Program, Natural Resources and Rights Program, Small Wood Program and various grants for selected conservation projects. Recent publications include *Floods of Fortune* and *Tales From The Jungle*, two excellent books on the Amazon. Their website is: http:www. rainforest-alliance.org

International Study Tours

225 W. 34th St., # 913, New York, NY 10122; ☎ (212) 563-1327; (800) 833-2111.

IST offers educational and cultural tours. Trips can be arranged for groups, including a rainforest expedition out of Manaus (or a combination including Manaus, the Pantanal, Iguaçu Falls, and Rio), "Carnaval of Cultures" 12-day tour of Rio, Salvador, and Recife to explore samba and Afro-Brazilian lore; and an "Art in Brazil" tour, including stops in Rio, Brasília, and Ouro Preto. Trips run from seven to 13 nights. Lecturers are Brazilian university professors. Inquire about single arrangements.

American Museum of Natural History Discovery Tours & Cruises

Central Park West at 79th Street, New York, NY 10024; ☎ (212) 769-5700.

The museum offers a cruise down the Amazon on the 98-passenger *Explorer* from April 11-21, 1997. Lectures will be given by a team from the museum. The price: $3,400-6,724 (no airfare).

New York Botanical Garden

Trav. pgrm/NY Botanical Gdn, Bronx, NY 10458-5126; ☎ (212) 220-8700, fax 6504.

Special Amazonian tours for groups of eight to 20 are planned for the early dry season of each year. Cruises are taken on a small river boat built especially for the program, accompanied by guides who lecture on the botanical aspects of jungle life. Fee, including roundtrip airfare from Miami to Manaus, all meals, transfers, expeditions, and reading material, is $2,495.

Brazilian Views, Inc.

201 East 66th Street, Suite 21G, New York, NY 10021, ☎ (212) 472-9539.

This specialty consulting firm has previously offered several types of expeditions, including a 10-day Pantanal birdwatching tour, a (four-day minimum) fishing expedition to the Pantanal, a garden tour of Brazil and Argentina sponsored by four South American garden clubs, and a decorative fiber arts and folk crafts tour of Belém, Recife, Salvador, Belo Horizonte, Rio de Janeiro, and São Paulo. Write for current information.

F & H Consulting

2441 Janin Way, Solvang, CA 93463; ☎ (800) 544-5503, fax (805) 688-1021.

This extremely reputable firm, co-owned by Claudio Heckmann, a native-born Brazilian, works only with five-star hotels and Brazilian-owned properties. Claudio is also the coordinator for the Brazilian Tourism Information Center. In the US, contact F & H for the most up-to-date information on resort facilities, spas, and private islands and the Ariau Jungle Tower outside Manaus.

Brazilian Roots

Rua do Riachuelo, 44, 4th floor (downtown). Rio de Janeiro, RJ Brasil 20.230-014; ☎ (21) 252-2759, fax 232-9643.

Owned and run by two black Brazilians prominent in video, radio, and politics, this is a service promotion company specializing in international trade and tourism. The agency designs, plans, and executes international events and also offers special "Ethnic Cultural Tours" featuring the Afro-Brazilian culture of Brazil. They are skilled in bringing large groups of Afro-American tourists to Brazil.

Travel Agencies & Tour Operators

Abreu Tours

317 E. 34th Street, New York, NY 10016; ☎ (212) 532-6550, fax (212) 532-7153.

Handles groups of 15 or more on custom basis. Also specializes in Portugal.

Go To Rio Tours

551 Fifth Ave., New York, NY 10176; ☎ (212) 682-5310, fax (212) 963-2398.

Arranges FITs and groups throughout Brazil, with 24-hour guides and special requests. Also Amazon packages. Carnaval packages, minimum five night, average is nine nights.

Equitable Travel

654 Madison Ave., New York, NY 10176; ☎ (212) 682-5310, fax (212) 486-0783.

Arranges trips for individuals, particularly businessmen.

Panavian Travel

25 W. 45th Street, New York, NY 10036; ☎ (212) 719-2270, fax (212) 719-2273.

Discount airfares available throughout the year.

Tourlite

551 Fifth Ave., New York, NY 10176; ☎ (212) 599-2727, fax (212) 370-0913.

Handles package tours. The Carioca package (New York-Rio) runs six nights, with airfare and three-star accommodations, for $1,339 in high season; $1,959 with five-star hotel. The "Ecological" packages include two days in Manaus, two days in a river lodge, and two days in Belém, including hotel, airfare, transfer, and half-day city tour (New York departure, $1,899).

Transbrasil

500 Fifth Ave;, New York, NY 10110; ☎ (212) 944-7374, fax (212) 944-7458.

Ocean Line Cruises

The following companies offer cruises that make port in various Brazilian cities, including Rio de Janeiro, Manaus, Recife, Salvador and Santarém.

Holland America Line
300 Elliott Avenue West
Seattle, WA 98119 . . . .   ☎ (206) 681-3535

Odessa America Cruise Company
250 Old Country Road
Mineola, NY 11501 . . . .   ☎ (516) 747-8880

Ocean Cruise Lines
1510 S.E. 17th St.
Fort Lauderdale, FL 33316 . . . .   ☎ (305) 764-3500
. . . .   or (800) 556-8850

Regency Cruises
260 Madison Avenue
New York, NY 10016 . . . .   ☎ (212) 972-4499

Royal Viking Line
95 Merrick Way
Coral Gables, FL 33134 . . . .   ☎ (305) 447-9660
. . . .   ☎ (800) 422-8000

Sun Line Cruises
1 Rockefeller Plz, # 315
New York, NY 10020. . . . .   ☎ (212) 397-6400
Outside New York City . . . .   ☎ (800) 872-6400

Also see *Travel Agencies* under the various Hands-On sections of each city in *Amazônia* and *The Pantanal*.

ONLINE INFORMATION

http://www.deltanet.com/brazil/og.ag.atm
Surf through this rainforest art exhibit offering native tribes, brightly colored birds and lots of green stuff.

http://www.embratur.gov.br/sBook/Poll/Lottery
EMBRATUR, Brazil's official tourist board, presents information on each state and city, with hotel guides and a calander of upcoming events. Win free trips!

http://sensemedia.net/sprawl/21672
A Brazilian goddess website featuring Iemanjá, ruler of the oceans. E-mail direct to a Bahian guide and get information on beaches and restaurants.

http://darkwing.uoregon.edu/~sergiok/brazil.html
Tour virtual street markets in Rio, behind the scenes of soccer teams, São Paulo and the Amazon jungle.

http://pasture.ecn.Purdue.edu/agentml/agenmc/brzil/recipes .html
Choice recipes from superb Brazilian cooks.

http://www.solution.net/rec-travel/hostels/sa.br.html
Brazilian hostels, addresses, etc., with international affiliations. America Online (keyword Travel Forum, Message Boards, World Traveler, Brazil). Chat with other Brazilophiles who will tell you how much they wish they were there – now!

RAINFOREST SUPPORT GROUPS

Arctic to Amazonia

P.O. Box 73, Stafford, VT 05072.

An educational organization devoted to constructive, non-violent change in the world by facilitating dialogue between indigenous and non-indigenous peoples, particularly regarding social justice and the environment. Publishes *Arctic to Amazonia Report*, available with a $25 annual membership.

Rainforest Action Network (RAN)

450 Sansome, Suite 700, San Francisco, CA 94111. ☎ (415) 398 4404.

A grass-roots activist environmental organization working with indigenous land-based peoples in struggles to protect their rainforest homelands and cultures from rampant destruction. Available with a $25 annual membership is *World Rain Forest Report* quarterly, with monthly action alerts.

Amanaka'a Amazon Network

339 Lafayette Street, #8, New York, NY 10012; ☎ (212) 253-9502, fax 274-1773.

A nonprofit organization that sponsors an annual Amazon Week to promote public dialogues between Amazon leaders and their US supporters. Amanaka also publishes a quarterly newsletter on Amazon-related issues. Volunteer programs are available for those who want to commit themselves to political and social activism. Letter-writing campaigns and civil protests initiated by Amanaka have already had far-reaching consequences in the region. Other organizations involved in saving tropical rainforests include:

Conservation International
1015 18th Street NW, Suite 1002
Washington, DC 20036

Friends of the Earth/U.S.
218 DD, SE
Washington, DC 20003

Greenpeace
1436 U Street NW
Washington, DC 20009

National Resources Defense Council
40 W 20th Street
New York, NY 10011

Rainforest Alliance
270 Lafayette St, Suite 512
New York, NY 10012

Sierra Club
730 Polk Street
San Francisco, CA 94109

World Wildlife Fund
Panda House, Godalming
Surrey GGU 7 1 XRR
England

COICA
(Coordinating Body for the Indigenous Peoples'
Organizations of the Amazon Basin)
Jiron Almagro 614, Lima 11, Peru

HEALTH KIT FOR THE TROPICS

Jet Lag

Overnight flights to Brazil (nine hours from New York to Rio) can easily cramp your style. The time change from the East Coast is only two hours, but it's the long hours spent cramped in a seat, the night of lost sleep, and the airline food and drinks that can get you down. Here are some tips to minimize discomfort:

- Drink as little alcohol as possible before and during the flight.
- Avoid large meals for several hours after landing to shrink your stomach to its normal size.
- Chew gum slowly to relieve ear discomfort.
- Avoid gas-producing and greasy foods.
- Eat small portions starting two hours before takeoff. Eat high-fiber foods to avoid constipation.
- Drink one pint of liquid for every three flying hours to counteract the dryness of the cabin; water and fruit juices are best.
- Use eyedrops for dry eyes and take off your contact lenses.
- Eat simply and sparingly the first few days in Brazil.

Sunburn

According to Dr. Howard Sobel, Clinical Attending Physician, Dept. of Dermatology, Lenox Hill Hospital (NYC), Rio de Janeiro (and let's add all of Brazil) is one of the top 10 "sizzle-'n'-fry hot zones in the world (others include Death Valley, California; Nairobi, Kenya; and Phoenix, Arizona). Primary factors that contribute to skin-cancer-producing conditions are hot temperatures, proximity to the equator, higher altitudes that are closer to the sun and have fewer atmospheric impurities to filter harmful rays (watch out for those Brazilian mountains), lack of natural shade, and closeness to large bodies of water, which reflect and amplify light.

As the daughter of a dermatologist, I have to say that the best way to ensure a great time in Brazil is first to protect your skin and hair from ultraviolet harm. My father would have told you that no tan is safe. Tanning is actually your skin's natural defense against ultraviolet rays. The pigment melanin helps to prevent radiation from altering the skin's cellular DNA. Over time, not all DNA damage is repaired, and the risk of skin cancer increases. Excessive UVA exposure also promotes premature aging of the skin.

To minimize hazardous exposure, Dr. Howard Soble suggests the following:

□ Plan outdoor activities for early morning or late after-noon, because the midday sun causes the most damage to your skin.

□ Administer sunblock at least 30 minutes before expo-sure, and always to dry skin since water dilutes it. UVA rays that burn are strongest at midday, but dangerous UVA radiation is present as long as the sun is up, even in a shadowed forest.

□ Limit your first exposure to the sun to a few minutes, and gradually increase.

□ Make sure you wear a strong enough sunblock to mini-mize the effects of the dwindling ozone layer. A sun-block with an SPF rating of 15 or higher should do the trick; reapply it after you perspire or swim. And don't neglect those easily forgotten places: neck, decolletage areas, hands, tops of feet, ears, lips, and bald spots.

□ Choose clothing with a tight weave – fabrics with natu-ral SPF are unbleached cotton, high-luster polyesters, and some silks. Wear a wide-brimmed hat and polariz-ing sunglasses.

□ Treat sunburn pain with aspirin and a lubricating oint-ment like petroleum jelly or 0.5% hydrocortisone. By nightfall your skin will feel dry and tight.

□ Do wear hair products that have sunscreen. (Fredric Fekkai, a famous New York hairstylist, suggests wear-ing botanical oil on your hair, then adding his Gel Coiffant and Texturing Balm to prevent it from drying out.)

Diarrhea

Traveler's diarrhea is not preordained, though few escape it. It's usually caused by ingesting contaminated food and water or by placing your contaminated fingers in your mouth. The rule for all travelers: Boil it, cook it, peel it, or forget it. Also:

- ☐ Avoid street foods, shellfish, salads, and any uncooked or undercooked foods. Do not eat raw foods. Be careful which restaurants you choose. Deluxe international hotels are usually your best bet, since most use modern refrigeration, purify local water, protect foods from insects, wash vegetables in chemical solutions, and cook food properly.
- ☐ Eat only fruit with thick skins that you peel yourself. Don't drink milk in Brazil after noon (since it is rarely refrigerated and is delivered only in the morning).
- ☐ Always wash your hands before eating. Germs are picked up through handling money, souvenir shopping, door knobs, sand, and the ocean, etc. In remote areas, carry your own soap, toilet tissue, and handiwipes.
- ☐ Drink only bottled water. The carbonation in water (*água com gas*) acidifies it and kills microorganisms that may have gotten into the water prior to boiling. Be suspicious of juices or fruit drinks not prepared in your presence.
- ☐ Minimize the water you swallow when swimming.
- ☐ Use bottled water when you brush your teeth (found in the mini-bar).

If you do get Montezuma's Revenge, minimize food intake for several meals and drinks lots of liquids. Medications that you should pack are Pepto Bismol and Immodium (both available over the counter), Bactrim (prescription), and Lomotil (prescription). If you have bloody stools or fever, feel unusually weak, or if your symptoms continue for three days, see a doctor immediately. Dehydration is a severe risk. Drink fruit juices, carbonated soft drinks, or mix eight ounces of carbonated or boiled water with a quarter-tablespoon of baking soda alternated with a mixture of orange juice, a half-teaspoon of honey or corn syrup and a pinch of salt. Drink alternately from each glass until thirst is quenched and supplement with carbonated beverages, water or boiled tea. *(Information courtesy of the Centers for Disease Control, Atlanta, GA.)*

Tips For Drinking Water

☐ Always order mineral water (*sem gás*, without gas, or *com gás*, with gas). Insist it be opened in front of you.

☐ Avoid ice cubes in any drink; they are usually made from tap water. If you must have ice, put them in a small, clean, leak-proof bag inside your glass.

☐ Tie a colored ribbon around the bathroom faucet to remind yourself not to drink tap water.

☐ Carry an electric immersion coil for boiling water – to brush teeth or make tea or coffee. You will most likely need a current converter and a plug adapter (available in department stores and travel boutiques).

☐ Carry a small (unbreakable) bottle of chlorine bleach or tincture of iodine to disinfect water when boiling is not feasible. Add two drops of 5% chlorine bleach or five drops of 2% tincture of iodine to a quart of clear water. Let stand for 30 minutes. Commercial tablets available in the US to disinfect water are Halazone, Globaline and Potable-Agua.

☐ Travelers using filters to purify river water may soon find them hopelessly clogged with sediment and thus be forced to drink river water straight – a perfect way to contract amebiasis. Best to take a safe water supply with you.

Immunizations

Yellow fever is endemic in the northern half of Brazil, Vaccines are recommended for those going to jungle or rural areas. Suggested, but not required, are hepatitis and typhoid immunizations when traveling to areas of sub-standard sanitation outside the usual tourist routes. Persons working extensively in the countryside and on working assignments in remote areas should be vaccinated. **Tetanus shots** should always be updated.

Malaria

Malaria is transmitted by the bite of the female anopheles mosquito, which feeds from dawn to dusk. You can also get malaria from blood transfusions, or from using contaminated needles and syringes. Not every mosquito carries malaria, but one bite can give you the disease. In 1995 the Centers for Disease Control stated that all travelers to the Amazon Basin will be exposed to what is called chloroquine-resistant malaria. The recommended prophylactic is **mefloquine**, taken weekly and continued for four weeks after leaving the malarious area. You can also carry a treatment of Fansidar or doxycycline alone, taken daily. If you are pregnant or are planning to fly a plane or undertake any task requiring fine coordination, you should not take mefloquine since small doses have been known to cause dizziness and/or gastrointestinal upset.

Other Bug-Transmitted Diseases

Dengue fever has flu-like symptoms, with rash, over in about a week. Antibiotics do not help and no vaccine is available. Beware of hemorraghing. *Lleishmaniasis* is usually caused by sandfly bites; they attack most frequently at dusk and dawn. *Filariasis* is caused by larvae of worms injected into the body through the bite of a mosquito; usually only heavier exposure causes symptoms. Treat with Hetrazan. *Onchocerclasis* is a form of *filariasis*, or river blindness, borne by flies that breed in rivers. If parasites invade the eyes, total blindness can occur. Treat with Ivermextin early. **Chagas' disease** is spread by the reduid bug, usually found on roofs and walls of native huts. For more information, see the *International Travel Health Guide* by Stuart R. Rose, M.D.

Prevention

Cut down on your chances of catching mosquito-transmitted diseases by protecting yourself. Search your sleeping quarters and bed for hidden insects. Use insecticides, preferably pyrethrum-based, in your living and sleeping quarters (RAID Formula II Crack and Crevice Spray is good). And protect your bed (if outdoors) with mosquito netting (spray the inside of the netting with RAID Flying Insect Spray).

Mosquito and tick bites can be reduced greatly by using the appropriate repellents. Insect repellents with a DEET percentage between 35 and 50 are recommended. Clothing may be sprayed with DEET-containing repellents and the insecticide permethrin, available in many states as Permanone, or PermaKill 4 Week Tick Killer. If you are using a mosquito net, spray it with the same product. A good, lightweight, compact mosquito net well suited for the vagabond traveler is "The Spider"; contact **Thai Occidental**, 5334 Yonge Street, Suite 907, Toronto M2N 6M2, Ontario, Canada; ☎ *(416) 498-4277;* price $69.95.

Cholera

Cholera is an acute diarrheal disease caused by bacteria found in water contaminated by sewage. Although there have been serious outbreaks of cholera during the last few years in many Latin American countries, including Brazil, few Western travelers ever get seriously ill. Most illness occurs in native people who are undernourished and who regularly ingest large amounts of contaminated water. The main symptom is explosive, though painless diarrhea, which, if left untreated, may lead to fatal dehydration. Treating loss of fluids immediately is primary to recovery. A good idea is to carry Oral Rehydration Salts mixture distributed by the World Health Organization, which you should mix with safe drinking water and consume after every loose stool. If you can't drink enough to replace lost fluid because of vomiting or weakness, get to a hospital immediately. The best prevention is to pay attention to what you eat and drink.

Other Diseases

Schistosomiasis

Wading or swimming in fresh water can put you at risk for this disease, caused by parasitic blood flukes called schistosomes. The tiny larvae of these creatures bore into the skin and mature within the body. Some people disregard the initial symptom – a rash at the site of penetration – but four to 12 weeks later, fever, malaise, and coughing, along with diarrhea, usually sets in abruptly. It's often curable, but if left untreated can progress to more severe stages.

Hepatitis A

This disease can be transmitted by person-to-person contact or by contaminated food, water, or ice. The flu-like symptoms don't appear typically for two to six weeks and are soon followed by jaundice. The CDC recommends a **gamma globulin** vaccination for each three-month period. There's no specific treatment and normally healthy people recover on their own, but do see a doctor.

Hepatitis B

Travelers to the Amazon basin are at high risk for hepatitis B. Vaccinations are not required, but the CDC recommends one for health-care workers, long-term travelers, or anyone expecting to have intimate relations with locals in rural areas. The virus is transmitted through the exchange of blood products, daily physical contact, and sexual intercourse. The vaccine involves a series of three intramuscular doses, which should be begun six months before travel.

Typhoid Fever

Travelers in Brazil are at risk for typhoid fever when in small cities, villages, and rural areas. Although not required, the CDC recommends a vaccination for those straying from the regular tourist itinerary or staying more than six weeks. The disease is transmitted through contaminated food and water. Currently, the vaccine only protects 70-90% of cases, so continue to drink only boiled or bottled water and eat well-cooked food, even if you've taken the vaccination.

AIDS

As of press time, Brazil does not require foreign travelers to take AIDS tests. For a free four-page leaflet on how to travel abroad and not bring home acquired immunodeficiency syndrome, write Global Programs on AIDS, World Health Organization, Avenue Appia, 1121, Geneva 27, Switzerland.

Information Sources

For the most current information on traveling to tropical countries, contact the **Centers for Disease Control**, ☎ (404) 332-4559, using a touch-tone phone 24 hours a day. A recorded voice will direct you through a menu of information.

For an extremely useful bimonthly newsletter on travel precautions, write *Traveling Healthy*, 108-48 70th Road, Forest Hills, NY 11375.

An excellent 51-page booklet published by the American Society of Tropical Medicine and Hygiene discusses such topics as pre-trip preparations, immunizations, malaria prevention, traveler's diarrhea, etc. Write: Karl A. Western, MD c/o **ASTMH**, 6436-31st Street N.W., Washington, D.C. 20015-2342. Price $4. Everything you need to know about the latest travel-health requirements worldwide (updated annually) can be found in *International Travel Health Guide*, by Stuart R. Rose, M.D. Published by Travel Medicine, Inc., 351 Pleasant Street, Suite 312, Northampton, MA 01060.

Post-Trip Checkups

Many specialists feel there is no reason to have a post-tropics checkup if you are feeling well. In some cases, however, symptoms don't appear for weeks, months, or a year after the trip; you may even suffer intermittent attacks followed by periods of subsidence. The incubation period for malaria varies from five days to a month, and longer in some cases. In its initial stages, it causes flu-like symptoms, and if treatment is delayed, it can become potentially fatal. If you have any of the following symptoms, don't delay seeking immediate medical attention:

- [ ] **Gastrointestinal distress** (if diarrhea, loose stools, abdominal pain, or excessive flatulence continues for a week or more, you could be harboring parasites).
- [ ] **Fever** (never ignore fever coming out of the tropics – it could be malaria, schistosomiasis, roundworms, hepatitis A, or a sign of tuberculosis).
- [ ] **Rashes**, change in skin pigmentation, or swelling.
- [ ] **Persistent coughs**, possibly due to parasitic worms in the lungs or tuberculosis.
- [ ] Unexplained **weight loss**.

In all cases, it is best to go to a tropical disease specialist straight away. To find one in your area, call the local health department or the tropical disease unit of a nearby hospital. The new **International Society of Travel Medicine**, Box 150060, Atlanta, GA 30333, ☎ *(404) 486-4046*, should have a list of specialists. To request a nationwide directory of tropical disease specialists, send a stamped, self-addressed business-size envelope to Dr. Leonard C. Marcus, 148 Highland Avenue, Newton, MA 02165.

BOOKS & FILMS

Books

Luso-Brazilian Books, Box 170286, Brooklyn, NY 11217; ☎ *(718) 624-4000, (800) 727-LUSO, fax (718) 858-0690.* This is one of the leading distributors of Brazilian and Portuguese-oriented material. Write for a free catalog.

Photography

Manor, Graciela, text, and Mann, Haus, photos. *The Twelve Prophets of Aleijadinho.* Austin and London: University of Texas Press, 1976. Black and white photos, a short text, and a poetic essay by Carlos Drummond de Andrade on the character of Minas Gerais as seen through the eyes of the baroque sculptor Aleijadinho.

Verger, Pierre. *Historical Center of Salvador* (Centro Histórico de Salvador) *1945-1950.* Rio de Janeiro: Câmara Brasileiro do Livro, 1989. Black and white photos by a French documentary photographer in the 1940s whose reminiscences are still fresh.

Bruce Weber. *O Rio de Janeiro.* New York: Knopf, 1986. A sensual photographic journal by one of the world's leading photographers.

History

Alden, Dauril., ed. *Colonial Roots of Modern Brazil.* Berkeley: University of California Press, 1973.

Burns, E. Bradford. *A History of Brazil.* New York: Columbia University Press, 1980. Perhaps the most readable history of Brazil readily available in bookstores.

Conrad, Robert Edgar. *World of Sorrow: The African Slave Trade in Brazil.* Baton Rouge & London: Louisiana State University Press, 1986. A rich resource of details and culture, particularly helpful for anyone writing an historical novel.

Diffie, Bailey W. *A History of Colonial Brazil 1500-1792.* Malabar, Florida: Robert E. Krieger Publishing Co., 1987.

Freyre, Gilberto. *Order & Progress: Brazil from Monarch to Republic.* Berkeley and Los Angeles: University of California Press, 1986. A three-volume masterpiece by the premier Brazilian sociologist.

Freyre, Gilberto. *The Mansions and the Shanty: The Making of Modern Brazil.* Berkeley and Los Angeles: University of California Press, 1986.

Freyre, Gilberto. *The Masters and the Slaves: A Study in the Development of Brazilian Civilization.* Berkeley and Los Angeles: University of California Press, 1986.

Maxwell, Kenneth. *Conflicts and Conspiracies: Brazil and Portugal 1750-1808.* Cambridge University Press, 1973. Interesting analysis explaining why Brazil adopted monarchical system of government instead of fragmenting into separate states.

Street Life

De Jesue, Maria. *Child of the Dark: The Diary of Carolina Maria de Jesus.* New York: Penguin, 1963. An extraordinary diary of a poor woman living in a São Paulo ghetto, originally written on scraps of paper. After her writings were discovered by a journalist, they were first serialized in the newspaper, then made into an instant bestseller. Nothing more honest and direct exists to describe the day-to-day struggle of living in a favela.

Dimenstein, Gilberto, introduction by Rocha, Jan. *Brazil: War on Children.* London: Latin America Bureau, 1991. One of Brazil's most outstanding journalists investigates the tragic world of underaged pimps, muggers, prostitutes, and petty criminals – all homeless children who live in fear of sudden death at the hands of vigilantes.

Trevisan, João, translated by Martin Forman. *Perverts in Paradise.* London: GMP Publishers, 1986. Written by one of the founders of the Brazilian gay movement, this is a fascinating, if severely biased, history of homosexuality in Brazil, from the Papal Inquisition to today's pop music idols. A provocative analysis of how homosexuality dovetails with the Brazilian traits of extravagance and social repression is followed by a startling interview with a candomblé priest. Write: GMP Publishers, Ltd., P.O. Box 247, London N15 6RW, England.

Native Peoples

Davis, Shelton H. *Victims of the Miracle: Development and the Indians of Brazil.* Boston: Cambridge University Press, 1977, reprint 1988. An anthropologist examines contemporary Indian policy in Brazil and discusses the devastation wrought on tribal life by highway construction and mining.

Hemming, John. *Amazon Frontier: The Defeat of the Brazilian Indians.* London: Macmillan London, Ltd., 1987. Covering the period from the mid-18th century to the early 20th century, this compelling analysis explains how and why the native cultures met their demise. The author is Director and Secretary of the Royal Geographic Society.

The Amazon

Head, Suzanne and Heizman, Robert, editors. *Lessons of the Forest.* San Francisco: Sierra Club Books, 1990. Essays from 24 leading authorities (biologists, ecologists, economists, and political activists), all committed to finding alternatives to rainforest decimation.

Hecht, Susanna and Cockburn, Alexander. *The Fate of the Forest: Developers, Destroyers and Defenders of the Amazon.* New York: Harper Perennial, 1990. A deeply researched and searing work exploring the history of the rainforest from the conquistadors to the gold miners to the military dictatorship. It also sheds new light on the role of Chico Mendes and other activists.

Lamb, F. Bruce. *Wizard of the Upper Amazon: The Story of Manuel Córdova-Rio.* Boston: Houghton-Mifflin, 1975. Written by a Peruvian healer held captive by Amazonian Indians, this is a mesmerizing document of life in a South American tribe, including descriptions of rituals using ayahuasca – a hallucinogenic tonic made from Amazonian plants.

Lewis, Scott, preface by Robert Redford. *The Rainforest Book: How You Can Save the World's Rainforests.* Los Angeles: Living Planet Press, 1990. An extremely easy-to-read book that explains how rainforests are being destroyed, why we should preserve them, and what we can do to save them from destruction.

Kane, Joe. *Running the Amazon.* New York: Knopf, 1989. A must-read for the armchair adventurer, this eyewitness account of traversing the Amazon River was written by a formerly office-bound journalist whose pre-trip naiveté was matched only by his unexpected fearlessness.

Matthiessen, Peter. *The Cloud Forest.* New York: Penguin, 1961, 1989. Zen master Matthiessen criss-crossed 20,000 miles of South American wilderness, from the Amazonian rainforests to Machu Picchu and Mato Grosso. Stylish, ironic, and insightful.

Plotkin, Mark. *Tales From A Shaman's Apprentice.* New York: Viking, 1993. One of the world's leading ethnobotanists recalls his harrowing adventure with some remote medicine men in the Amazon. Great to read before, during, and after your trip.

Popescu, Petru. *Amazon Beaming.* New York: Viking, 1991. When world-class photographer Loren McIntyre was kidnapped by an Amazonian tribe, he found himself descending, unwillingly, into another level of perceptual reality that ultimately changed his life. This amazing Twilight Zone story is told by Romanian filmmaker Petru Popescu.

Shoumatoff, Alex. *The Rivers Amazon.* San Francisco: Sierra Club Books, 1978 and 1986. A staff writer for *The New Yorker* and a premier commentator on Brazilian affairs resolved to spend his 30th birthday in the Amazon. His reminiscences of negotiating headwaters, mosquitoes, exotic vegetation, and wildlife, as well as all manner of bureaucratic red tape, lie somewhere between poetry and science.

Pantanal

Banks, Vic. *The Pantanal: Brazil's Forgotten Wilderness.* San Francisco: Sierra Club Books, 1991. Photojournalist and cinematographer Vic Banks chronicles his lively adventures in the Pantanal, accompanied by photos. Also included is a good overview of the political dilemmas of the region.

Art & Architecture

Epstein, David. *Brasília: Plan and Reality. A Study of Planned and Spontaneous Urban Development.* Berkeley: University of California Press, 1973.

Holston, James. *Brasília: The Modernist City. An Anthropological Critique.* Chicago & London: University of Chicago Press, 1989.

Music

McGowan, Chris and Ricardo Pessanha. *The Brazilian Sound.* New York: Billboard Books, 1991.

Perrone, Charles. *Master of Contemporary Brazilian Song: MPB 1965-1985.* Austin: University of Texas Press, 1989.

Roots & Culture

Amado, Jorge. *Bahia de Todos Os Santos (Guia de ruas e mistérios).* A mystical guide to Salvador's streets and icons by Brazil's foremost novelist (Portuguese).

Religion

Brumana, Fernando Giobellina and Elda Gonzales Martinez. *Spirits from the Margin: Umbanda in São Paulo.* Stockholm: Wicksell International, 1989.

Bastide, Roger, translated by Helen Sebba. *The African Religions of Brazil: Toward a Sociology of the Interpretation of Civilizations.* Baltimore and London: Johns Hopkins Uniiversity, 1960. The leading analysis of Brazilian religious cults by a noted French social scientist.

Galembo, Phyllis. *Divine Inspiration: Benin to Bahia.* New Mexico: University of Albuquerque Press, 1993. An exquisite photo album with a foreword by David Byrne and various essays celebrating the ritualistic "theater" of African and Afro-Brazilian trance cult religions. The folkloric-rich photos help explain how African traditions, as living elements transmitted orally, were adapted in Brazil without losing their sacred fire.

McGregor, Pedro. *Jesus of the Spirits.* New York: Stein & Day, 1966. An interesting analysis of African myths and rituals and their influence on the religious beliefs of Brazilians.

O'Gorman, Frances. *Aluanda: A Look at the Afro-Brazilian Cults.* Rio de Janeiro: Livraria Francisco Alves Editora S.A., 1979.

St. Clair, David. *Drum & Candle.* New York: Doubleday, 1971. An American journalist made a personal investigation into the psychic/spiritual side of Brazil and came out a believer.

Wofer, Jim. *The Taste of Blood: Spirit Possession in Brazilian Candomblé.* Philadelphia: University of Pennsylvania Press, 1991.

Samba/Carnaval

Guillermoprieto, Alma. *Samba.* New York: Random House, 1990. A marvelous account of one year in the life of Rio's Mangueira samba school, written by a former journalist with the soul of a poet.

Gardel, Luis. *Escolas de Samba.* Rio de Janeiro: 1967. Subtitled "A Descriptive Account of the Carnival Guilds of Rio," this book is a bit out of date, but the historical details of Carnaval are interesting. (The English edition is available in Rio's best book stores; try the one next door to the Copacabana Palace Hotel.)

Dance

Bira, Almeida. *Capoeira: A Brazilian Art Form: History, Philosophy, and Practice.* Berkeley: North Atlantic Books, 1986. The student of one of the great capoeira masters of the 20th century and now a master teacher himself in California, the Brazilian-born author writes poignantly about the history, philosophy, and form of the country's premier martial art. The book is filled with legends, songs, and tricks of the trade – valuable for anyone interested in ethnocultural studies.

Cuisine

Rojas-Lombardi, Felipe. *The Art of South American Cooking.* Harper Collins, 1991. Innovative Latin cooking by the late Peruvian owner of The Ballroom restaurant in New York City. Superb Brazilian delicacies.

Health

Rose, Stuart R., MD. *International Travel Health Guide.* Northampton: Travel Medicine, Inc., 1991. Written by a physician who is a member of the AMA and the American Society of Tropical Medicine and Hygiene, this book gives excellent advice about traveling in third-world countries and tropical jungles. Specific guidelines for individual countries, including Brazil, are denoted in detail.

Guides

The Best Of São Paulo. Hard-cover pocket-size guide written by a native Paulistano. Price, including shipping and handling, is $10. Write to: Editora Marca D'Agua, Avenida Cidade Jardim, 427 #124, São Paulo, Brazil 01453; ☎ *(11) 881-0753, fax (11) 883-5965.*

Humor

O'Rourke, P. J. *Holidays in Hell.* New York: Vintage, 1989. An irreverent and world-weary foreign correspondent for Rolling Stone reports from hellholes around the world. His chapter about driving on third-world roads is required reading for anyone heading to the Amazon or Pantanal.

Films

Black Orpheus. Directed by Marcel Camus, with music by Antônio Carlos Jobim and Luis Bonfá, this stunning movie retells the Orpheus tale through the eyes of a carioca streetcar conductor who figuratively descends into hell to save the woman he loves. A lush, if fantastical, view of Carnaval during the 1960s. Portuguese with English subtitles. (Available from Luso-Brazilian Books; see address above.)

At Play in the Fields of the Lord. Directed by Hector Babenco, this 1991 film preserves the moral intelligence of Peter Matthiessen's 1965 novel, but loses some of the adventure. Aidan Quinn plays a nerdy evangelist sent to convert an Amazonian tribe, which is also being invaded by a half-Cheyenne mercenary with his own savior complex. The footage of the jungle near Belém is colossal.

Medicine Man. New York magazine called this film "the most enjoyable bad movie in some time" – a big, messy emotional drama starring Sean Connery as a research scientist obsessed with finding a cure for cancer in the Amazon jungle. The shots of Connery and his sidekick, Lorraine Bracco, swinging over the forest on cables are exciting, but her jungle attire is all wrong.

Blame It on Rio. Michael Caine plays a businessman in São Paulo seduced by the nubile virgin daughter of his best friend. The film gives a beautiful view of Grumari Beach, but the token toplessness is not authentic to the region. Anyone going to Rio for the first time might tolerate the horrible script for the cultural glimpses of candomblé, capoeira, and samba.

Flying Down to Rio. This 1933 music and dance extravaganza featuring Fred Astaire and Ginger Rogers is unabashedly fun, especially the chorus line dancing samba on the wings of the airplane. Unfortunately, the music is more mariachi than Brazilian.

The Emerald Forest. A marvelous, near-mythical tale of an Amazonian Indian who tries – literally – to save civilization. The score alone is superb, and the clash between the white and native cultures is thought-provoking.

SELECTED DISCOGRAPHY

The following is an extremely subjective list of some of the best recordings ever. Stars (★) represent the music I cannot live without. Large stores in major US cities carry good selections; ask for a catalog. Do set aside time in Brazil to visit record stores, where you can listen before you buy.

Singer/Songwriters

★ Ben, Jorge. *Benjor*. Tropical Storm/WEA, 1989.
Ben Jorge and Gilberto Gil. *Gil Jorge*. Polygram/Verve, 1975.
Ben, Jorge. *Live in Rio*. Warner Bros., 1992.
★ Bethânia, Maria. *Alibi*. BR/Philips, 1988 (rpt.)
Bethânia, Maria. *Memória de Pele*. BR/Philips, 1989.
Bethânia, Maria. *Personalidade*. Polygram/Brazilian Wave.
Biglione, Victor. *Baleia Brazil*. Tropical Storm/WEA, 1989.
★ Bonfá, Luis. *Non Stop to Brazil*. Chesky Records, 1989.
Bosco, Joäo. *Dá licença meu senhor*. Song Discos, 1996.
Buarque, Chico. *Construção*. BR Philips, 1980.
Buarque, Chico. *Malandro*. Barclay, 1985.
Buarque, Chico. *Personalidade*. Polygram/Brazilian Wave, 1987.
Buarque, Chico. *Vida*. BR/Philips, 1980.
Carlos, Roberto. *Roberto Carlos*. BR/CBS, 1986.
Djavan. *Lilás*. CBS, 1984.
★ Djavan. *Luz*. BR/CBS, 1982.
Djavan. *Não é Azul, Mas é Mar*. CBS, 1987.
Djavan. *Seduzir*. World Pacific, 1990 (rpt).
★ Gil, Gilberto. *Dia Dorim Noite Neon*. Tropical Storm/WEA, 1985.
Gil, Gilberto. *Parabolic*. Tropical Storm, 1992.
Gil, Gilberto. *Raça Humana*. Tropical Storm/WEA, 1984.
★ Gil, Gilberto. *Realce*. Tropical Storm, 1979.
Gil, Gilberto. *Um Banda Um*. Tropical Storm, 1982.
Gilberto, João. *Chega de Saudade*. BR/EMI, 1959.
Gilberto, João. *Interpreta Tom Jobim*. BR/EMI, 1985.
★ Gilberto, João. *The Legendary João Gilberto*. World Pacific, 1990.
Gilberto, João. *Live in Montreux*. Elektra/Asylum, 1987.
★ Gonzaga, Luiz. *0 Melhor de Luiz Gonzaga*. BR/RCA, 1989.

Gonzaguinha. *É*. World Pacific, 1990 (rpt.).

★ Horta, Toninho. *Diamond Land*. Polygram/Verve, 1988.

Horta, Toninho. *Moonstone*. Polygram/Verve, 1989.

Joyce. *Language and Love*. Verve, 1991.

Joyce. *Music Inside*. Verve, 1991.

Lins, Ivan. *Awa Yiô*. *Reprise*, 1991.

Lins, Ivan. *Harlequin*. GRP, 1986.

Lins, Ivan. *Love Dance*. Reprise, 1989.

★ Lins, Ivan. *0 Talento de Ivan Lins*. EMI. Maria, Tânia. Bela Vista. Capitol, 1990.

Maria, Tânia. *Love Explosion*. Concord, 1984.

Nascimento, Milton. *Amigo*. Warner Bros., 1995.

★ Nascimento, Milton. *Anirna*. 1982.

★ Nascimento, Milton. *Ao Vivo*. Polygram. 1983.

★ Nascimento, Milton. *Clube da Esquina 2*. BR/EMI, 1978.

★ Nascimento, Milton. *Geraes*. BR/EMI, 1976.

★ Nascimento, Milton. *Milagre dos Peixes*. Intuition Records, 1992 (reissued).

Nascimento, Milton. *Missa dos Quilonibos*. Polygram/Verve, 1982.

Nascimento, Milton. *Txai*. CBS, 1992.

Toquinho. *Canta Brasil*. CGD, 1989.

Toquinho. *Made in Coração*. Elektra, 1990.

Toquinho e Vinícius. *Personalidade*. Polygram/Brazilian Wave.

Valença, Alceu. *7 Desejos*. EMI, 1992.

★ Veloso, Caetano. *Cinema Transcendental*. BR/Philips, 1979.

★ Veloso, Caetano. *Circuladô*. Elektra. 1992.

Veloso, Caetano. *Estrangeiro*. Elektra/Musician, 1989.

★ Veloso, Caetano. *Personalidade*. Polygram.

★ Veloso, Caetano. *Totalmente Demaiis*. Verve, 1987.

Vila, Martinho da. *Martinha da Vida*. CBS, 1990.

Viola, Paulinho da. *0 Talento de Paulinho da Viola*. EMI Odeon.

Singers

Alcione. *Emoções Reais*. RCA, 1990.

Alcione. *Fogo da Vida*. RCA, 1985.

Andrade, Leny. *Embraceable You*. Timeless Records, 1991.

Barbosa, Beto. *Beto Barbosa*. BR/Continental, 1988.

Belém, Fafá de. *Atrevida*. BR/Som Livre, 1986.

★ Calcanhoto, Adrians. CBS Discos, 1992.

Caram, Ana. *Rio After Dark*. Chesky Records.

Carvalho, Beth. *Das Bêncãos que virão com os novos amanhã*. RCA, 1985.

Carvalho, Beth. *O Carnaval de Beth Carvalho and Martinho da Vila.* BMG, 1990.

Caymmi, Nana. *Atrás da Porta.* BR/CID, 1977.

Costa, Gal. *Bem Bom.* RCA, 1985.

★ Costa, Gal. *Gal Canta Caymmi.* Verve, 1976.

Costa, Gal. *Personalidade.* Polygram/Brazilian Wave.

Gilberto, Astrud. *Astrud Gilberto Plus the James Last Orchestra.* Polydor, 1987.

Kenia. *Initial Thrill.* MCA, 1987.

Leão, Nara. *Personalidade.* Polygram/The Best of Brazil.

Lee, Rita. *Rita Lee.* BR/Som Livre, 1986 (rpt.).

Matogrosso, Ney. *Matogrosso & Mathias, vol. 14.* Chantecler.

Menezes, Margareth. *Kindala.* Mango, 1991.

Menezes, Margareth. *Elegibo.* Mango, 1989.

Mercury, Daniela. *Samba.* Sony, 1994.

Miranda, Carmen. *Carmen Miranda.* BR/RCA, 1989.

★ Monte, Marisa. *Marisa Monte.* BR/EMI, 1988.

Purim, Flora. *Midnight Sun.* Virgin Records, 1988.

Purim, Flora. *Queen of the Night.* Sound Wave Records, 1992.

Ramalho, Elba. *Personalidade.* Polygram/The Best of Brazil series.

Regina, Elis. *Elis.* BR/Philips, 1988 (rpt.).

★ Regina, Elis. *Elis & Tom.* Verve, 1974.

★ Regina, Elis. *Essa Mulher.* WEA Latina, 1988.

★ Regina, Elis. *Fascinação.* BR Philips, 1988.

Regina, Elis. *Falso Brillhante.* BR/Philips, 1988 (rpt.).

Regina, Elis. *Nada Será Como Antes.* Fontana, 1984.

Regina, Elis. *Personalidade.* Polygram/Brazilian Wave, 1987.

★ Regina, Elis. *Samba Eu Canto Assim.* 1983.

★ Sá, Sandra. *Sandra!* BMG Ariola Discos, 1990.

Simone. *The Best of Sinione.* Capitol Records, 1991.

Rock

Baby Consuelo. *Sem Pecado E Sem Juizo.* BR/CBS, 1985.

★ Cazuza. *Burguesia.* BR/Philips, 1989.

Kledir. *Kledir Ao Vivo.* Som Livre, 1991.

Lobão. *Sob 0 Sol de Parador.* BMG/RCA, 1989.

Paralamas do Successo. *Bora Bora.* Capitol/Intuition, 1989.

Paralamos do Successo. *Selvagem?* EMI, 1989.

RPM. *Rádio Pirita Ao Vivo.* BR/CBS, 1986.

Gaúcho

Borghetti, Renato. *Renato Borghetti.* BR/RCA, 1987.

Gaucho da Fronteira. *Gaitero, China e Cordena.* Chantecler.

Gildo de Freitas. *Successos Imortais de Gildo Freitas.*

Minas School

Azul, Paulinho Pedra. *Sonho de Meniio.* 1988.
Azul, Paulinho Pedra. Uma Janela Dentro dos Meus Olhos, 1984.
Franco, Tadeu. *Captivante.* Barclay, 1983.
★ Franco, Tadeu. *Animal.* Barclay, 1989.
Guedes, Beto. *Viagem das Mãos.* EMI, 1987.
Guedes, Beto. *Alma de Borracha.* EMI, 1986.

Instrumentalists

Airto, Moreira. *Saniba de Flora.* Montuno Records, 1988.
★ Moreira, Airto. *Identity.* Arista, 1975.
★ Moreira, Airto & Flora Purim. *The Colors of Life.* W. Germany/In +
    Out, 1988.
★ Assad, Sérgio and Odair. *Alma Brasileira.* Elektra/Nonesuch, 1988.
Alameida, Laurindo & Carlos Barbosa-Lima, Charlie Byrd. *Music
    of the Brazilian Masters.* Concord Picante, 1989.
Alemão (Olmir Stocker). *Longe dos Olhos, Porto do Coração.*
    Happy Hours Music.
Banda Savana. *Brazilian Movements.* Libra Music (Denmark).
Barbosa-Lima, Carlos & Sharon Isbin. *Brazil, with Love.* Concord,
    1987.
Biglione, Victor. *Victor Biglione.* Tropical Storm, 1987.
★ Castro-Neves, Oscar. *Maracujá.* JVC, 1989.
★ Castro-Neves, Oscar. *Oscar! Living Music.* 1987.
Cayymi, Dori. *Brasilian Serenata.* Qwest/Warner, 1991.
★ Elias, Eliane. *Eliane Plays Jobim.* Blue Note, 1990.
Elias, Eliane. *So Far So Close.* Blue Note, 1989.
★ Favero, Alberto. *Classical Tropico.* Tropical Storm/WEA Latina,
    1989.
★ Gandelman, Leo. *Leo Gandelman.* Secret Records, 1989.
★ Geraissati, André. *Dadgad.* Tropical Storm/WEA, 1989.
Gismonti, Egberto. *Amazônia.* EMI, 1991.
★ Gismonti, Egberto. *Dança das Cabeças.* ECM, 1977.
Gismonti, Egberto. *Dança das Escravos.* ECM, 1989.
★ Gismonti, Egberto. *Sol do Meio Dia.* ECM, 1978.
Gismonti, E. & Nana Vasconcelos. *Duo Gismonti-Vasconcelos.* Jazz
    Bühne Berlin/Repertoire Records, 1990.
★ Jobim, Antônio Carlos. *Passarim.* Polygram/Verve, 1987.
Jobim, Antônio Carlos. *Personalidade.* Polygram/Brazilian Wave.
Jobim, Antônio Carlos. *Urubu.* BR/WEA, 1985 (rpt.).

★ Jobim, Antônio Carlos & Gal Costa. *Rio Revisited*. Verve, 1989.
Lyra, Carlos. *Carlos Lyra: 25 Anos de Bossa Nova*. 3M, 1987.
Tiso, Wagner. *Baobab*. Antilles/Island, 1990.
Silveira, Ricardo. *Sky Light*. Polygram/Verve, 1989.
Uakti. *I Ching*. Point, 1993.
Vasconcelos, Naná. *Storytelling*. EMI, 1995.

Compilations

Alô Brasil. Tropical Storm/WEA Latina, 1989.
Afro Brasil. Verve, 1990.
Bahia Black Ritual Beating System. Island Records, 1992.
Black Orpheus (soundtrack). Verve, 1990 (rpt.).
Brazil Classics 1: Beleza Tropical, compiled by David Byrne. Luaka
  Bop/Sire, 1989.
Brazil Classics 2: O Samba, compiled by D. Byrne. Luaka
  Bop/Warner, 1989.
Brazil Classics 3: Forró, etc., compiled by David Byrne. Luaka
  Bop/Warner, 1989.
Brazil Classics 4: The Best of Tom Zé, compiled by David Byrne.
  Luaka Bop/Warner, 1989.
Luaka Bop. Sire, 1990.
Brazil is Back. Braziloid Records, 1987.
Brazilian Groove: Melting Pot. Lux Music Corp., 1994.
Djavan, João Gilberto, Toninho Horta. Capitol Records, 1990.
Lambada Brazil, featuring Caetano Veloso & Margareth Menezes.
  Polygram, 1990.
Nordeste Brazil. Verve, 1991.
Samba Brazil. Verve, 1991.
Sampler '89. Tropical Storm/WEA, 1989.
Sounds of Bahia Volume 2. Sound Wave Records, 1991.
★ *Violões*. Banera. (São Paulo), 1991.

Best Samba Recordings

Escolas de Samba Enredo. Sony Music. Collection with 10 CDs,
each dedicated to one of the great samba schools in Rio – from
Portela to Beijo Flor, with famous interpreters like Beth Carvalho,
João Bosco, and others.

Olodum, O Movimento. Continental/Warner. The famous
percussion band from Bahia, which made international headlines
with Paul Simon.

A História da Musica de Carnaval. Collector's. Eight cassettes
with rare recordings of sambas and marches extracted from 78s,

compiled by the famous musicologist José Maria Manzo. For more information, call in Rio, ☎ (21) 239-6367.

For Brazilian-influenced recordings by non-Brazilians, check out the releases of **Stan Getz, Pat Metheny, Basia, Chick Corea, Ella Fitzgerald, Manhattan Transfer, Dave Grusin, Lee Ritenour, Sara Vaughan, Weather Report,** and **Paul Winter,** among others.

The best cities to buy and hear music in Brazil are Rio and São Paulo (all genres), Belo Horizonte (especially the Mineiro School), Fortaleza (*forró* and *lambada*), Salvador (*afoxé*), Recife/Olinda (*forró*).

LANGUAGE

It's often been said that Portuguese is one of the sexiest languages in the world. If you are planning to spend any time in Brazil, it's well worth studying it seriously, even for a few months. Those who do are usually deeply moved by the sensuosity of the cadences and the vibrant vowel sounds – surely the secret behind the beauty of Brazilian music. Accents notwithstanding, continental Portuguese (spoken in Portugal), varies only slightly in word usage, although natives from Portugal are constantly lamenting the damage Brazilians have wrought on the mother tongue over their 500-year history. (Brazilians, for their part, consider their contributions enlivening.) Among other things, Brazilians have usurped a lot of Tupi, Arabian, and French words, not to mention English phrases, particularly in the field of advertising. Don't be surprised if, in the middle of a whirl of Portuguese, you suddenly hear more familiar words like "know-how," "marketing," "design," "outdoor," and "brainstorm" – all somewhat mangled by the Brazilian accent.

The easiest way to reap a smile from a Brazilian is to learn one choice phrase of slang and use it at just the right time.

Slang

Cool, neat (literally, legal)	*Legal! (leh-gow)*
How great!	*Que legal!*
Really, really great!	*Tri-legal!*
How neat!	*Bacana!*
What a joy! Neat! Cool! Fantastic!	*Jóia!*
Wow! No kidding.	*Puxa! (or Puxa vida!)*
Oh, my gosh (literally, Our Lady)	*Nossa Senhora (Nossa).*
Keep cool.	*Fica frio.*
Keep it going. Chill out.	*Fica numa nice.*
expert (adjective)	*craque*
You said it!	*Falô!*

Super (and even hiper, which is bigger and better) can be added to any word in Portuguese, i.e., *supermercado* (supermarket), *hipermercado* (even bigger supermarket), *super legal* (better than great), and *super bonita* (really beautiful).

These three proverbs should cover almost any situation.

Don't create a tempest in a teacup
Não fazer tempestade em copo d'água.

One who doesn't have a dog hunts with a cat (in other words, make do with what you have).
Quem não tem cão caça com gato!

A man is a devil that no woman can deny, but every woman wishes to be taken away by him.
O homem é um diabo não há mulher que o negue, mas toda mulher deseja que um diabo a carregue.

Airplane/Customs

Have you anything to declare?	*Tem alguma coisa a declarar?*
One suitcase of mine is missing.	*Faltame uma mala.*
Smoking is not allowed.	*É proibido fumar.*
I feel air-sick.	*Sinto-me enjoado(a).*

Common Questions & Phrases

Where is the bathroom?	*Onde fica o toilete (banheiro)?*
Flirting Hello	*Alô*
Hi, hey	*Oi*
Oops	*Opa*
Bye	*Tchau (as in ciao)*
Good-bye (until later)	*Até logo*
Good morning	*Bom dia*
Good afternoon	*Boa tarde*
Good night (good evening)	*Boa noite*
What's your name?	*Qual é seu nome?*
My name is . . .	*Meu nome é . . .*
How are you?	*Como vai?*
I'm fine, thank you.	*Bem, obrigado(a).*
Thank you (very much).	*Obrigado (muito).*
You're welcome.	*De nada.*
Excuse me (apology).	*Desculpe.*
Where are you from?	*De onde você é?*
I'm from . . .	*Sou de . . .*

Do you speak Portuguese/ English/Spanish?	*Você fala português/inglês/ espanhol?*
I don't speak Portuguese.	*Não falo português.*
Do you understand?	*Você entende?*
I don't understand.	*Não entendo.*
Please speak more slowly.	*Por favor, fale mais devagar.*
How do you say . . . ?	*Como se diz . . . ?*
What do you call this in Portuguese?	*Como se chama isto em português?*
What does " – " mean in Portuguese?	*Que quer dizer " – "?*
Want to go out with me?	*Quer sair comigo?*
Want to have a drink?	*Quer tomar alguma coisa?*
You're very beautiful.	*Você é muito bonito (a).*

UP CLOSE TIP: *Gosto de você is perhaps the most misunderstood phrase in Brazilian Portuguese. Depending on the tone, the body gesture, and the look in the eye, it can variously mean I like you (you're a nice person), I like you a lot (I hope we see each other again), I really like you a lot (let's be friends for life), or I really, really like you a lot (do you want to go to bed with me?).*

Directions

left	*esquerda*
right	*direita*
there (where you are)	*aí*
over there or yonder	*lá*
pull	*puxe*
push	*empurre*
here	*aquí*

Brush-Offs For Street Punks

Leave me alone	*Deixe-me em paz.*
Go away.	*Vá embora.*
Don't touch me.	*Não me toque.*
Don't bother me.	*Não me chateie.*
Don't bother me (stronger).	*Não enche.*
Help!	*Socorro*

Dates

Monday	*segunda-feira*
	(written as 2a)
Tuesday	*terça-feira* (3a)
Wednesday	*quarta-feira* (4a)
Thursday	*quinta-feira* (5a)
Friday	*sexta-feira* (6a)
Saturday	*sabado*
Sunday	*domingo*
weekend	*fim de semana*
yesterday	*ontem*
today	*hoje*
tomorrow	*amanhã*
the day	*o dia*
the month	*o mês*
the year	*o ano*

Numbers

Numbers in Portuguese use periods instead of commas, and commas instead of periods. For example, cr $3.500,75.

1	*um/uma*	17	*dezessete*
2	*dois/duas*	18	*dezoito*
3	*três*	19	*dezenove*
4	*quatro*	20	*vinte*
5	*cinco*	21	*vinte e um*
6	*seis*	30	*trinta*
7	*sete*	40	*quarenta*
8	*oito*	50	*cinquenta*
9	*nove*	60	*sessenta*
10	*dez*	70	*setenta*
11	*onze*	80	*oitenta*
12	*doze*	90	*noventa*
13	*treze*	100	*cem*
14	*quatorze*	101	*cento e um*
15	*quinze*	500	*quinhentos*
16	*dezesseis*	1000	*mil*

Time

What time is it?	*Que horas são?*
At what time?	*A que horas?*
How long does it take?	*Leva quanto tempo?*
When?	*Quando?*
Which day?	*Que dia?*

Official time in Brazil (buses, airplanes, etc.) is reported on a 24-hour system. Midnight is *meia noite*; one, two, three o'clock in the morning is *uma hora, duas horas, três horas*, etc., until noon, which is *meio dia*. One o'clock in the afternoon is reported as *treze horas*, two o'clock as *quatorze horas*, etc. In general conversation, use the 12-hour system (i.e., you'll meet for dinner at *oito horas* (eight o'clock).

at 1 a.m.	*a uma hora*
at 3 p.m. (official)	*às quinze horas (15:00 hours)*
an hour from now	*daqui a uma hora*
yesterday	*ontem*
today	*hoje*
tomorrow	*amanhã*
this week	*esta semana*
last week	*semana passada*

Dining

Waiter/Maitre d'	*Garçon/Maitre*
The menu, please.	*O cardápio, por favor.*
What's the specialty?	*Qual é a especialidade da casa?*
I don't eat meat/fish.	*Não como carne/peixe.*
A little more.	*Um pouco mais.*
The bill, please.	*A conta, por favor.*
Is service included?	*O serviço está incluido?*
I want a receipt.	*Quero recibo, por favor.*
The meal was superb.	*A refeição estava ótima!*
I'm full.	*Estou satisfeito (a).*
breakfast/lunch/dinner	*café da manhã/almoço/jantar*
a napkin	*um guardanápio*
a plate	*um prato*
a glass	*um copo*
a cup	*uma xícara*

Beverages

mineral water	*água mineral*
carbonated/noncarbonated	*com gás/*sem gás
coffee	*café*
tea	*chá*
milk	*leite*
black coffee in demitasse	*cafezinho*
soda pop	*refrigerante*
beer/draft beer	*cerveja/chopp*
wine	*vinho*
red wine	*vinho tinto*
white wine	*vinho branco*
with ice	*com gelo*
without ice	*sem gelo*

Cover/Condiments/Hors d'Oeuvres

cover	*couvert*	bread	*pão*
butter	*manteiga*	salt	*sal*
pepper	*pimenta*	sugar	*açúcar*
oil	*azeite*	vinegar	*vinagre*
without sugar	*sem açúcar*	sauce	*molho*

Fruits

fruits	*frutas*	apple	*maçã*
banana	*banana*	grapes	*uvas*
lemon	*limão*	melon	*melão*
orange	*laranja*	pear	*pêra*
orange juice	*suco de laranja*	strawberries	*morangos*

A smoothie with fruit, juice, and often milk and sugar is a *vitaminas*.

Seafood

seafood	*frutos do mar*	codfish	*bacalhau*
crab	*siri*	lobster	*lagosta*
octopus	*polvo*	oysters	*ostras*
shrimp	*camarão*	sole	*linguado*
squid	*lula*		

Beef

beef	*bife*	all-you-can-eat	*rodízio*
chops	*costeletas*	goat	*bode*
ham	*presunto*	lamb	*carneiro*
pork	*porco*	rabbit	*coelho*
sausage	*linguiça*	turkey	*peru*
veal	*vitela*	barbecue	*churrasco*
chicken	*frango/galinha*		

Vegetables, Beans & Pasta

salad	*salada*	carrot	*cenoura*
cucumber	*pepino*	green beans	*vagens*
lettuce	*alfaçe*	tomato	*tomate*
bean	*feijão*	pasta	*massa*

Cooked vegetables are referred to as *legumes cozidos*.

Money

cash	*dinheiro*
credit card	*cartão de crédito*
traveler's check	as is, or *cheque de viagem*
exchange house	*câmbio*
I want to exchange money.	*Quero trocar dinheiro.*
Do you exchange money?	*Você troca dinheiro? (dólares)*
What is the exchange rate?	*Qual é o câmbio?*
Can you cash a traveler's check?	*Pode trocar um traveler's check (cheque de viagem)?*

Getting Around/Directions

Where is the . . . ?	*Onde é o (a) . . . ?*
I want to go to . . .	*Quero ir para . . .*
How can I get to . . . ?	*Como posso ir para . . . ?*
Does this bus go to . . . ?	*Este ônibus vai para . . . ?*
Please, take me to . . .	*Por favor leve-me para . . . ?*
airport	*aeroporto*
bathroom	*toilete*
beach	*praia*

bus station	*rodoviária*
bus stop	*ponto de ônibus*
embassy/consulate	*embaixada/consulado*
gas station	*posto de gasolina*
supermarket	*supermercado*
market/street market	*mercado/feira*
street arts fair	*feira hippie*
movies	*cinema*
police station	*delegacia de polícia*
post office	*correio*
subway station	*estação de metrô*
theater	*teatro*
train station	*estação de trem*
Please stop here.	*Por favor pare aqui.*
Please wait.	*Por favor espere.*
I want to rent a car.	*Quero alugar um carro.*

Driving

Danger	*Perigo*
Dangerous bend	*Curva perigosa*
Service station	*Posto*

At the Doctor's Office

Call for the doctor.	*Chame o médico.*
I have a . . .	*Estou com dor . . .*
headache	*de cabeça*
sore throat	*de garganta*
stomach ache	*de estômago*
toothache	*de dente*
backache	*nas costas*
I have a bad sunburn.	*Estou queimado(a) do sol.*
sunstroke	*insolação*
food poisoning	*intoxicação alimentar*
I sprained my arm/ankle.	*Torci o braço/o tornozelo.*
I have a fever.	*Estou com febre.*
injections	*injeções*
cough medicine	*xarope*
aspirin	*aspirina*
tablets	*comprimidos*
ointment	*pomada*

tonic	*tônico*
vitamins	*vitaminas*
I need to go to the hospital.	*Preciso ir ao hospital.*

At The Hotel

I have a reservation.	*Tenho uma reserva.*
I need a reservation.	*Quero fazer uma reserva.*
I want to see the room.	*Quero ver o quarto.*
I want to see the manager.	*Quero falar com o gerente.*
a single room	*um quarto de solteiro*
a double	*um quarto de casal*
double room with bath	*quarto de casal com banheiro*
triple	*triplo*
with air conditioning	*com ar condicionado*
mini-bar	*frigobar*
safe	*cofre*
key	*chave*
What time is breakfast served?	*A que horas é o café da manhã?*
Can you wake me up at seven?	*Pode me acordar às sete horas?*
I need another pillow/blanket.	*Preciso de outro travesseiro/ cobertor.*
Where can one hire a car?	*Onde se pode alugar um automóvel?*
The air conditioning/heat doesn't work	*O ar condicionado/aquecimento central não está funcionando.*
Does that include all service & taxes?	*Estão incluídos o serviço e o imposto?*
Where is the manager?	*Onde está o gerente?*
I enjoyed my stay.	*Gostei da estadia.*
Thank you for your help.	*Obrigado/a pela sua ajuda.*

Shopping

Brazilian salespeople, especially those barely out of their teens, are sometimes overly eager to help. To have some breathing space, it's absolutely necessary to learn the password *Só olhando*, or "just looking." Other helpful phrases are:

How much?	*Quanto?*
How much does it cost?	*Quanto custa?*
That's too expensive.	*É muito caro.*

I want something cheaper.	*Quero alguma coisa mais barata.*
Can I try this on?	*Posso provar?*
I want to buy (this).	*Quero comprar (isto).*
Do you sell film?	*Vende filme?*
batteries	*pilhas*
cassette	*fita cassete (K-7)*
Where can I buy . . . ?	*Onde posso comprar . . . ?*
postcards	*cartões postais*
soap/shampoo	*sabonete/xampu or champoo*
toothpaste/sunscreen	*pasta de dente/filtro solar*
stamps	*selos*
condom	*camisinha*
newspaper	*jornal*
shoe store	*sapataria*
These shoes do not fit me.	*Estes sapatos não me servem.*
What size do you take in shoes/clothes?	*Qual é o tamanho/número que calça/que veste?*
This color does not suit me.	*Esta cor não me fica bem.*
This coat is tight on me.	*Este paletó está apertado.*
silk	*seda*
cotton	*algodão*

Clothes

suit	*terno*
skirt	*saia*
jacket	*casaco*
dress	*vestido*
trousers	*calça*
swimsuit/bikini	*maiô/fio dental/tanga*
blouse	*blusa*
raincoat/umbrella	*capa de chuva/guarda-chuva*
girdle/stockings/panties/bras	*cinta/meias/calcinha/soutien*
socks/nightgown	*meias/camisola*
tie/shirt	*gravata/camisa*

INDEX

Accommodations: *Alta Floresta,* 218; *Alter de Chão,* 146; *Belém,* 172-173; *Chapada dos Guimarães,* 271-272; *costs, v; Cuiabá,* 259-260; *Manaus,* 197-204; *Santarém,* 149-150

AIDS, *291*

Alenquer, *148-149*

Alta Floresta, *215-219; accommodations, 218; culture, 216-218; hands-on, 218-219*

Alter de Chão, *144-146*

Amazon: *conquest of, 8-12; health kit, 285-292; river travel, 169, 195; travel quiz, ix; voices from, 73-114, 227-231*

Amazônia, *1-219; Alta Floresta, 215-219; Belém, 158-182; bird's-eye view, 3-4; cuisine, 115-122; culture, 115-124; destinations, 137-219; facts, myths and legends, 5-7; fauna, 34-60; flora, 34-39, 60-64; history, 8-17; Indian issue, 18-28; Manaus, 183-214; map, 3; quick rainforest tour, 29-33; Santarém, 138-157; survival kit, 132-135; travel options, 125-131*

Anaconda *(boa constrictor),* 50, *134-135,* 234

Anhinga, *242-243*

Anteater, *39*

Ants, *59-60*

Balsam copal, *64*

Bass, peacock, *53*

Bats, *38*

Beaches, *Manaus,* 190, 193

Bees, *252*

Belém, *158-182; accommodations, 172-173; bird's-eye view, 159; excursions, 166-172; hands-on, 180-182; history, 158-159; jungle* adventure, *166-169; nightlife, 177-178; restaurants, 174-176; shopping, 162-163, 178-179; sights,* 160-169

Birds: *Amazônia,* 46-48; *Pantanal,* 236-244

Bittern, *35-36*

Boa constrictor (anaconda), *50, 134-135,* 234

Books, *293-298*

Botels and boat cruises, *Pantanal, 250*

Bushmaster, *49, 134-135*

Butterflies, *37*

Caiman, black, *49*

Candirú açu, *55, 135*

Capuchin, white-faced, *45*

Capybara, *38, 43, 232*

Caracará, crested, *242*

Catfish, *55*

Cattle, Pantanal, *234*

Centers for Disease Control, *291*

Centipedes, *57-58*

Chapada dos Guimarães, *266-275; accommodations, 271-272; bird's -eye view, 267-268; hands-on, 274-275; healers, 273; history, 267; restaurants, 272-273; shopping, 273; sights, 268-271*

Chichá, *64*

Cholera, *290*

Coati, ring-tailed, *42-43*

Cock-of-the-rock, *47*

Cockroaches, *58*

Contacts, *277-282; health information, 291-292; ocean line cruises, 281-282; online information, 282-283; travel agencies and tour operators, 280-281*

Copaiba, *71*

Cormorants, *242-243*

Cowboys, Pantanal, 227-228
Crafts: Amazônia, 123-124; Museums, Manaus, 192-193; see also Shopping
Crajiru, 71
Crickets, 58
Cruises: botels and, 250; ocean line, 281-282; river, Manaus, 194-195; river, Santarém, 146-149
Cuiabá, 256-265; accommodations, 259-260; bird's-eye view, 257; hands-on, 262-265; healers, 262; museums and zoo, 258-259; nightlife, 261; restaurants, 260; shopping, 261-262; sights, 257-259
Cuisine: Amazônia, 115-122; dainty morsels and sweets, 122; dishes of Amazonas, 119; dishes of Pará, 115-118; fruits of the Amazon, 119-122
Culture, Amazônia, 115-124; Alta Floresta, 216-218; cuisine, 115-122; festivals, 122-123; handicrafts, 123-124
Culture, Pantanal, 227-231; cowboys, 227-228; Indians, 228-231
Curassow, 47

Deer, 43, 232
Dengue fever, 289
Diarrhea, 287-288
Discography, 300-305
Diseases, see Health kit; Survival kit
Dogfish, 52-53
Dolphins, 35, 53
Dourado, 235
Drinking water, 288
Ducks, 243-244

Eagle, harpy, 242
Eco alert, mercury, 30-32
Ecotourism, interactive, vii, 32
Egrets, 237

Facts, myths and legends, 5-7
Fauna: Amazônia, 34-60; amphibians, 51; birds, 46-48, 236-244; fish, 51-55, 196-197,
235-236; insects, 56-60, 133-134; mammals, 39-43, 232-233; Pantanal, 232-244; primates, 43-46; reptiles, 49-51, 233-234; spiders, 56
Felines, 34, 39-40, 233
Festivals, Amazônia, 122-123
Films, 298-299
Fish: Amazônia, 51-55; ornamental, 196-197; Pantanal, 235-236
Fishing: equipment, 131; fly-fishing in Amazônia, 126-131; mercury alert, 32; packages, Manaus, 195; tips, 129-130; tours, 131
Flora: Amazônia, 34-39, 60-64; medicinal plants, 70-72; Pantanal, 244-245; trees, 62-64
Frogs, 38, 51
Fruit sales, 103-114
FUNAI, 22, 230

Gold miner, 217-218
Guaranà, 61, 70

Handicrafts: Amazônia, 123-124; Museums, Manaus, 192-193; see also Shopping
Hands-on: Alta Floresta, 218-219; Belém, 180-182; Chapada dos Guimarães, 274-275; Cuiabá, 262-265; Manaus, 210-214; Santarém, 154-157
Hawks, 241-242
Healers: Chapada dos Guimarães, 273; Cuiabá, 262
Health kit, 285-292; AIDS, 291; cholera, 290; diarrhea, 287-288; disease prevention, 289-290; drinking water, 288; hepatitis, 290, 291; immunizations, 134, 288; information sources, 291-292; jet lag, 285; malaria, 134, 219, 288-289; other bug-transmitted diseases, 289; other diseases, 290-291; post-tropics checkups, 292; sunburn, 285-286; symptoms, 292; see also Survival kit
Hepatitis, 290, 291
Herons, 48, 237-238

History: *Amazônia, 8-17; Belém, 158-159; Chapada dos Guimarães, 267; conquest of the Amazon, 8-12; gold rush, 16-17; Indians, 18-22; Manaus, 186-187; Pantanal, 225-226; rubber boom and bust, 12-15; Santarém, 139-140*
Hitchhiking, 224
Hoatzin, 36, 48
Horse, Pantanal, 235
Hummingbirds, 37

Ibises, 238-239
Immunizations, 134, 288
Indians, 18-28; *fruit sales of, 103-114; FUNAI, 22, 230; history, 18-22; initiation rite, 97-101; linguistic heritage, 86-88; and medicinal plants, 68-69; Pantanal, 228-231; recent events, 22-28; ritual dances, 87-88; shaman's apprentice, 73-84; travel to Indian reserves, 28, 33; Yanomami tribe, 24-28*
Information sources, 291-292
Initiation into sacred science, 85-102
Insect repellents, 289
Insects, 56-60, 133-134; *and disease, 289-290*

Jaçaná, 35, 241
Jacaré, 233
Jaguar, 39-40, 233
Jet lag, 285
Jungle adventures, *Belém, 166-169*
Jungle lodges outside Manaus, 200-204
Jungle survival training course, 196
Jungle tours, *Manaus, 195*

Kapok ceiba, 62
Kingfisher, 36
Kite, sail, 242

Language, 306-315; *Indian heritage, 86-88*
Lapwings, 241

Lizards, 36-37, 234
Lungfish, 54-55

Mahogany, Brazilian, 63
Malaria, 134, 219, 288-289
Manatee, 40
Manaus, 183-214; *accommodations, 197-204; beaches, 190, 193; bird's-eye view, 185-186; cruise packages, 194-195; excursions, 196-197; hands-on, 210-214; history, 186-187; jungle lodges outside the city, 200-204; jungle survival training course, 196; museums, 190-193; nightlife, 207-208; restaurants, 204-207; shopping, 208-210; sights, 187-193*
Maps: *Amazônia and Pantanal, 3; Pantanal, 222*
Marajó Island, 171-172
Marmoset, 44
Medical emergencies, *Pantanal, 252*
Medicinal plants, see *Pharmaceuticals*
Mercury contamination, 30-32
Money, *v*
Monkeys, 43-46
Monte Alegre, 148
Mosqueiro Island, 170-171
Mosquitoes, 133-134, 212, 219
Mosquito nets, 289-290

Nightlife: *Belém, 177-178; Cuiabá, 261; Manaus, 207-208; Santarém, 152*
Nut tree, Brazilian, 64

Ocean line cruises, 281-282
Online information, 282-283
Orchids, 60
Otter, giant, 40
Owls, 243

Packing tips, 133, 253
Pacu, 235
Pantanal, 221-275; *bird's-eye view, 221-224; botels and boat cruises, 250; Chapada dos Guimarães, 266-275; climate, 252; Cuiabá,*

256-265; culture, 227-231; destinations, 256-275; fauna, 232-244; flora, 244-245; history, 225-226; independent travel, 251; Indians, 228-231; lodges/fazendas, 246-250; maps, 3, 222; medical emergencies, 252; survival kit, 252-253; Transpantaneira Highway, 222-224, 250; travel options, 246-251

Parrots, 38, 46
Passerines, 239-240
Pau-de-tucano, 62
Peccary, 41-42
Pharmaceuticals, 65-72; economic challenges and, 67-68; ethics and, 68-69; Indians and, 68-69; medicinal plants, 70-72
Piranha, 52, 135, 235
Pirarucu, 52
Pit viper, 49-50
Post-tropics checkups, 292
Potoo, 39
Prices, v
Puma, 41

Quiz, ix

Rainforest: Belém jungle adventure, 166-169; future of, 65-72; jungle survival training course, 196; mercury contamination, 30-32; preservation of, 29-30, 32-33; quick tour, 29-33; sensual art of, 88-90; spirits of the forest, 216-217; support groups, 283-284
Restaurants: Alter de Chão, 146; Belém, 174-176; Chapada dos Guimarães, 272-273; costs, v; Cuiabá, 260; Manaus, 204-207; Santarém, 150-151
Riverboat and jungle tours: Belém, 166-172; Manaus, 195
River cruises: Manaus, 194-195; Santarém, 146-149
Roseate spoonbill, 239
Rubber tree, 62-63

Salinas, 172
Santarém, 138-157; accommodations, 149-150; bird's-eye view, 140-141; excursions, 144-149; hands-on, 154-157; history, 139-140; lodge expeditions, 149; nightlife, 152; restaurants, 150-151; river cruises, 146-149; shopping, 153-154; sights, 141-144
Sapucaia, 63
Sateré-Mawés tribe, 85-102; expedition with, 95-97; initiation rite, 97-101; travel to, 88-90
Schistosomiasis, 290
Shaman's apprentice, 73-84
Sharks, 54
Shopping: Alter de Chão, 146; Belém, 162-163, 178-179; Chapada dos Guimarães, 273; Cuiabá, 261-262; Manaus, 208-210; Santarém, 153-154
Sinimbu, 234
Skunk, Amazonian, 42
Sloth, 41
Snakes, 49-50, 134-135, 234
Specialty tours, 277-282; ocean line cruises, 281-282; travel agencies and tour operators, 280-281
Spiders, 56
Spirits of the forest, 216-217
Spoonbill, roseate, 239
Sting ray, 53-54
Storks, 238
Sunburn, 285-286
Survival kit: Amazônia, 132-135; clothing, 132; disease prevention, 289-290; drinking water, 288; malaria, 134, 219, 288-289; mosquitoes and bugs, 133-134; photographic gear, 133; preparation, 132; vaccinations, 134, 288; warnings, 134-135; see also Travel alerts; what to pack, 133; see also Health kit
Survival kit, Pantanal, 252-253; bees, 252; climate, 252; disease prevention, 289-290; drinking

water, *288; medical emergencies,*
252; what to pack, 253
Survival training course, *196*
Swallows, *36, 38-39*

Tapir, *42, 233*
Termites, *58-59*
Terns, *240-241*
Tetras, *54*
Ticks, *57*
Toucans, *47*
Tours, specialty, *277-282*
Transpantaneira Highway, *222-
224, 250*
Travel   agencies   and   tour
operators, *280-281*
Travel alerts: *bees, 252; candirú açu
(fish), 55; fire ants, 59-60;
hitchhiking, 224; Indian reserves,
28, 33; malaria, 134, 219, 288-289;
market thefts and photos, 163;
medical   emergencies,   252;
mosquitoes and bugs, 133-134, 212,
219; piranha, 135; rainforest
preservation, 32-33; snakes, 50,*

*134-135; vaccinations, 134, 288;
yellow fever, 134, 212*
Travel options: *Amazônia, 125-131;
Pantanal, 246-251*
Trees, *62-64, 245*
Tuiuiú, *238*
Turtles, *50-51*
Typhoid fever, *291*

Urucu, *71-72*

Vaccinations, *134, 288*
Vultures, *35, 48, 242*

Water, drinking, *288*
Water lilies, *61*
Water vines, *61*
Where to eat, see *Restaurants*
Where to stay, see *Accommodations*
Wolf, maned, *40-41*

Yanomami tribe, *24-28*
Yellow fever, *134, 212*

Zoo, Cuiabá, *258-259*